PQ 2285. C8. Z5 NAS

QM Library

D0321791

DATE DUE FOR RETURN

WITHDRAWN
FROM STOCK
QMUL LIBRARY

LES CONTEMPLATIONS OF

VICTOR HUGO

Les Contemplations of Victor Hugo

An Allegory of
the Creative Process

BY SUZANNE NASH

Princeton University
Press

187843

Copyright © 1976 by Princeton University Press

Published by Princeton University Press, Princeton, New Jersey
In the United Kingdom:
Princeton University Press, Guildford, Surrey

ALL RIGHTS RESERVED

Library of Congress Cataloging in Publication Data
will be found on the last printed page of this book

Publication of this book has been aided by a
grant from The Andrew W. Mellon Foundation

This book has been composed in Linotype Granjon

Printed in the United States of America
by Princeton University Press, Princeton, New Jersey

QUEEN MARY
COLLEGE
LIBRARY

To

my parents

PREFACE

Although Victor Hugo was recognized early in his own lifetime as one of the great literary geniuses of the nineteenth century and has continued to live in the popular imagination as France's poet laureate, he has not always fared well at the hands of the critics. Before Hugo was even dead, Edmond Biré, in his four-volume biography, began deflating the legend Hugo had so artfully created for himself. Almost immediately after his death there set in, both in France and abroad, a reaction against the "hugolatrie" that had reigned for over fifty years and had turned Hugo's funeral into a gaudy national holiday.

For the first fifty years of this century Hugo scholarship in France centered mainly on his social, religious, and political ideology, very little attention being paid to his work as a formal achievement. In English-speaking countries, even to this day, Hugo is primarily known as a novelist, probably because the difficulties of translating his poetry are almost insurmountable. Swinburne, George Saintsbury, and Tennyson were among the rare nineteenth-century critics who appreciated his genius for language, and when French poetic theory began to interest the English poets at the beginning of this century, critics turned resolutely to the symbolists for inspiration, stressing the mediocrity of Hugo's thought and the bombastic nature of his rhetoric. Most importantly, perhaps, Hugo's formal innovations, crucial to the development of French poetic diction, did not affect English poetry because many of them were relevant only to French problems of versification. This book is an effort to fill the gap in English criticism by clarifying Hugo's contribution to the development of modernist poetics through a detailed study of one of his best-known mature works.

Since the 1950's there has been a vital resurgence of Hugo studies in France, and in the last decade particular interest has been paid the later, visionary works which characterize the sixth book of the *Contemplations*. I have found Michael Riffaterre's short studies of Hugo's visionary style especially stimulating and suggestive. Although there is no full-length study of *Les Contemplations* as a unified whole, I am indebted to many great Hugo scholars who have written about this work. René Journet and Guy Robert have produced an updated examination of the manuscript based on Joseph Vianey's critical edition of 1922 and have collated all the materials from the Hugo dossier related to the composition of the collection. Their three books, *Autour des 'Contemplations,'* *Le Manuscrit des 'Contemplations,'* and *Notes sur 'Les Contemplations,'* have been indispensable tools in the writing of this study. In their introductions to various recent editions of *Les Contemplations*, Pierre Albouy (Pléiade, 1964), Jacques Seebacher (Cluny, 1964), Léon Cellier (Garnier, 1970) have all emphasized the importance of the larger narrative and of Léopoldine as a key figure in its unfolding. One of the most provocative studies of Hugo's poetic creation during the period surrounding the composition of *Les Contemplations* (1830-1860) is Jean Gaudon's monumental *Le Temps de la contemplation* (Flammarion, 1969). His book has served as a demanding and inspiring interlocutor, forcing me to question my own apprehension of Hugo's work with greater rigor. Finally, the new *Club français du livre* edition of Hugo's complete works, published under the direction of Jean Massin, has been a mine of information for every aspect of Hugo scholarship. I will refer the reader to Jean Gaudon's fine edition of *Les Contemplations* in Vol. IX of Massin throughout this work.

The inspiration for this study, which was in its original form my doctoral dissertation, belongs, in the first place, to the teaching of Paul de Man, whose lectures on Romantic and symbolist poetry I attended while a graduate student at Cornell University. I am grateful to him for reading my manuscript in an earlier form and for making suggestions which I have only imperfectly been able to fulfill.

I wish to thank my dissertation advisor at Princeton University, Léon-François Hoffmann, for his clear-minded counsel and for allowing me the freedom to pursue my own course. Special thanks go to Karl D. Uitti and Eloise Goreau for their painstaking readings of early drafts, and their consistently perceptive critical advice.

It is due in large part to the interest and encouragement of my colleague, Alban Forcione, that I decided to revise and enlarge my original study to its present form. His willingness to listen, and his tactful and discriminating observations provided a vital dialogue throughout the writing of this book. I am further indebted to the many other friends and colleagues who were kind enough to read portions of the manuscript at various stages and offer valuable suggestions—notably, Sylvia Molloy, Albert Sonnenfeld, John Logan, Laura Curtis, Stanley Corngold, and Barbara Guetti. My thanks go as well to Jerry Sherwood and Joanna Hitchcock of Princeton University Press for their patience and expert advice. Finally, my greatest debt is to my husband and children for their loving support and most especially for being my link to the creature world.

CONTENTS

LES CONTEMPLATIONS OF

VICTOR HUGO

INTRODUCTION

W̲HE̲N̲ Victor Hugo died in 1885, "France unburdened itself of a man, a literary movement, and a century." Thus, in terms implying an almost visceral relief, Roger Shattuck describes the beginning of a new era of conscious modernism in French poetry.[1] Cynical admiration often characterizes the tone modernists adopt when referring to this poet who was for them too prolific, too popular, too much the official poet of the Republic. They cannot reconcile the dazzling originality of Hugo's art and the adulation he always enjoyed from the crowd and officialdom alike. Critics have consistently struggled to split Hugo in two, to separate man from poet and message from expression, in their evaluations of him. Baudelaire liked to see Hugo's immense popularity as a sign of dangerous simplemindedness. Thus, in *L'Art romantique,* he began his essay on Hugo with typically ambivalent condescension:

> Je me souviens d'un temps où sa figure était une des plus rencontrées parmi la foule; et bien des fois je me suis demandé, en le voyant si souvent apparaître dans la turbulence des fêtes ou dans le silence des lieux solitaires, comment il pouvait concilier les nécessités de son travail assidu avec ce goût sublime, mais dangereux, des promenades et des rêveries? Cette apparente contradiction est évidemment le résultat d'une existence bien réglée et d'une forte constitution spirituelle qui lui permet de travailler en marchant, ou plutôt de ne pouvoir marcher qu'en travaillant.[2]

When asked who was the greatest French poet who ever lived,

---

[1] *The Banquet Years* (New York, 1955), p. 5.
[2] *Oeuvres complètes*, ed. Le Dantec (Paris: Bibliothèque de la Pléiade, 1956), p. 1082.

Introduction

André Gide replied for all modern French writers when he answered: "Victor Hugo, hélas!"

Nevertheless, despite their disdain for Hugo as a social reformer and religious philosopher, precursors or practitioners of modernism have all been aware of Hugo's profound contribution to the resources of French poetic diction. Baudelaire, Rimbaud, Valéry, Breton, Aragon—each an exemplar of some form of profound literary change—have all cited Hugo as the writer whose experimentation with language, quite simply, made their work possible. More acutely than Hugo's undiscriminating popular audience, they recognized that from the very beginning of his career, Hugo had struggled to liberate poetic language from the ossified restrictions of a worn-out neoclassical aesthetic which had held France in its grip longer than any other European country.

An assessment of Hugo as a genuinely original poet did not come easily to his literary heirs, virtually all of whom felt driven to distinguish between the generative influence of his art and the stultifying effects of his philosophical pretensions and public reputation. Force-fed on Hugo, Rimbaud is a good example of the rebellious schoolboy who, when he wished to ridicule his austerely religious mother, called her "La Bouche d'ombre," but who also wrote to Paul Demeny: "Hugo, *trop cabochard*, a bien *vu* dans les derniers volumes."

Recognition of Hugo's genius was perhaps most painful for his younger contemporary, Baudelaire, who felt overshadowed throughout his lifetime by the kind of popular acclaim which the constant and prodigious flow of Hugo's writing seemed to produce and who sought, almost pathetically, until he died, to win the master's recognition and approval for his own neurotically restricted work. The public's relatively easy acceptance of Hugo's artistic innovations seemed to preclude any critical awareness of the value of these experiments and hence of the experiments in which Baudelaire was at that time engaged.

4

Baudelaire's understandable resentment caused him repeatedly to question, indeed to attack Hugo's critical intelligence, all the while acknowledging and even extolling his creative genius. Even though Baudelaire complained about the virtual dictatorship that Hugo had exercised over literary activity in France in the 1830's, he insisted that Hugo alone was responsible for the revitalization of poetry which had been dead or dying in France for over 100 years:

> Quand on se figure ce qu'était la poésie française avant qu'il apparût, et quel rajeunissement elle a subi depuis qu'il est venu; quand on imagine ce peu qu'elle eût été s'il n'était pas venu; combien de sentiments mystérieux et profonds, qui ont été exprimés, seraient restés muets; combien d'intelligences il a accouchées, combien d'hommes qui ont rayonné par lui seraient restés obscurs, il est impossible de ne pas le considérer comme un de ces esprits rares et providentiels qui opèrent, dans l'ordre littéraire, le salut de tous, comme d'autres dans l'ordre moral et d'autres dans l'ordre politique. (*L'Art romantique*, p. 1084)

Baudelaire's ironic use of Hugo's own religious vocabulary reflects the ambivalent attitude he has adopted throughout his essay in *L'Art romantique*, where he insidiously underscores the seemingly miraculous nature of Hugo's inventions:

> Je vois dans la Bible un prophète à qui Dieu ordonne de manger un livre. J'ignore dans quel monde Victor Hugo a mangé préalablement le dictionnaire de la langue qu'il était appelé à parler; mais je vois que le lexique français, en sortant de sa bouche, est devenu un monde, un univers coloré, mélodieux et mouvant. Par suite de quelles circonstances historiques, fatalités philosophiques, conjonctions sidérales, cet homme est-il né parmi nous, je n'en sais rien. . . . (p. 1086)

Baudelaire thus makes the mistake of distinguishing spontaneous creation from reflective consciousness by suggesting that Hugo *unwittingly* touched upon all the resources of French poetic diction, leaving his heirs the task of rationalizing his achievement.[3]

It was Paul Valéry, one of the most cerebral and technically meticulous of all modern French poets, who was to place Baudelaire's jaundiced assessment of Hugo into question. "Hugo, comme tout véritable poète, est un critique de premier ordre," he says in a lecture significantly entitled, "Victor Hugo, créateur par la forme."[4] Valéry distinguishes Hugo from the other Romantic poets (Lamartine, Vigny, Musset), who, he felt, sought above all to give vent to their emotions, and thus to overcome the formal restrictions which poetic language necessarily imposes upon spontaneous feeling. Hugo, Valéry claims, did just the opposite: form, not feeling, was the source of his inspiration:

> Ce qu'on nomme la Pensée devient en lui . . . le moyen et non la fin de l'expression. Souvent le développement d'un poème est visiblement chez lui la déduction d'un merveilleux accident de langage qui a surgi dans son esprit.
> (p. 589)

[3] Baudelaire's biased distinction became a cliché of Hugo criticism and has only recently been challenged. René Wellek, for example, begins his discussion of Hugo in *A History of Modern Criticism*, Vol. II, "The Romantic Age" (New Haven, 1955), p. 252: "It has been the fashion to dismiss Hugo as an intellect and as a critic, but this understandable reaction against the excesses of his rhetoric has surely gone too far, as has the wholesale dismissal of his poetry. Both need rectification. Much has been done for the reinstatement of his last 'apocalyptic' poems; something can be done for his criticism, which among much verbiage, contains profound insights and brilliant formulas for age-old problems."

[4] *Oeuvres*, ed. Jean Hytier, Vol. I (Paris: Bibliothèque de la Pléiade, 1962), p. 587.

For Valéry, Hugo is the father of modern French poetry because he was the first to grasp the crucial truth that form is meaning. Hugo sought to resolve all of his problems, artistic and philosophical, through the artifice of rhetoric. Contrary to Shattuck, Valéry insists that Hugo did not die in 1885 and that France will never be free of his meteoric presence as long as his work continues to excite impassioned debate amongst poets. The extent of his genius, Valéry says, can be measured by the innovations his work has required of his successors:

> Pour le *mesurer*, il suffit de rechercher ce que les poètes qui sont nés autour de lui, ont été *obligés* d'inventer pour exister auprès de lui. Le problème capital de la littérature, depuis 1840 jusqu'en 1890, n'est-il pas: Comment faire autre chose que Hugo? Comment être visible malgré Hugo? Comment se percher sur les cimes de Hugo? On l'a cherché du côté de la perfection technique, du côté de la bizarrerie des sujets, du côté des sentiments, du côté des dimensions du poème, etc., etc.[5]

Hugo's critical awareness of the difficulties of translating perception into language is clear from the very beginning of his career and is, I believe, responsible for the increasingly complex structure of his linguistic universe in the very works Baudelaire most admired. I have chosen to analyze one of those later works, *Les Contemplations*, because it dramatizes the relationship between spontaneity and reflectiveness in an especially crucial and highly self-conscious manner. Hugo wrote most of the poems in the collection during the traumatic early years of his exile (1851-1856), at a time when he began to look back upon his life and perceive in it the outlines of a larger, metaphysical pattern. For Hugo, as for Coleridge, revelation

---

[5] Letter from Valéry to Paul Souday, *Oeuvres*, Vol. I, p. 1715.

is rooted in self-consciousness.[6] The book is organized in such a way as to reflect simultaneously the evolution of his personal, historical existence and that of his poetical and religious consciousness. *Les Contemplations* successfully realizes the blurring of distinctions between genres that Hugo laid down in his preface to *Cromwell* in 1827 as the revolutionary aim of great Romantic art. It is a collection of separate lyric poems that, if taken together, act out the drama of their own creation. Understanding the complex superstructure within which each poem occupies a place is a necessary task for any serious exegete of this work.

An examination of the thematic and structural patterns in *Les Contemplations* should help to resolve a paradox central to all Hugo's later, visionary works. At the same time that he was developing an increasingly schematized account of the cosmogony and man's place within it, his own creations appear—but only appear—to become more unstructured and digressive—even monstrous in their proportions. This apparent contradiction between message and form became obvious for the first time with the publication of *Les Contemplations*. The sheer weight and variety of the collection would seem to defy any attempt to establish a clear-cut order; yet Hugo says in his preface that the reader will find mirrored in his book, not only Hugo's own life, but the story of human destiny as well. He seems to be saying that to read this work is to read all his works; to understand his achievement is to understand the Divine Logos itself. His organization of the collection into six parts, each one with a chapter heading referring to some stage

6 ". . . the act of self-consciousness is for *us* the source and principle of all *our* possible knowledge. . . . We begin with the *I know myself*, in order to end with the absolute *I am*. We proceed from the self, in order to lose and find all self in God." *Biographia Literaria*, ed. J. Shawcross, Vol. 1 (Oxford: Clarendon Press, 1907), p. 186.

in his life, reinforces the messianic tone of the preface and sets the stage for a narrative and, in my view, an essentially allegorical experience.

Hugo announces at the outset that *Les Contemplations* is arcane and initiatory. A careful reading of the work reveals that its formal irregularity is consciously designed to obscure a unity that Hugo wishes his reader to perceive *in a particular way*. During his years of exile he became increasingly convinced that he had been chosen to lead mankind toward reform by effecting its spiritual conversion. Thus, as the architect of his imaginary universe, he felt justified in imposing upon the reader a sequence of steps by which he must ascend to the cosmic height necessary for a panoramic view of the total vision. Hugo wanted the task of the decipherer of that fundamental unity to be a difficult one, but there can be no doubt that the reader has failed to enter Hugo's world on his terms if he does not seek to discern a providential order behind the apparent chaos.

Hugo's use of allegory as late as 1856, one year before the publication of *Les Fleurs du mal*, is particularly significant in view of the controversy over the relative value of symbol and allegory that had been the subject of debate in Germany and England since the turn of the century. Goethe was the first to redefine the terms, giving preference to the symbol, which permits one to grasp the ineffable immediately, through a particular form, whereas allegory, he said, never moves beyond the level of rational analysis. Like Goethe, Coleridge believed that symbolic language could reveal Divinity directly:

> Now an allegory is but a translation of abstract notions into a picture language, which is itself nothing but an abstraction from objects of the senses; the principle being more worthless even than its phantom proxy. . . . On the

other hand, a symbol . . . is characterized above all by the translucence of the eternal through and in the temporal. . . .[7]

Hugo too believed in the power of symbolic language to reveal Divine Presence, but not before a prolonged initiation that requires the active participation of the reader in the creation of that language. Allegory was the trope most suited to Hugo's utopian purpose. Because allegory both constitutes and contains a prolonged, narrative experience, it involves the historical consciousness of the reader, who is forced to move sequentially through the text and to become involved in a dialectical relationship with the writer, who himself is figural. Hugo's belief in poetry—a belief that must be understood in its total context—implies a concomitant belief in progress and man's ability to alter the course of human history. He was bent upon breathing new life into a rhetorical form which could articulate that belief.

Hugo's purpose seems to have been apparent to Baudelaire, for in 1861 he dedicated to Victor Hugo "Le Cygne," a poem which implicitly redefines allegory as the rhetorical statement of man's hopeless imprisonment within the flux of time and thus poetically suggests the naiveté of Hugo's idealism. "Paris change! mais rien dans ma mélancolie / N'a bougé . . . / . . . tout pour moi devient allégorie." Baudelaire's response to Hugo's work reflects an awareness of the philosophical implications of the use of such rhetorical devices that would later become the very subject of Mallarmé's po-

[7] *The Statesman's Manual*, ed. W.G.T. Shedd (New York, 1875), pp. 437-38, quoted in Angus Fletcher's *Allegory: The Theory of a Symbolic Mode* (Ithaca, 1964), p. 16. For a brilliant discussion of the function of these tropes for certain Romantic poets see Paul de Man's "The Rhetoric of Temporality," in *Interpretation, Theory and Practice*, ed. Charles S. Singleton (Baltimore, 1969).

etry. Thus an appreciation of Hugo's use of allegory in *Les Contemplations* should help to establish his position within the debate regarding figurative language that began toward the end of the eighteenth century and has yet to be resolved.

Current, post-structuralist critics, for example, tend to view all literary discourse as an endless deferment of sense, a deferment that they in turn equate with a loss of plenitude traditionally associated with natural man; and they see the use of such rhetorical figures as allegory or metonymy as signs of the poet's awareness of the failure of language to move beyond its own hollow constructs. Hugo certainly understood poetic language and the natural experience that inspired its creation to be radically cut off from one another ("*Autrefois, Aujourd'hui. Un abîme les sépare, le tombeau*," preface to *Les Contemplations*), yet he repeatedly affirmed that this language constitutes a new, supernatural Presence in its own right, one to be experienced empirically by the reader. Although there are moments throughout Hugo's work when we sense his awareness of the problematical basis of his faith in the mediating power of language, they do not undercut the rationalized intentions that forcefully determine the architecture of his world. Indeed, the skepticism that appears to subvert his messianic pretensions is, as we shall see, an essential part of a larger, redemptive pattern. Such moments of ironic deconstruction serve, then, entirely different functions in the works of Hugo and Baudelaire.

This study will propose a new reading of *Les Contemplations* as a unified, allegorical whole; only in this way, I am convinced, is it possible to demonstrate properly the relationship between Hugo's thought and the complex structure of his linguistic universe. Because he organized his book so as to reflect his own development as a poet, the work constitutes a key document for understanding Hugo's perception of the poetic process and hence of his other works as well. By remaining within the boundaries of this single work, I hope to define the cosmic scope of Hugo's visionary consciousness; by examining the monstrous complexity of its formal structure, to discover the fundamental simplicity of his belief: "La création est un palimpseste à travers lequel on déchiffre Dieu."

I

THE ALLEGORICAL NATURE AND
CONTEXT OF HUGO'S WORK

Hugo's intention that *Les Contemplations* represent a work greater than the sum of its lyric parts is immediately apparent from a reading of his preface and a glance at the narrative format: Part I—Autrefois, 1830-1843; Part II—Aujourd'hui, 1843-1855. Each part contains a further, tripartite division: in Autrefois I—*Aurore*, II—*L'Ame en fleur*, III—*Les Luttes et les rêves*; followed by IV—*Pauca meae*, V—*En marche*, and VI—*Au bord de l'infini* in Aujourd'hui.[1]

The reader is informed in the preface to *Les Contemplations* that he is to read the collection as a *book* ("Ce livre doit être lu comme on lirait le livre d'un mort") that is both "Mémoires d'une âme" and the book of human destiny. Mirrored in Hugo's own life we are to find written the story of the Human Spirit:

> L'auteur a laissé pour ainsi dire, ce livre se faire en lui. La vie, en filtrant goutte à goutte à travers les événements et les souffrances, l'a déposé dans son coeur. Ceux qui s'y pencheront retrouveront leur propre image dans cette eau profonde et triste, qui s'est lentement amassée là, au fond d'une âme.

Hugo repeatedly sketches the linear, progressive direction

---

[1] For a general résumé of changes made in the arrangement of the poems within each section before the publication of *Les Contemplations* in 1856, see René Journet and Guy Robert, *Autour des 'Contemplations.' Annales littéraires de l'université de Besançon*, 1955, pp. 47-51.

of this universalized biography, urging us to read it from be-ginning to end.

> C'est l'existence humaine sortant de l'énigme du berceau et aboutissant à l'énigme du cercueil; c'est un esprit qui marche de lueur en lueur en laissant derrière lui la jeunesse, l'amour, l'illusion, le combat, le désespoir, et qui s'arrête éperdu 'au bord de l'infini'. Cela commence par un sourire, continue par un sanglot, et finit par un bruit du clairon de l'abîme.
>
> Traverser le tumulte, la rumeur, le rêve, la lutte, le plaisir, le travail, la douleur, le silence; se reposer dans le sacrifice, et, là, contempler Dieu; commencer à Foule et finir à Solitude, n'est-ce pas, les proportions individuelles réser-vées, l'histoire de tous?
>
> La joie, cette fleur rapide de la jeunesse, s'effeuille page à page dans le tome premier, qui est l'espérance, et dis-paraît dans le tome second, qui est le deuil.

A further internal evidence of Hugo's concern that the text be read as a continuous narrative is reflected in the dates and places at the end of each poem. It is by now a well-known fact that on the manuscripts destined for publication in *Les Con-templations* Hugo scratched out most of the original dates and substituted dates of symbolic significance.[2] For example, many seemingly light-hearted poems placed in *Aurore* and dated prior to 1843 were actually written in the 1850's, contemporane-ously with poems like "Horror," "Pleurs dans la nuit," or even "Ce que dit la bouche d'ombre."[3]

[2] For a list of real and fictional dates of all of the poems in the col-lection, see Léon Cellier's edition of *Les Contemplations* (Paris: Gar-nier, 1969), pp. xxxix-xliv or the *Oeuvres complètes*, ed. Jean Massin, Vol. ix (Paris: Club français du livre, 18 volumes, 1967-1970), pp. 51-7.

[3] Among these are: I,xii ("Vere novo"): I,xiv ("A Granville, en 1836"): I,xv ("La Coccinelle"): I,xvi ("Vers 1820"), I,xix ("Vieille

It has been suggested that Hugo changed dates in the published version in order to keep his private life secret from Madame Hugo or Juliette Drouet, or to alter the public's notion of his political evolution toward republicanism in order to show himself in a more favorable light. It seems more likely, however, that the Hugo-allegorist of *Les Contemplations* considered himself quite separate from and indeed superior to the poet-dreamer of the individual works. In fact, the separation of the lyric narrator from the visionary and their eventual reintegration is a leading theme in the book. By altering the dates, Hugo could organize his work around a specific biographical event and then fill it with providential significance. In this way he poeticizes his personal history so that it gains a superior dimension worthy of the reader's attention. Events such as his affair with Léonie d'Aunet thus take on metaphysical significance. The dates and places assigned to the poems in the manuscript are signs within some universal evolutionary process toward an expanded consciousness through which the reader-initiate must be guided. The lyric poetry of the first person gives way to the dramatic experience of a representative human spirit.

Final internal evidence of the structural unity of the poems is the key position Hugo ascribes to his daughter, Léopoldine, throughout the work. The first and last poems of AUTREFOIS ("A ma fille" and "Magnitudo parvi") are addressed directly to her. The central biographical year, 1843 (cf. *Préface*: "Vingt-cinq années sont dans ces deux volumes"), is the year of her drowning. Many poems are dated the anniversary of her death. *Pauca meae* is devoted entirely to her memory, and in 1855 Hugo decided to end the collection with an epilogue entitled

---

chanson du jeune temps"): I,xxi ("Elle était déchaussée, . . ."). *Les Contemplations*, ed. Massin, pp. 31-399. Henceforth all quotations from Hugo's work will be taken from this edition.

"De l'absent à l'absente," later to be changed to "A celle qui est restée en France." It is clear that in order to understand the narrative message, one must understand Léopoldine's role in Hugo's poetic scheme.

There is also a good deal of external evidence that points to Hugo's concern with a narrative reading of his work. In 1854 and 1855, when he was assembling *Les Contemplations* for publication, he insisted upon its structural integrity in both letters and conversations, just as Baudelaire was to do for *Les Fleurs du mal.* A letter Hugo wrote to Emile Deschanel insisting upon the sacred architecture of the book is striking evidence of this:

> *Les Contemplations* sont un livre qu'il faut lire tout entier pour le comprendre. . . . Le premier vers n'a de sens complet qu'après qu'on a lu le dernier. Le poème est une pyramide au dehors, une voûte au dedans. Pyramide du temple, voûte du sépulcre. Or dans des édifices de ce genre, voûte et pyramide, toutes les pierres se tiennent.[4]

We find another example in Adèle Hugo's diary. She recounts a conversation between her father and Auguste Vacquerie about two poems of Part VI, "Horror" and "Dolor." In response to Vacquerie's criticism that Hugo was attacking those who doubt too strongly, the poet answered:

> Vous ne connaissez pas tout mon livre. Ne jugez pas mon livre sur un détail. Ces deux pièces de vers—elles n'attaquent pas les douteurs, elles blâment les rieurs.[5]

[4] The discovery of this unpublished letter inspired Francis Pruner to write a fervent monograph in which he argues that a secret mathematical order apparent to anyone familiar with Masonic ritual governs *Les Contemplations.* "*Les Contemplations,* 'pyramide-temple,' ébauche pour un principe d'explication," *Archives des lettres modernes,* 43, 1962.

[5] René Journet and Guy Robert, *Notes sur 'Les Contemplations,'* *Annales littéraires de l'université de Besançon,* 1958, p. 189.

16

The ideal of writing a long allegorical poem was in no way alien to current Romantic thought. During the first half of the nineteenth century—especially before the abortive revolution of 1848—the notion of a utopian world to be realized through the inspired teaching of the poet was a popular one in France. Hugo, Lamartine, and Vigny were all dedicated to the belief in the redemptive power of language as a means of altering the course of history. Unlike traditional metaphysical poets, the younger generation of Romantics believed that once man understood his place within the Divine Scheme, he would and should alter his conduct in such a way as to help realize the city of God in the here and now. For them politics was very much a part of the poet's domain. It is not surprising to see that both Lamartine and Hugo were active in French government or that they read Lamennais and de Maistre with as much care as they did Shakespeare or Schiller.

Lamartine, like Hugo, dreamed of writing "the great predestined poem of the nineteenth century which was to explain man to himself, by throwing onto the poetic screen the birth, the growth, the vicissitudes of the destinies of the human race."[6]

> Elle [la poésie] ne sera plus épique; l'homme a trop vécu, trop réfléchi pour se laisser amuser ... la poésie sera de la raison chantée, voilà sa destinée pour longtemps; elle sera philosophique, religieuse, politique, sociale, comme les époques que le genre humain va traverser.
>
> (Cited by Hunt, p. 154, from *Des Destinées de la poésie, Les Méditations*)

The resemblance of this passage to Hugo's preface to *Les Contemplations* is striking. The Romantic exaltation of self leads to a communion with a collective, historical self. These

---

[6] Herbert J. Hunt, *The Epic in Nineteenth-Century France* (Oxford, 1941), p. 154.

are messianic poets dedicated to preparing the public for a utopian future.[7]

With *Les Contemplations*, then, Hugo places himself intentionally within a didactic allegorical tradition. In his preface he informs the reader that he is telling the story of human destiny and describes the traditional allegorical theme of man's voyage from life to death and redemption. In AUTREFOIS he invokes two important allegorists whom we know from his poem "Les Mages" he considered to be his literary ancestors: Milton in I,iv and Dante in III,i. That he sees himself as the nineteenth-century French reincarnation of Dante is evident from the key position of this poem at the beginning of *Les Luttes et les rêves*, the book that describes the hell of contemporary existence. Its title, "Ecrit sur un exemplaire de la Divina Commedia," implies that the poem was dictated to Hugo by Dante's own spirit.[8] The identification of Hugo with Dante

---

[7] Herbert J. Hunt and Jacques Roos in *Les Idées philosophiques de Victor Hugo* (Paris, 1958) have pointed out the debt that the younger Romantics owe to the social and religious mysticism of Ballanche, whose theory of the continuity of perfectible creation was outlined in *Essais de palingénésie sociale*, (*1829-30*), pp. 79, 80:

> There are certain moments in history when measurable advance is possible: they are the "époques palingénésiques," and each palingenetic age has its Moses, its Prometheus, its Heracles, its Oedipus, its Servius Tullius, etc., under whose guidance, or by whose agency an old "expiation" is concluded and a new "initiation" begun. . . .
> . . . man will have become completely a creator when he shall have thrown off the yoke of fatality or destiny, and achieved full liberty. The achievement of such liberty is both the process of perfectibility and assigns a limit to that perfectibility.

For a comprehensive study of the messianic consciousness in England and Germany, see M. H. Abrams' *Natural Supernaturalism, Tradition and Revolution in Romantic Literature* (New York, 1971).

[8] For a while Hugo planned to make *La Vision de Dante*, written in February 1853, but not published until 1883, the final book of *Les Châtiments*. In his study of the allegorical mode, Edwin Honig notes: "That Dante at the beginning of his quest cannot pass beyond even the least forbidding obstacles and must have Virgil's aid through Hell

is further strengthened by the theme of the transmigration of souls and the final triumphant line: "Maintenant, je suis homme, et je m'appelle Dante." This dependence upon another human but prophetic guide is a theme of traditional allegory and reflects the relationship Hugo has already set up between himself and the reader in the preface, where he insists that his life is really our life as well. "Prenez donc ce miroir et regardez-vous-y." The prefatory poem of *Les Contemplations* dramatically introduces the traditional daemonic[9] or divinely inspired agent, who will be our guide, as the poet. The hero of the Romantic quest is not only a man of action, but a contemplative consciousness as well. In fact, for the Romantic recasting of the allegorical tale, redemption lies in the hero's image-making powers.

> Un jour je vis, debout au bord des flots mouvants,
> Passer, gonflant ses voiles,
> Un rapide navire enveloppé de vents,
> De vagues et d'étoiles;
>
> Et j'entendis, penché sur l'abîme des cieux,
> Que l'autre abîme touche,
> Me parler à l'oreille une voix dont mes yeux
> Ne voyaient pas la bouche:

---

and Purgatory indicates the didactic and emulative character of the quest. The path through the unknown is partly opened up by the counsel and guidance of his fellow poet, who previously has gone most of the way." *Dark Conceit; The Making of Allegory* (Evanston, 1959), p. 75.

[9] In speaking of the "daemonic agent" present in all allegorical fiction, Honig says: "The hero's physical appearance is often so cogently portrayed as a declaration of what he is that this description suffices for identification without further amplification. His typicality, observed immediately from external signs, is enough to stamp him, as it does the first appearance of an actor on the stage, with an intensely dramatic presence. In this way the personified forces in allegory carry something of the traditional authority not only of *dramatis personae* but also of sacred figures in myths," p. 85.

"Poète, tu fais bien! Poète au triste front,
        Tu rêves près des ondes,
Et tu tires des mers bien des choses qui sont
        Sous les vagues profondes!

La mer, c'est le Seigneur, que, misère ou bonheur,
        Tout destin montre et nomme;
Le vent, c'est le Seigneur; l'astre, c'est le Seigneur;
        Le navire, c'est l'homme."[10]

The three levels of existence—individual, historical, and meta-physical—are all evoked by the age-old figure of the ship. The poet, like the sails of the ship, has been filled with the breath of Divinity. Thus the literary voyage the reader is about to undertake must be viewed as an act of faith. As Hugo later says in *La Contemplation suprême*: "L'héroisme est une affirmation religieuse."[11]

Thus if one is to take Hugo's chapter organization, preface, and poeticized dates seriously, *Les Contemplations* as a whole seems to constitute a narrative that affirms the providential nature of creation. It is a sacred book, a kind of new scripture, in that it claims to reveal that obscure but ideal order to us. The meaning of individual poems is deciphered by the or-dering consciousness of 1855. Mythic chronology emerges from under historical chronology as the poet-decipherer scratches away at the palimpsest of his own life. The poet of 1855 is able to see that order because he is "dead"—that is to say he himself has passed through all stages of human destiny and has turned back to tell the tale.

[10] Northrop Frye, *The Anatomy of Criticism* (New York, 1957), p. 90: "We have actual allegory when a poet explicitly indicates the relationship of his images to examples and precepts, and so tries to indicate how a commentary on him should proceed. A writer is being allegorical whenever it is clear that he is saying 'by this I also (*allos*) mean that.'"

[11] *Oeuvres complètes*, ed. Massin, Vol. ii, p. 121.

... c'est une âme qui se raconte dans ces deux volumes.
Autrefois, Aujourd'hui. Un abîme les sépare, le tombeau.
(*Préface*)

If it is plausible, then, that Hugo's collection constitutes an integrated allegorical narrative rather than a loosely bound assortment of separate works, it is important to determine more precisely the nature of the quest. I have already suggested that the daemonic guide is a contemplative consciousness rather than a man of action. The title Hugo chose for his collection emphasizes at the outset the focus of the work.

The individual poems, or, by extension, the six books, are to be understood as separate contemplative experiences which together lead to the revelation of an Ideal Logos; hence the plural, Les Contemplations. The abstract notion of contemplation is thus objectified and naturalized into a series of perceivable experiences. Each book focuses on a new level of an evolving spiritual and poetic awareness: Book i—organic nature, Book ii—earthly love, Book iii—society, Book iv—personal suffering, Book v—prophetic duty, and Book vi—supernatural reality. Thus the collection begins and ends with the world outside the subjective consciousness (nature–surnature), but the metaphysical significance of that world cannot be felt until the poetic imagination has acted upon it. Hence the Romantic inwardness characteristic of Chateaubriand or Rousseau, for example, is merely an important stage in the quest that leads beyond the alienation of human thought. Hugo's presenting the reader with the poet as his guide would suggest that the reader is being introduced into a structure that reflects the image-making process itself, that is to say, into an allegory of the poetic process.[12] There is external evidence to support this view.

[12] Hugo's vision could be said to be the mirror image of that of modern-day structuralists, who would say with Lévi-Strauss that myths sig-

21

A few years after the publication of *Les Contemplations*, Hugo wrote a series of prose works in which he discussed the steps in the creative process. In *Philosophie, commencement d'un livre* he divides the experience of metaphysical contemplation into three stages: "observer," "penser," "prier." First one can observe with the naked eye the magnificence of creation. After this period of enthusiastic observation, there follows a terrible sense of alienation:

> Une fois l'éblouissement de cette quantité de soleils passé, le coeur se serre, l'esprit tressaille, une idée vertigineuse et funèbre lui apparaît . . . l'état normal du ciel, c'est la nuit. . . . Cet immense monde que nous voyons et dont nous sommes, serait donc l'enfer? (ed. Massin, Vol. xii, pp. 30-1)

The final stage, that of prayer, is described as the rediscovery of natural order and the communication of it to the alienated world of men. That order is now "supernatural" and the contemplator is reborn as a kind of cosmic self:

> Le cerveau s'écroule; ceci s'en va. Où? Dans le prodigieux réceptacle du moi impérissable, dans la solidarité pensante de la création, dans le rendezvous des consciences, distinctes, quoique en communion; dans le lieu d'équilibre des libertés et des responsabilités; dans la vaste égalité de lumière universelle où les âmes sont les oiseaux des astres, dans l'infini. (Ibid., p. 50)

These three stages which result in the birth of a visionary work correspond to the "sourire," "sanglot," "bruit du clairon" evolution outlined in the preface to *Les Contemplations*. One

---

nify the spirit that elaborates them. For Hugo, the process by which patterns are inscribed into poetic language by the creative consciousness points toward a transcendental signifier of which he is the earthly reflection. "Le Verbe, c'est Dieu."

can find them represented in Books I-II, III-IV, and V-VI respectively. The work Hugo put together from the poetic fragments of his past is both a spiritual way and a poetic *grimoire*.

That *Les Contemplations* is really a religio-poetic allegory becomes clearer when one compares its formal organization to the metaphysical system as it is described in the final revelatory poem, "Ce que dit la bouche d'ombre." It is no accident that the reader is not given this key until the very end of the initiatory experience, for otherwise he would suffer no transformation. He would remain fixed in the alienated stage of "penser" in his relationship to the work. Angus Fletcher has commented upon the cryptic nature of all allegorical literature:

> If the style was and still remains difficult, that puts it in
> the main tradition of prophetic literature. . . . The poet
> can always justify his obscurity . . . because he claims to
> be presenting an inspired message. This is not mere al-
> legorical cleverness. It is the attitude of the prophet who
> in turn is reading the mind of some higher Being. . . .
> *Allegory thus would reach its highest plane in a symbolism*
> *that conveys the action of the mind.* (my italics)[13]

Very briefly, then, here is a description of the metaphysical system outlined in "Ce que dit la bouche d'ombre."[14] At the moment of Creation, imperfection or evil is born. Otherwise Creation would be indistinguishable from God or Perfect Unity. Nevertheless, at the very beginnings of Creation, this

---

[13] Fletcher, *Allegory*, pp. 277-78.

[14] Hugo's system is inspired by a very ancient tradition beginning with the radical monism of Plotinus. For a description of the philosophical history of emanation-metaphysics, see Abram's *Natural Supernaturalism*, pp. 146ff. The message of Hugo's "bouche d'ombre" is similar in many respects to that of Balzac's Swedenborgian mystic, Louis Lambert.

imperfection is nearly invisible. Matter consists of diaphanous angelic forms through which Divinity shines forth. Yet it is the nature of Creation that imperfection create more imperfection, and that the increasing weight of matter pull it further and further away from original purity. Thus there is established a ladder of being: angels or spirits are at the top, and the heaviest, mute forms at the bottom. Man exists somewhere in the middle, and he is distinguished by his consciousness which is a reflection of the original, Divine Logos. Thus, within Hugo's scheme of things, the cause of the Fall—the desire to know—is the source of man's potential redemption. He is in fact free to choose between a life devoted to the material existence, which reflects his fallen condition, and a life devoted to the contemplation of that superior and immaterial reality from which he issued. His soul is the reflection of that reality. Indeed, all things in the chain of being have souls and hence must be treated lovingly, but only man is capable of bringing about his own transcendence. Contemplation of his own essence and contemplation of God are synonymous. By turning material reality into communicable thought, that is to say by poeticizing his life, man moves closer to those divine origins. Thus God can be perceived by the highly developed contemplative genius through his imperfect and imprisoned material self.

This ideated reality (the poem or work) takes its place in the objective universe and serves as a medium through which the reader can be led in his turn to a superior level of experience. Indeed, once assimilated into the reader's imagination, it will become part of some future symbolic construct. For Hugo each chapter in this continuing narration, passed on from consciousness to consciousness, adds a new step up from the depths of the original Fall symbolized by Léopoldine's death.

The importance Hugo places upon individual freedom within a divinely ordered universe helps to explain further his deliberate attempt to obscure the lines of the narrative and hence to render impossible any "this means that" reading. Like Dante's pilgrim, the reader "awakes to find himself in a dark wood." Book I (*Aurore*) is by far the most confusing. Besides narrative complexities there are many other obscuring devices, which I will describe in Chapter IV on *Aurore*. It is only after he completes the entire journey that the reader can see the typological significance of that first book. AUTREFOIS and AUJOURD'HUI are temporal words which suggest the historical dialectic of the Old and New Testaments. But in the mid-nineteenth century Divine Order is even more mysterious and distant than it was for Dante's reader in 1300:

> The unquiet heart of the Christian pilgrim has grown quiet, and the very notion of a journey of the mind and heart to God in this life now requires such an effort of the historical imagination as would have been a veritable scandal to the medieval mind.[15]

Society can no longer recognize the spiritual quality of its own heroes. Quasimodo, Gilliatt, Gwynplaine are monstrous to the profane eye.

Although intentional mystification is true of much allegorical fiction,[16] in Hugo's case the shrouding of truth is directly related to his notion of freedom. The reader is expected to achieve insight into a larger, Cosmic Order through his own existential experience. Hugo's use of complex allegory assures the active intellectual and emotional participation of the reader, who is forced to make constant interpretive choices in order to find his way. Never is he offered the direct explanation provided by the abstractions of simple allegory.

Hugo as nineteenth-century allegorist obscures his meaning

[15] Charles Singleton, "The Allegorical Journey," *Dante Studies 2, Journey to Beatrice.* (Cambridge, Mass., 1958), p. 8.
[16] See Fletcher, *Allegory*, pp. 310, 330.

not just in order to prod his reader into an active interpretive role. He does so because chaos and disorder characterize the particular historical reality in which he finds himself. Thus his work assumes the *form* of history. One of his last great efforts was to bring meaning to the seemingly most mon-strous year of all—*Quatrevingt-Treize*. Disappearings, rifts, and darkenings proliferate throughout Hugo's work. In the last pages of *Les Misérables* we are told that the words on Jean Valjean's gravestone were eventually erased by time; in the first chapter of *Les Travailleurs de la mer*, that Gilliatt's name written in the snow by Déruchette had fallen into "une pro-fondeur obscure." The mysterious architecture of *Notre Dame de Paris* is built upon a word long since effaced from the wall of the cathedral. Yet none of these are final endings, but rather moments of apocalypse, promising a new, utopian world to come. Time repeatedly and persistently wipes away the origi-nal message. Every century must find a poet to reconstruct that message according to the reality within which he lives. Hugo imagined himself to be the scribe chosen for the nine-teenth century. Every one of his works after 1851 is an elaborate allegorical structure within which he inscribes the providential significance of historical reality.

Chateaubriand, Hugo, and Baudelaire all used allegory with a high degree of self-consciousness. Their relationship to one another and to French Romanticism generally can, perhaps, be grasped in terms of their use of this trope.

When Hugo mentions in the preface to *Les Contemplations* that his book could just as well have been called "*Les Mémoires d'une âme*, si le mot n'avait quelque prétention," he alludes to a Romantic genre represented by Rousseau's *Confessions* or Chateaubriand's *Mémoires d'outre-tombe*, a genre that by its very nature stresses the importance of individual genius. Yet despite his boyhood statement, "Je veux être Chateaubriand ou rien!" it is apparent that by the 1850's Hugo considered his ideology more fully evolved than that of his early hero. A comparison of Hugo's preface with Chateaubriand's "Avant-propos" to *Les Mémoires d'outre-tombe* reveals his intention to move beyond the cult of the idiosyncratic and personal toward the realization of a mystical and universal self. Chateaubriand was loath to give himself up to history:

> La triste nécessité qui m'a toujours tenu le pied sur la gorge, m'a forcé de vendre mes Mémoires. Personne ne peut savoir ce que j'ai souffert d'avoir été obligé d'hypothéquer ma tombe . . . . Par un attachement peut-être pusillanime, je regardais mes Mémoires comme des confidents dont je ne m'aurais pas voulu séparer. . . .

Hugo says:

> Nul de nous n'a l'honneur d'avoir une vie qui soit à lui. Ma vie est la vôtre, votre vie est la mienne, vous vivez ce que je vis; la destinée est une. Prenez donc ce miroir et regardez-vous-y.

That he had Chateaubriand in mind is clear when one compares the diction of the two introductions:

Chateaubriand:

> . . . les rayons de mon soleil, depuis son aurore jusqu'à son couchant, se croisant et se confondant, ont produit une sorte d'unité indéfinissable; mon berceau a de ma tombe, ma tombe a de mon berceau.

Hugo:

> C'est l'existence humaine sortant de l'énigme du berceau et aboutissant à l'énigme du cerceuil; c'est un esprit qui marche de lueur en lueur en laissant derrière lui la jeunesse, l'amour, l'illusion, le combat, le désespoir, et qui

s'arrête éperdu 'au bord de l'infini'. Cela *commence* par un sourire *continue* par un sanglot, et *finit* par un bruit du clairon de l'abîme. (my italics)

The tragic circularity of the first gives way in the second to a mystical progression toward salvation.

A study of the typological relationship of *Atala* and *René* reveals that Chateaubriand's use of allegory reflected his growing disillusionment. *Atala* can be read as a contemporary rewriting of *Genesis*. The book begins with the narrator's description of what was once a "new" paradise:

> La France possédait autrefois, dans l'Amérique septentrionale, un vaste empire qui s'étendait depuis la Labrador jusqu'aux Florides, et depuis les rivages de l'Atlantique jusqu'aux lacs les plus reculés du haut Canada.
>
> Quatre grands fleuves, ayant leurs sources dans les mêmes montagnes, divisaient ces régions immenses. . . . Ce dernier fleuve, dans un cours de plus de mille lieues, arrose une délicieuse contrée que les habitants des Etats-Unis appellent le nouvel Eden, . . .[17]

The action itself is, of course, postlapsarian. The reader watches Atala fight against the notion of sinfulness that is her maternal heritage as she and Chactas wander through the wilderness in search of a new beginning. Chateaubriand takes his characters further and further from that Original Oneness, even repeating their tragedy of separation in a yet more distorted form in *René*. In the end we hear from one of the last survivors of Chactas' tribe that René died a witness of "civilized" man's destruction of the "new Eden." René is characterized in the second novel as even more hopelessly alienated than Chactas, for

[17] *Atala, René, Le Dernier Abencérage*, ed. Letessier (Paris: Garnier, 1962), pp. 29-30.

he has become a prisoner of his own imagination, utterly incapable of connecting with anyone outside of himself. Chateaubriand's use of allegory, which points toward an endless spiral away from Paradise into pure subjectivity, will find a parallel in Baudelaire's work.

Hugo, on the other hand, would take language beyond the necessary stage of inwardness characterized by the genre of the memoir, or the incestuous introspection of Chateaubriand's quest, to a direct apprehension of Divinity. This ultimate stage of enlightenment that he later calls "la contemplation suprême" reunites the alienated human soul with a heightened or supernatural world beyond the restrictions of time and space.

It is the second-generation Romantic poets' belief in the redemptive potentiality of human consciousness that separates them dramatically from Baudelaire and that inspires Hugo's letter written after Baudelaire's publication of his essay on Gautier:

Vous ne vous trompez pas en prévoyant quelque dissidence entre vous et moi. Je comprends toute votre philosophie . . . je fais plus que la comprendre, je l'admets; mais je garde la mienne. Je n'ai jamais dit: l'art pour l'art; j'ai toujours dit: l'art pour le progrès. Au fond, c'est la même chose, et votre esprit est trop pénétrant pour ne pas le sentir. En avant! C'est le mot du progrès; c'est aussi le cri de l'art. Tout le verbe de la poésie est là. *Ite*. . . . L'art n'est pas perfectible, je l'ai dit, je crois, un des premiers; donc je le sais; personne ne dépassera Eschyle; personne ne dépassera Phidias; mais on peut les égaler; et, pour les égaler, il faut déplacer les horizons de l'art, monter plus haut, aller plus loin, marcher. Le poëte ne peut aller seul, il faut que l'homme aussi se déplace. Les pas de l'humanité

29

sont donc les pas mêmes de l'art.—Donc, gloire au Progrès. C'est pour le progrès que je souffre en ce moment. . . .[18]

Baudelaire utterly rejects this utopian optimism, later to be so vigorously expressed in *Les Misérables*. For him man is tainted once and for all with the sin of existence.

Hélas! du Péché Originel, même après tant de progrès depuis si longtemps promis, il restera toujours bien assez de traces pour en constater l'immémoriale réalité.[19]

The younger and more disillusioned poet sees man frozen within his own alienated imagination, forever dreaming about an unattainable ideal. Like the swan's or Andromaque's nostalgic dreaming in "Le Cygne," allegory no longer expresses the power of human consciousness to communicate redemptively and to alter the course of human events, but rather enunciates the poet's resignation before the ultimate failure of language to carry us beyond its own self-referential constructs. Poetic language with its dizzying, infinitely allusive character signifies for Baudelaire man's state of permanent exile within the pure temporality of impermanence.

Paris change! mais rien dans ma mélancolie
N'a bougé! palais neufs, échafaudages, blocs,
Vieux faubourgs, tout pour moi devient allégorie,
Et mes chers souvenirs sont plus lourds que des rocs.

Aussi devant ce Louvre une image m'opprime:
Je pense à mon grand cygne, avec ses gestes fous,
Comme les exilés, ridicule et sublime,
Et rongé d'un désir sans trêve! et puis à vous,

[18] "Victor Hugo à Charles Baudelaire," 6 Oct. 1859, *Oeuvres complètes*, ed. Massin, Vol. x, p. 1327.
[19] "Les Misérables par Victor Hugo," *Oeuvres complètes*, p. 1149.

Andromaque, des bras d'un grand époux tombée,
Vil bétail, sous la main du superbe Pyrrhus,
Auprès d'un tombeau vide en extase courbée;
Veuve d'Hector, hélas! et femme d'Hélénus!

Hugo, the exiled poet to whom Baudelaire dedicates his poem, is for him one of those sublime but ridiculous fools who continue to believe in an absent Presence.

Baudelaire's nostalgic despair recalls that of Chateaubriand, the very poet beyond whom Hugo tried to move. Baudelaire's admiration for that other great dandy seems to be unrestricted.[20] "Chateaubriand a chanté la gloire douloureuse de la mélancolie et de l'ennui," he says in *Théophile Gautier*. The ennui that pervades *Les Fleurs du mal* is curiously akin to the paralyzed brooding upon the past of "le grand René." Both poets are like the swan, their necks twisted backward toward an idealized past.

Whereas Hugo would have the bouquet of verses he sends to Villequier from his island of exile carry with them the mediating power of prayer, Baudelaire's verses remain flowers born out of the imperfection of existence ("les fleurs maladives") symbols of the tomb of language itself. To contemplate them is to contemplate one's own mortality: "Auprès

---

[20] One of the reasons Baudelaire loathed Villemain was that he had dared to criticize the *Mémoires d'outre-tombe*. See "L'Esprit et le style de M. Villemain," *Oeuvres complètes*, pp. 1153-54:

"C'est bien la jugeote d'un pédagogue, incapable d'apprécier le grand gentilhomme des décadences, qui veut retourner à la vie sauvage.
A propos des débuts de Chateaubriand au regiment, il lui reproche son goût de la parure. Il lui reproche l'inceste comme source de génie. Eh! que m'importe à moi la source, si je jouis du génie!
Les Villemain ne comprendront jamais que les Chateaubriand ont droit à des immunités et à des indulgences auxquelles tous les Villemain de l'humanité ne pourront jamais aspirer."

d'un tombeau *vide* en extase courbée." The movement away from temporal existence—*anywhere out of this world*—toward a moment of ideal harmony, a kind of musical-pictorial stasis, and the fall back to an ironic awareness of the solipsistic nature of his quest constitute the structure of a significant number of Baudelaire's poems and of the first part of *Les Fleurs du mal* ("Spleen et Idéal"). The mane of hair, the cadaver, the swan, are all symbols that postulate an order greater than themselves and begin the voyage by which the poet hopes to attain to that Ideal Order. But the symbol, despite its power to point toward an Ideal Unity, reveals itself in a seductive sensual form ("comme une femme lubrique"), and thus inevitably draws the poet back to the evanescent world of his own fallen condition from which he hoped to escape. Like the dog in "Une Charogne" he returns to sniff the intoxicating odor of mortality. The last stanza of that poem is spoken in the mode of the sixteenth-century *carpe diem* love poem, but with the irony of the disillusioned post-Romantic poet:

> Alors, ô ma beauté! dites à la vermine
> Qui vous mangera de baisers,
> Que j'ai gardé la forme et l'essence divine
> De mes amours décomposés!

Thus form (composition) in Baudelaire's work contains within it, as its subject, the worm of time, the destruction ("décomposition") of idyllic duration.

It is paradoxical that allegory is the mode that translates both Hugo's messianic poetics and Baudelaire's disillusioned idealism. Unlike symbol, allegory does not attempt to render divinity incarnate. Its apprehension involves the reader in an experience of temporality fundamentally different from that which attends his enjoyment of symbolic expression. Allegory requires a sequential reading of the text and hence the reader's historic consciousness—his ability to recognize the allusive and

32

conventionalized nature of art. The use of allegory, then, reflects for both writers preoccupation with the inescapability of the temporal dimension.[21] Hugo sees the present within a meaningful continuum emerging from the past and moving toward the future; Baudelaire sees duration as an ideal state, with death and disillusionment as an inescapable conclusion to that ideal. Whereas Baudelaire uses allegorical diction to state poetically the failure to achieve transcendence through symbolic language, Hugo's allegorical narrative encloses within it the assertion of Unity, of Divine Duration. The difference between the two poets, then, is that for Baudelaire the recognition of man's temporal nature constitutes a fall from the ideal promised by the symbol, and for Hugo it begins man's struggle toward spirituality within the framework of a poeticized history, a struggle that can be communicated allegorically —from consciousness to consciousness—and is the subject of the following chapters.

[21] Paul de Man, "The Rhetoric of Temporality," points out that the switch from metaphoric to allegorical diction in *La Nouvelle Héloïse* poetically reflects Rousseau's recognition of man's temporal nature. His conclusion is helpful to our consideration of Hugo and Baudelaire: "Whether it occurs in the form of an ethical conflict, as in *La Nouvelle Héloïse*, or as an allegorization of the geographical site, as in Wordsworth, the prevalence of allegory always corresponds to the unveiling of an authentically temporal destiny. This unveiling takes place in a subject that has sought refuge against the impact of time in a natural world to which, in truth, it bears no resemblance." Hugo can be said to be a precursor of modernism in that he understands that signification lies in the structures of language itself, but he differs dramatically from Baudelaire and other post-Romantic poets in that he believes that this power to signify affirms the truth of Being, of an ontological Presence that exists prior to and outside of poetic creation, but that can be perceived through it.

II

THE STRUCTURE OF
HUGO'S ALLEGORY

L IKE THE metaphysical scheme described in "Ce que dit la
bouche d'ombre," the chapters in *Les Contemplations* move
from the light of *Aurore* (Genesis) to the darkness and imprisoned forms of *Les Luttes et les rêves* (Sodom and Gomorrah) and back to the light of the final revelation in *Au
bord de l'infini* (Salvation).[1]

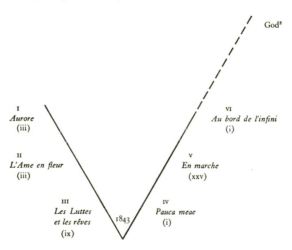

[1] Jacques Roos in *Les Idées philosophiques de Victor Hugo* has
pointed out this direction in Ballanche's cosmogony: rupture with
original unity leads to division and dispersion and through expiation
back to original unity. Roos supplies a detailed breakdown of simi-
larities between Ballanche's and Hugo's religious ideas.

[2] God or the Ideal is never reached without the annihilation of consciousness. This is what happens at the end of *Dieu*. His presence,
however, is perceived and asserted.

This is the structure of the new Romantic mythology that posits the redemptive power of language. It also corresponds visually to Léopoldine's symbolical drowning-descent, which Hugo placed at the center of the book.

Dante (iii,i) leads the narrator into the death experience, announced in the preface. The inward descent is necessary for the birth of the disembodied angelic forms of Book vi. The spirit-forms in turn lead him back up toward a visionary state corresponding to the Original Creation, when God's presence could still be felt. Book vi is in fact characterized at once by the absence of restricting material boundaries and by its rhythmic force.

The evolution of the Léopoldine figure (i,iii; ii,iii; etc.), which I will analyze in more detail in the next chapter, follows the same pattern. Her presence undergoes a series of transformations that make her less and less recognizable in a biographical sense. (I refer to Léopoldine rather than to any of her sister forms because Hugo himself ordered the work around the date of her drowning, thus demonstrating the historical origins of his poetic vision.) In ii,iii she appears as Europa, in iii,ix, a sacrificial virgin, in iv as a mediating angel. Thus from the innocent childhood of *Aurore* one moves to the ambivalent, highly sensual sacrificial figure of *Les Luttes et les rêves* to the symbolical drowning-death. In the final book of the collection, *Au bord de l'infini*, she becomes an angelic reflection of the poet's own divine soul.

Since Hugo's narrative operates on several levels simultaneously, it may be helpful to sum up as concisely as possible what these levels are. From the visionary's point of view the work can be compared to the pattern a pebble makes when thrown into a pond. Contemporary man, who stands on the farthermost ring of the widening gyre of creation, is blind to his own significance. He is not able to discern from his limited temporal standpoint that his ring or life parallels all past and

35

future rings—that the beginnings of Creation and the course of universal consciousness reflect one another. It is the role of the visionary, be he poet, scientist or philosopher, to bring that pattern into focus for the rest of mankind. Since each man, each period in history, and each planet occupies a different position within the Divine Scheme, the language of this revelation must change. Greek mythology and lyric poetry, for example, were no longer meaningful for the medieval mind. The Christian mass and epic poetry ceased to be revelatory for the eighteenth-century rationalist. The Romantic visionary, in turn, had to invent a new set of mediating symbols for post-revolutionary man.

Hugo's poem is intended to contain that new set of signs. It operates on at least three levels, and each of these three levels is composed of further subdivisions. On the first level, that of argument, the poet wishes to describe to his reader, indeed to *teach* him, the nature of the Ideal, and to show him the parallel between his own seemingly absurd individuality and this Divine Scheme. Hugo does this by using the events in his own life as steps in a universal metaphysical Order. The pattern of that Order, clearly outlined in the last poem ("Ce que dit la bouche d'ombre"), is not very different from that of traditional Christian theology: birth, fall from innocence, recognition, suffering, and redemption. This pattern applies both to Original Creation and to the creation of man; that is to say, Lucifer's fall is reflected in the exile of Adam from Paradise, which in turn is reflected in every individual's coming of age, including that of Léopoldine, Hugo, or the reader himself. The poet as constitutive (allegorizing) consciousness then traces the events of his life for us according to this scheme. He is at once Lucifer, postlapsarian Adam, Everyman, and a particular nineteenth-century man with a specific biography. The six books of the collection all operate on each of these levels. *Aurore* is at once the beginning of Creation, the beginning of Hugo's own life, the beginning of Léopoldine's life, and the first step in an ever-renewing creative process. *L'Ame en fleur* is the ripening of Creation, Adam's discovery of Eve, a sensually awakened Léopoldine, and a "primitive" consciousness enthralled with lyric form. *Les Luttes et les rêves* is the Fall or the revelation of evil on all levels and the breakdown of the poetic voice into rhetorical imprecations and rigidly conventionalized forms. In *Pauca meae* Léopoldine's drowning figures the divine punishment visited upon Lucifer, Adam, Christ, and Hugo himself. It relegates all previous experience of creation (birth, sensual awakening, and recognition of evil) to the past. From Book IV on, the poet-narrator must draw his inspiration from the inwardness of his own memory. *En marche* reveals the possibility of redemption through that exiled consciousness and *Au bord de l'infini*, the visionary experience itself. These steps, represented by the six books, are also reflected in the thematic ordering of the poems within each book and even within individual poems themselves. Thus each element is both Genesis and the entire Scripture. In *Aurore*, for example, which was, after all, conceived by a fallen consciousness, innocence and joy are replaced by a mounting apocalyptic tone. The chapter ends with the redemptive symbol of Christ's shining hair in the hand of his executioner, yet this symbol is contained within the idyllic surroundings of a country inn—just as the apocalypse is contained within the birth of Creation (*Aurore*) itself. In *L'Ame en fleur*, the joyous lovers gradually retreat from nature into the tight circle of their own shadows, yet their uneasiness is contained within a lyric form. Thus each chapter is a microcosm of the entire work.

Hugo's purpose in presenting the general metaphysical pattern simultaneously as both part and totality becomes clearer after a consideration of the second level on which the work operates. The Romantic visionary is not content merely to describe the Divine Order to us as he imagines his poetic ancestors (Milton, Dante) did. He would make visionaries of his readers as well. Indeed, the difference between the medieval allegorist's and Hugo's Romantic use of the trope is that Hugo believes that he can and should influence the course of history. The poet, then, is both Lucifer and the Creator, as he is in the myth of Prometheus. It is his satanic awareness that provides him with the means for reconstructing the mythic pattern and hence for communicating it redemptively. An educated humanity, a humanity that has undergone the visionary experience and possesses thereby an expanded consciousness, will be closer to the angelic forms from which it has fallen, and social evils will in part disappear. Hugo thus conceives of his own exile (from which he wrote in rapid succession *Les Châtiments* and *Les Contemplations*—at one point he even planned to publish them under the same cover) as both a political and a poetic statement. Since he wishes to involve the reader in his narrative, he arranges the poems in such a way as to assure the reader's vicarious and repeated experience of the Divine Scheme (innocence, sensuous awakening, fall, and redemption). Like Adam or Everyman, the reader is at first seduced by his own sensuous involvement in the poetic creation. An awakened consciousness must, however, follow if he is to understand the redemptive message. The critic, who is the counterpart of the poetic visionary, discovers that the subject-object paradox applies to him as reader as well as to the poet as writer. He, like the poet, is both Lucifer and Creator. He is acted upon by the text and he acts upon it. Again the order of the six parts and the arrangement of the poems within each part reflects Hugo's concern with the reader's experience. The language of the lyric poems of *L'Ame en fleur* seems much more familiar than that of the long visionary works of *Au bord de l'infini*. This may explain why the vast majority of casual readers of Hugo proclaim their enthusiastic appreciation of the first half of *Les Contemplations* and their dislike of the long, apocalyptic verse. In *Aurore, L'Ame en fleur,* or *Pauca meae,* for example, one is touched by the poeticized biography of the man's life. The poems are generally not long, and either one feels no need for a sustained narrative reading (as in the case of *Aurore*) or the narrative focus is superficially apparent. Yet within these books, Hugo makes certain that the reader is from time to time jolted out of his conventionalized reading and his passive role of observer. Abrupt changes in rhythm, a sudden shift in point of view, or the introduction of an unexpected event such as the Titan's fall in "Eglogue" (ii,xii) occur throughout Book i. Whenever this unsettling effect takes place, the reader's reaction to the surrounding poems, however innocent they may appear, is influenced by an ironic distancing. I shall examine in more detail in the following chapters how the arrangement of the poems within each book is artfully designed to awaken the reader's critical consciousness. What must be kept in mind is that the reader is as much a questing hero as the narrator is, and that as he progresses through the allegory, he gains a critical perspective that imitates the *felix culpa* of the mythic scheme.

Any discussion of the means by which the poet seeks to influence the reader's experience of his work leads directly to the third level on which the poem operates, that of language itself. The new creation in which the fallen reader finds mirrored the redemptive pattern leading back to original Creation is a purely formal construct. Certain changes in Hugo's use of poetic tropes reflect the same determination to use the very condition of man's fallen state—his historicity—to transcend that condition. If allegory and metonymy are tropes that, because of their sequential nature, depend upon and hence assert man's temporality for their proper interpretation, metaphor, and—even more dramatically—symbol could be said to be tropes of simultaneity by means of which a superior, atemporal level of reality can be perceived. Their use reflects the poet's belief in the mediating power of language—that is, its power to conjure forth Divinity directly. A more detailed examination of *Les Contemplations* will reveal that Hugo is aware of the philosophical implications of the use of these tropes. Since he believes that man can achieve divine insight through his fallen condition (*felix culpa*), he uses tropes that require a temporal relationship—metonymy and allegory—in order to assert the timeless (symbolic) nature of the universe.

Hugo's intentionality in regard to his use of certain poetic devices is made clear in the evolution of Léopoldine as a figure for poetic language. Since she was Hugo's daughter in real life—that is, a metonymic and temporal extension of himself—she provides the perfect parallel for the subject-object paradox the poet establishes on the levels of argument and experience. His fallen creation in real life becomes the creating medium through which the reader experiences the redemptive pattern. Her drowning dissolves her limited material form and makes her a sacred vessel for the questing hero. In general, the figure evolves, again according to the mythic pattern, from a pictorially described image of real life out of which a metaphor is born (i,iii, "Mes deux filles") to a metonymic presence charged with symbolic traceries (ii,iii, "Le Rouet d'Omphale") and then to an allegorical figure whose every attribute has symbolic significance (iii,ix). In Part ii (AUJOURD'HUI) she is an ever-present mythological persona in the narrator's increasingly dramatic journey toward revelation. Thus the sensuous appeal of the descriptive image gives way to an intellectually contrived emblem that in turn gives way to the mythic figures of the fully awakened consciousness—the "observer," "penser," "prier" of the evolution of human consciousness itself. Léopoldine is not a *single* symbolic form through which one can glimpse eternity, but rather a *changing* allegorical persona who guides us along the way. If the reader remains transfixed by any one of her presences, as her creator is tempted to do in *Aurore* or *Pauca meae*, he negates the very condition—his existential reality—that permits ultimate salvation and fails to respond to the sacred call.

I have said that Hugo's poetic and metaphysical universe can be compared to the widening circles a pebble makes when thrown into a pond. Each poem in *Les Contemplations* reflects more or less clearly, depending upon where it has been placed in the narrative scheme, the redemptive pattern I have described in the preceding pages. Thus, Hugo's poetic universe is both metonymic and analogical; each part points to a whole that is beyond itself, but that it contains. Before going on to look at the more obscure or buried pattern of the Léopoldine poems and from there to the themes and techniques governing the six books of *Les Contemplations* as a whole, it may be useful to illustrate Hugo's redemptive order with one of these metonymic analogues.

"Pasteurs et troupeaux" could be described as a parable of Hugo's metaphysical scheme. Both technically and thematically it is a concentrated dramatic rendering of the larger development within which it stands. Significantly, "Pasteurs et troupeaux" is found in Book v, where, as we shall see in chapter VIII, the poems take on a metapoetic dimension as reflections upon the reflections of the earlier books. Thus the work as an allegory of its own creation is strikingly clear.

Pasteurs et Troupeaux

A madame Louise C

Le vallon où je vais tous les jours est charmant,
Serein, abandonné, seul sous le firmament,
Plein de ronces en fleurs; c'est un sourire triste.
Il vous fait oublier que quelque chose existe,

41

Et, sans le bruit des champs remplis de travailleurs,
On ne saurait plus là si quelqu'un vit ailleurs.
Là, l'ombre fait l'amour; l'idylle naturelle
Rit; le bouvreuil avec le verdier s'y querelle,
Et la fauvette y met de travers son bonnet;
C'est tantôt l'aubépine et tantôt le genêt;
De noirs granits bourrus, puis des mousses riantes;
Car Dieu fait un poëme avec des variantes;
Comme le vieil Homère, il rabâche parfois,
Mais c'est avec les fleurs, les monts, l'onde et les bois!
Une petite mare est là, ridant sa face,
Prenant des airs de flot pour la fourmi qui passe,
Ironie étalée au milieu du gazon,
Qu'ignore l'océan grondant à l'horizon.
J'y rencontre parfois sur la roche hideuse
Un doux être; quinze ans, yeux bleus, pieds nus, gardeuse
De chèvres, habitant, au fond d'un ravin noir,
Un vieux chaume croulant qui s'étoile le soir;
Ses soeurs sont au logis et filent leur quenouille;
Elle essuie aux roseaux ses pieds que l'étang mouille;
Chèvres, brebis, béliers, paissent; quand, sombre esprit,
J'apparais, le pauvre ange a peur, et me sourit;
Et moi, je la salue, elle étant l'innocence.
Ses agneaux, dans le pré plein de fleurs qui l'encense,
Bondissent, et chacun, au soleil s'empourprant,
Laisse aux buissons, à qui la bise le reprend,
Un peu de sa toison, comme un flocon d'écume.
Je passe, enfant, troupeau, s'effacent dans la brume;
Le crépuscule étend sur les longs sillons gris
Ses ailes de fantôme et de chauve-souris;
J'entends encore au loin dans la plaine ouvrière
Chanter derrière moi la douce chevrière,
Et, là-bas, devant moi, le vieux gardien pensif
De l'écume, du flot, de l'algue, du récif,

Et des vagues sans trêve et sans fin remuées,
Le pâtre promontoire au chapeau de nuées,
S'accoude et rêve au bruit de tous les infinis,
Et, dans l'ascension des nuages bénis,
Regarde se lever la lune triomphale,
Pendant que l'ombre tremble, et que l'âpre rafale
Disperse à tous les vents avec son souffle amer
La laine des moutons sinistres de la mer.

Jersey, Grouville, avril 1855.

The title illustrates the relatedness of the naive and visionary voices characteristic of Hugo's art. The pastoral setting announced by shepherds and their flocks is inevitably enriched for the Christian reader by associations with the Holy Shepherd and the Sacrificial Lamb. One can, in fact, see how, in typical Hugolian fashion, the apparently clear-cut "pasteur-troupeau" opposition will be transformed into a relationship of sacred interdependence.

As in *Les Contemplations* as a whole, the general dramatic movement in "Pasteurs et troupeaux" is from the particular to the general, from the familiar to the cosmic, from multiplicity to unity. Like AUTREFOIS and AUJOURD'HUI, the poem is divided into three parts or steps, and in each one the reader experiences an enlarging of his vision. The sunlit happiness and naiveté one associates with the first chapters of the collection, *Aurore* and *L'Ame en fleur,* characterize the first eighteen lines of the poem. Multiplicity of objects, enumeration, repetition ("tantôt," "tantôt," "là," "là," "là"), and metonymically related oppositions ("bouvreuil"-"verdier"; "aubépine"-"genêt"; "granits bourrus"-"mousses riantes"; "mare"-"océan") create a chaos of forms through which the narrator wanders. In this first part of the poem he is closer to the carefree lyric dreamer figured in *Aurore*: "Le poète s'en va dans les champs . . ." (I,ii) than to the prophet of Book VI. But, just as in many

43

Aurore poems, the dominating light-hearted tone disguises a number of disturbing elements that announce the storm to be unleashed at the end of the poem. The same unsettling effects that jolt the reader out of his passive enjoyment of the lyric poetry of *Aurore* operate here. The poet reminds one from the outset that this conventionalized setting is a fool's paradise: "Il vous fait oublier que quelque chose existe," and "On ne saurait plus là si quelqu'un vit ailleurs." The "charming" events described contain their own potential explosion—birds quarrel, a pond teases an ant—and words with postlapsarian connotations proliferate: "ronces," "triste," "travailleurs," "querelle," "de travers," "bourrus," "prenant des airs," "ignore," "grondant." But most disturbing for the reader are the highly literary or artificial terms the narrator uses to describe natural phenomena: "L'idylle naturelle / Rit" (the enjambement adds to our malaise); "Car Dieu fait un poème avec des variantes, / Comme le vieil Homère, il rabâche parfois," culminating with the metaphorical transformation of an aspect of nature into an alienated attitude of the mind:

> Une petite mare est là, ridant sa face,
> Prenant des airs de flot pour la fourmi qui passe,
> Ironie étalée au milieu du gazon,
> Qu'ignore l'océan grondant à l'horizon.

Irony is repeated on many levels. Just as the little pond imitates the great ocean, Hugo appears to be imitating La Fontaine, only to make a striking formal departure from classical prosody by introducing two examples of the forbidden hiatus when irony is named: "Ironie étalée au. . . ." By telling us that the pond reflects more than it thinks it does, the narrator asserts himself as decipherer of hidden meanings and the poem as parable for some larger truth.

The same dramatic development from calm to storm, reflected in the first eighteen lines and finally in the poem as a whole, is also felt on the level of poetic diction in the first sentence of "Pasteurs et troupeaux." Once again it is evident that the reflection of the whole in the part is crucial to Hugo's vision. The first line sounds like nothing more than a cliché observation, closer to the devitalized language of everyday discourse than to the privileged language of seers: "Le vallon où je vais tous les jours est charmant." There follows, however, in rapid succession such a piling up of modifying elements in the second and third lines that the sentence loses its place within conventional discourse and becomes increasingly strange, i.e., poetic. Whereas "charmant" has lost all poetic value from overuse, the three adjectives that constitute the second line of the poem: "serein," "abandonné," "seul sous le firmament" personify the valley in stronger and stronger terms by evoking a threatening but invisible "other" which is somehow responsible for the valley's state of being. The contradictory implications of "serein" and "abandonné, seul sous le firmament," on a semantic or referential level, are glossed over, however, by the alliterative cohesion of the phrase on a purely phonological level. A new poetic language, it would seem, is struggling to be born out of prose in these first few lines. The tension between appearance and reality, meaning and form, is finally stated as the truth hidden in the valley—first naturalistically and finally metaphorically: "Plein de ronces en fleurs; c'est un sourire triste." Thus poetic diction bursts forth, appropriately in the form of oxymoron. It will be the role of the poet, whose observing presence we see reflected ironically in the landscape he describes, to reveal the correspondences that link and structure a seemingly chaotic external reality. Already, in the metaphorizing consciousness, opposites are overcome, but not without a note of suffering and sacrifice: "c'est un sourire triste."

The second dramatic development in the poem is the encounter of the narrator with another human awareness in this "abandoned" landscape that is a conventionalized projection of his own literary heritage. She is an innocent but pubescent shepherdess who is both frightened by and drawn to the narrator, who names himself "sombre esprit." She is, quite literally, nature personified. A familiar poetic device used throughout the first part of the poem is given life, transformed into a flesh-and-blood presence, naturalized and objectified. The thirteen lines of this second part are divided into two sentences. The first focuses on the shepherdess, and the second on her flock. Thus the dramatic event of encounter is reflected in the binary nature of the syntax. Everything in this part, however, works to reinforce the conflicting, antithetical *appearance* of reality. Meter and syntax are far more disturbing here than they were in the first eighteen lines. Two different durations are established—one syntactic and one rhythmic. The development of an idea may be concluded in the middle of a line, and a new notion may be introduced in the second hemistich, and then extended into the next line. Thus a tension is created between referential and non-referential levels of discourse:

> J'y rencontre parfois sur la roche hideuse
> Un doux être; quinze ans, yeux bleus, pieds nus, gardeuse
> De chèvres, habitant, au fond d'un ravin noir,
> Un vieux chaume croulant qui s'étoile le soir;
> . . .
> Chèvres, brebis, béliers, paissent; quand, sombre esprit,
> J'apparais, le pauvre ange a peur, et me sourit;

This rent in the formal texture of the poem is paralleled by an interruption in the dramatic unity of the scene with the introduction in line 23 of the shepherdess's sisters: "Ses soeurs sont au logis et filent leur quenouille." Since they are invisible to the natural eye, unlike the other aspects of the landscape thus far, their presence here seems gratuitous. It is, of course, their very gratuitousness that endows the landscape with mysterious, mythological significance. The temporal specificity of such words as "tous les jours" (l. 1) and "parfois" (l. 19), begin to lose their reassuring function of anchoring us to everyday reality. This encounter, which only *sometimes* occurs in the valley where the narrator goes *daily*, has something of the marvelous ("charmant") about it. The very specific "roche hideuse" where it takes place becomes a sacred locus. The blue-eyed child-woman who shyly but sensuously wipes her bare feet on the reeds over which the "mare-étang-océan" has washed, is approaching her expulsion from paradise; she is the muse who will unleash the storm of visionary experiences that follow. She is the angel touched with human frailty at the center of Hugo's book; Europa etched on the plinth of Omphale's spinning wheel (II,iii), horrified to see the monstrous ocean lick at her toes; the sacrificial virgin of poem ix of *Les Luttes et les rêves*, around whom Don Juan hovers.

The effect of the encounter between the innocent muse and the satanic apprehending consciousness is felt immediately. The second sentence, focusing on the lambs, is charged with symbolic, sacrificial value and begins the dynamism that will also characterize Hugo's ultimate visionary expression in Book VI. Verbal forms proliferate and are placed strategically within the sentence so as to overcome traditional boundaries for poetic duration: "Bondissent, et chacun, au soleil s'empourprant, / Laisse aux buissons, à qui la bise le reprend." Alliteration (*s,b*) and internal rimes ("Bondissent," "buissons," "toison," "flocon") help carry the couplets beyond themselves. By comparing the bits of fleece left on the naturalistic bushes to "flocons d'écume" the poet reminds his reader of the almost forgotten oceanic presence which he had mentioned casually in line 18. The poem moves, from now on, irrevocably forward both in space and time toward the final vision.

Je passe, enfant, troupeau, s'effacent dans la brume;
. . .
J'entends encore au loin dans la plaine ouvrière
Chanter derrière moi la douce chevrière,
Et, la-bas, devant moi. . . .

The idyll is behind him (the backward-glancing rhyme, "che-vrière"-"derrière," tells us that poetically), effaced ("s'effacent") before a new beginning in the creative process. The unity of vision is formally complemented by the single complex sentence of these final fifteen lines. The chaos of forms and multiplicity of images that characterized the early part of the poem give way to one strikingly concrete figure that rises up in front of the narrator: "Le pâtre promontoire au chapeau de nuées / S'accoude et rêve au bruit de tous les infinis." As in Book VI, the narrator-decipherer has been transformed for the reader into a porous vessel, a perceiving awareness through whom he can know without fully understanding. The image of poet as shepherd is not expressed as a metaphor implying some distance between the poeticizing consciousness and external reality, as in the title or the first part of the poem: "sourire triste," "Ironie étalée." Hugo does not write "Le promontoire qui, pâtre," but rather presents the reader with a concrete image bringing man and nature ("pasteurs et troupeaux") into an inextricably interdependent relationship. It is impossible to say which of these nouns carries more adjectival value. For Hugo, the tension between tenor and vehicle characteristic of metaphoric language has thus been overcome. He would represent in a single symbolic figure the analogical relationships uniting Man, Nature, and God. The rationally impossible concept of "tous les infinis," where plurality and singularity are indistinguishable, can now replace the mundane and temporal "tous les jours" that began the adventure. Hugo's own historical reality—"Jersey, Grouville, avril 1855"—is thus filled with mythological importance.

Something of the same movement from metaphoric to symbolic diction takes place with the fleece imagery. "Comme un flocon d'écume" (l. 31) becomes "La laine des moutons sinistres de la mer" in the final line of the poem. Clichés or metaphors deadened from overuse both begin and end the poem ("charmant," "mouton de la mer"), but at the end they have been revitalized, rendered "other" by the dramatic enactment of the poeticizing process which has gone before.[3] The valley is "charming" in its original etymological sense; it is a place from which song (carmen) will be born. The lambs are "sinistres," strange, other-worldly in the way that a deconventionalized poetry is "sinistre." One could say, then, that in this poem, just as in the collection as a whole, Hugo enacts the rebirth of language itself. Its meaning is the process of its own coming into being. Man's ability to name is what distinguishes him from the animal: "Le vallon où je vais tous les jours *est* charmant." In this sense all language is a symbolizing process. But words become empty, self-referential signs from overuse; signs of absence rather than presence, like Léopoldine's tomb, to which Hugo ultimately dedicates his book. He seeks to fill each word with a generative presence, to resurrect the life for which it was substituted, to turn mere

---

[3] The Russian formalist, Victor Shklovsky, defines poetic language as a process of defamiliarization: "And art exists that one may recover the sensation of life; it exists to make one feel things, to make the stone *stony*. The purpose of art is to impart the sensation of things as they are perceived and not as they are known. The technique of art is to make objects "unfamiliar," to make forms difficult, to increase the difficulty and length of perception because the process of perception is an aesthetic end in itself and must be prolonged. *Art is a way of experiencing the artfulness of an object; the object is not important.*" "Art as Technique," *Russian Formalist Criticism*, ed. by Lee T. Lemon and Marion J. Reis (Lincoln, 1965), p. 12.

signs into symbols pointing beyond themselves. In the epilogue poem, "A celle qui est restée en France," he will send his book, figured as a bridegroom, back to the grave at Villequier, which has now been transformed into a marriage bed:

Que ce livre, du moins, obscur message, arrive,
. . .
Qu'il entre en ce sépulcre où sont entrés un jour
Le baiser, la jeunesse, et l'aube, et la rosée,
Et le rire adoré de la fraîche épousée,
. . .
Qu'elle dise: Quelqu'un est là; j'entends du bruit!
Qu'il soit comme le pas de mon âme en sa nuit!

At the end of "Pasteurs et troupeaux" a movement of ascension representative of the final chapter of *Les Contemplations* replaces the Dantesque descent into the valley which began the journey: "Et, dans l'ascension des nuages bénis, / Regarde se lever la lune triomphale." This redemptive image is followed immediately by a final view of the tumultuous sea to which the lambs, like Léopoldine, have been sacrificed, thus ending the poem on a seemingly sinister note. Each sentence in "Pasteurs et troupeaux," like each chapter in *Les Contemplations* as a whole, builds toward a larger, more all-encompassing vision, then recedes, but never quite so far back as before, until the final vision in which opposites are reconciled: the sea and "L'Océan d'en haut" are revealed as the same thing. Hugo's poetic language is the medium that has made real the relationship between God, the unique, light-giving circular moon, and Creation, the oceanic chaos from which all things are born and to which they inevitably return. A single divine principle ("la lune triomphale") governs the flux and reflux of creation on all levels.

In the following chapter we shall see how the redemptive structure of "Pasteurs et troupeaux" is repeated in the evolution of the Léopoldine figure through the six books. Every path in *Les Contemplations* leads ultimately to the same end, and the constant repetition of the narrative pattern ensures for the reader a temporal experience of Hugo's redemptive message.

III

LEOPOLDINE—MEDIATING ANGEL

THE REAL, historical origins of his allegorical message are inscribed into the very center of Hugo's book. "4 SEPTEMBRE 1843," the date of Léopoldine's drowning, is the "poem" around which *Les Contemplations* is structured. An examination of Léopoldine's transposition from a figure in Hugo's life into the fictional space of his work demonstrates how the poet's perception of his daughter's death began the creative process that ended with *Les Contemplations*.

The choice of Léopoldine as the real-life source for his central poetic figure must have been largely due to the configuration of events that surrounded her drowning and Hugo's subsequent exile. The circumstances of her death are well known, but their curiously providential significance cannot be sufficiently stressed.[1] On February 15, 1843, the day of Léopoldine's marriage, Hugo wrote a poem to her during the private ceremony: "Adieu! sois son trésor, ô toi qui fus le nôtre!" This is the poem he places directly before the apocalyptic date, September 4, 1843, in *Pauca meae*. Léopoldine sent Juliette Drouet, Hugo's mistress, who, to quote Maurois, "could not decently be present," the missal she carried during the wedding ceremony. In March *Les Burgraves* failed miserably, thus ending Hugo's career as a dramatist. It is a play that interests the Freudian critic, Charles Baudouin, because of Hugo's elaborate, almost phobic, treatment of the Oedipal theme.[2] On July 9 Hugo

---

[1] André Maurois is sensitive to the mythic chronology of these events. My summary follows his narrative. See chapter 27, "A Villequier," of *Olympio ou la vie de Victor Hugo* (Paris, 1954).

[2] *Psychanalyse de Victor Hugo* (Geneva, 1943). See chapter 1, "Caïn: le motif des frères ennemis."

visited Léopoldine, now three months pregnant, before he left for his annual summer trip with Juliette.[3] He decided to go south—away from the Germanic north of *Les Burgraves*— to Spain, where long ago with his mother and brothers he had gone in search of his father, a womanizing general in Napoleon's army. Baudouin considers this early trip a turning-point in the boy's psychological formation. Not only did he find his missing father, but it was there that he attended his first play, *Les Ruines de Babylone*, and was first awakened to sexual desire. His career as a dramatist and his illicit but highly spiritualized relationship with Juliette, whom he first met as an actress in one of his own plays, seem to have been foreshadowed during that first trip to Spain. Some thirty years later Hugo set out with the highest hopes of rediscovering the lost paradise of his youth, but the trip was riddled with disappointments from the beginning. He saw everything from the alienated perspective of the grown man:

> Hélas, Irun n'est plus Irun. Irun est maintenant plus empire et plus acajou que Paris. Ce ne sont que maisons blanches et contrevents verts. . . . Irun a perdu toute sa physionomie. O villages qu'on embellit, que vous devenez laids! Où sont les souvenirs? Irun ressemble aux Batignolles.[4]

On the twenty-fourth of August Juliette and Hugo explored the mountains and came across the beautiful glacial Lake Gaube. The setting could not have failed to evoke Rousseau's novel for them. On a rock overlooking the lake they read a prophetic inscription on a tomb. Hugo was so touched that he copied the epitaph:

[3] The guilt associated with this trip is made clear in "Amour" (iii,x), fictively dated Juillet 1843.

[4] Hugo, *Voyage aux Pyrénées, Oeuvres complètes*, ed. Massin, Vol. vi, p. 861.

Léopoldine

A La Memoire
De
William Henri Pattison, Ecuyer,
Avocat de Lincoln's Inn, à Londres,
Et de Sarah Frences, Son Epouse,
Agés L'Un De 31 Ans et L'Autre De 26 Ans,
Mariés Depuis Un Mois Seulement.
Un Accident Affreux Les Enleva A Leurs Parents
Et A Leurs Amis Inconsolables.
Ils Furent Engloutis Dans Ce Lac
Le 20 Septembre 1842
Leurs Restes Transportés En Angleterre
Reposent A Wilham Dans Le Comté D'Essex.[5]

Léopoldine read the account of this event in a letter addressed to her brother on September 3, the day before she and her new husband drowned together.

Hugo was especially anxious to visit the Island of Oléron; yet, despite his good spirits of the day before he was overcome by a sense of terrible foreboding when he and Juliette visited there on September 8, 1843, four days after Léopoldine's drowning, still unknown to them. The island was in the throes of a smallpox epidemic and the passengers with whom Hugo and Juliette traveled spoke constantly of death.

Aucun bruit au large. Aucune voile, aucun oiseau. Au bas du ciel, au couchant, apparaissait une lune énorme et ronde qui semblait dans ces brumes livides l'empreinte rougie et dédorée de la lune.

J'avais la mort dans l'âme . . . ce soir-là tout était pour moi funèbre et mélancolique. Il me semblait que cette

[5] Yvan Delteil, *La Fin tragique du voyage de Victor Hugo en 1843 d'après le journal de voyage autographe de Juliette Drouet (1843)* (Paris, 1970), p. 38.

île était un grand cercueil couché dans la mer et que cette lune en était le flambeau.[6]

Finally, on September 9, when he and Juliette stopped in a tavern on their return home, Hugo read in *Le Siècle* of September 7 (the mystical value of the date would not have escaped him) an account of his own daughter's drowning and of her young husband's futile attempts to save her until he finally allowed himself to sink with her in his arms.

> M. Charles Vacquerie était un habile nageur; quatre fois il a reparu à la surface de l'eau, soutenant sa jeune femme; puis ils ont disparu entrelacés dans les bras l'un de l'autre. Les vêtements de Mme Vacquerie étaient déchirés en plusieurs endroits et témoignent des efforts que, dans son désespoir, son mari avait fait pour la sauver, efforts impuissants auxquels il ne devait pas survivre! (Cited by Delteil, p. 145)

Like the couple in the tomb at Lake Gaube, Léopoldine and Charles were buried in the same coffin at Villequier. In a letter to his wife on September 9, Hugo cried out: "O mon Dieu, que vous ai-je fait!" Subsequent articles were written by Hugo's own friends: Alphonse Karr for *Le Siècle*, September 10, 1843 and Jules Janin for *Débats*, September 11, 1843.[7] Thus

---

[6] *Voyage aux Pyrénées*, p. 940. This is the last entry in the account of his trip that summer.

[7] Janin's article was particularly poetic and touched Hugo deeply. His friends knew that he would read about the tragedy in the newspaper and hoped that they could soften the blow. Unfortunately, Hugo did not see their articles until after he had read the rather crude "Faits divers" account in the paper of Sept. 7. As a refrain throughout his article Janin repeats: "Laissez-moi vous parler d'elle. . . ." "Laissez-moi vous parler d'elle. . . . Devant elle, sous ses yeux, se balançait mollement la barque fatale; la barque était toute blanche, toute parée et elle bondissait avec tant de grâce et de légèreté! Ainsi se balançait la

his knowledge of the event was fictionalized at the outset. Yet the significance of the experience of death on the island of Oléron was not to be appreciated and "read" until after 1851, when Hugo chose the island of Jersey for his own death-in-life exile.

The theme of the two brothers that Baudouin points out in *Les Burgraves* is also present in the *figurants* of the Villequier-Jersey dramas. Poetically it appears as the subject-object paradox upon which Hugo constructs *Les Contemplations*. There are Charles and Auguste Vacquerie (iv,xvii; v,i)—the practical and the romantic brothers. Charles was to drown, Auguste to accompany Hugo into exile. The latter was a perfect model for the Romantic hero. He was a would-be poet, yet more famous as Hugo's faithful disciple and chronicler. There are Léopoldine and Adèle Hugo of "Mes deux filles." Adèle, like Auguste, was the lonely recorder of her father's exile, a composer of music and would-be writer who secretly imagined herself the betrothed of a handsome but crass English lieutenant stationed on Guernsey. Finally, there are the two sons—Charles and François-Victor, one something of a man-about-town, the other a sensitive writer and translator of Shakespeare, his father's disciple. The other two "faithfuls" on the island-tomb are, of course, Madame Hugo and, in a separate house, Juliette.

Léopoldine's appearance at a séance of the turning tables in the fall of 1853 confirmed once and for all for Hugo her mediating powers. The first spirit which spoke to a skeptical Hugo identified itself as "Ame Soror" and "Morte." Vacquerie reports that though everyone present understood Léopoldine, her name was never mentioned. (Hugo was to observe the same discretion in *Les Contemplations*.) Hugo was an immediate believer:

---

blanche nef quand périt dans le même Océan toute la famille du roi d'Angleterre, Henri, que rien depuis n'a fait sourire." (Delteil, p. 146)

Ici, la défiance renonçait: personne n'aurait eu le coeur ni
le front de se faire devant nous un tréteau de cette tombe.
Une mystification était déjà bien difficile à admettre, mais
une infamie! Le soupçon se serait méprisé lui-même.[8]

The events of 1843 later served as organizing principles for
the first half (AUTREFOIS) of *Les Contemplations*. *Aurore* is
the recollection of an awakening sensuous awareness in much
the same way that the Pyrenees trip is the mature poet's re-
experience of the birth of desire. *L'Ame en fleur*, which Hugo
called "Juliette's chapter," is addressed uniquely to the loved
and desired woman. These poems carry with them both the
belief in the mediating power of spiritualized love and also
the guilt of original sin and the lost innocence of *Aurore*. The
fact that Hugo secretly inserted some poems written to Léonie
d'Aunet into Juliette's chapter unquestionably reflects the guilt
that threatened the seemingly idyllic love of Charles and Léopoldine. Yet *L'Ame en fleur* could be said to represent not
only the illicit relationship with Juliette that Hugo was en-
joying at the very moment of his daughter's drowning and
Charles' devoted suicide, but also Léopoldine's own life between February 15 and September 4. Sexual love and consciousness of death are clearly synonymous in the arrangement of the
poems in Book IV. Hugo's cryptic identification with Léopoldine's husband is clear both in *Pauca meae* and in the theme
of incest which appears in "A celle qui est restée en France."[9]

[8] Auguste Vacquerie, *Les Miettes de l'histoire* (Paris, 1863), p. 384.

[9] Jacques Séebacher discusses the theme of incest in "Poétique et
politique de la paternité," *Oeuvres complètes*, ed. Massin, Vol. XII, p.
xxiii. Abrams, *Natural Supernaturalism*, pp. 148-49, cites a neo-Platonic
source from which such a theme may have sprung: "At times Plotinus
makes graphic the longing of the separated part (man) from its source
(God or unity), in the figure of the soul as lover and the One as the
beloved (VI.V.10); and this metaphor is elaborated into a distinction
between the errant soul (which has fixed its desire on the things of
the material world) as a harlot and the faithful soul as the heavenly

The repetition of certain patterns of good and evil in Hugo's own life implied for him the presence of a greater ordering consciousness supplying him with the signals for a new book of revelation. He, in turn, arranged the Léopoldine poems as iconographical markers for the reader to contemplate along a spiritual way. Thus, the evolution of the Léopoldine figure constitutes an allegory of the changing form of poetic language as it realizes its redemptive function. A closer look at the diction in representative poems from four books (i,iii; ii,iii; iii,ix; v,xxv)[10] reveals the value of certain rhetorical devices within Hugo's scheme.

Léopoldine is present throughout *Aurore*. The first poem, "A ma fille," is addressed directly to her and establishes the identification between reader and fictionalized child that poe-

---

Aphrodite . . . Alternating with this erotic figure for the relation of the separated soul to the One is a familial figure, in which the soul is a daughter who 'takes up with another love, a mortal, leaves her father and falls. But one day coming to hate her shame, she puts away the evil of earth, once more seeks the father, and finds her peace'" (VI, ix, 9; also V, i, 1).

[10] The numbers of these poems are striking for their symbolic value. Three is an organizing principle of *Les Contemplations* and symbolizes spiritual synthesis. Nine, or three times three, is the "symbolic number *par excellence*, for it represents triple synthesis, that is, the disposition on each plane of the corporal, the intellectual, and the spiritual." J. Cirlot, *A Dictionary of Symbols* (New York, 1962), p. 223. One is unity or perfection, and Seven ($25 = 2 + 5 = 7$) is also symbolic of perfect order—the time it took God for creation. Charles Singleton has demonstrated the importance of 7 (70,25,151); 3 (33,99); and 1 (10,145,100) in *The Divine Comedy*. "The Poets' number at the center," *MLN*, Vol. 80, Jan. 1965, pp. 1-11. See also Balzac's *Louis Lambert*: "*Trois* est la formule des Mondes créés. Il est le signe *spirituel* de la création comme il est le signe *matériel* de la circonférence. . . . L'homme qui pressent l'infini la reproduit-il dans ses oeuvres. *Deux* est le Nombre de la génération. *Trois* est le Nombre de l'existence, qui comprend la génération et le produit. Ajoutez le Quaternaire, vous avez le *sept*, qui est la forumule du ciel. Dieu est au-dessus, il est l'Unité." *La Comédie humaine*, Vol. x (Paris: Bibliothèque de la Pléiade, 1955), p. 455.

tically unveils the providential nature of human destiny. In this
opening poem the father seems to prepare his child for a religious vocation:

> O mon enfant, tu vois, je me soumets.
> Fais comme moi: vis du monde éloignée;
> Heureuse? non; triomphante? jamais.
> —Résignée!—
> Sois bonne et douce, et lève un front pieux.
> Comme le jour dans les cieux met sa flamme,
> Toi, mon enfant, dans l'azur de tes yeux
> Mets ton âme!

Like Dante's Beatrice she will become, as we know, the new
martyr through whom Divinity will be revealed.

In the last poem of *Aurore*, "Halte en marchant," she appears only briefly as a blonde child filling her water jug at a
well[11] outside a country inn. That she is somehow sacred,
however, is again made clear. The inn reminds the narrator
of the Nativity setting, and immediately after seeing the child's
eyes ("yeux de firmament") reflected in the fountain, he has
a vision of a martyred Christ shining with godliness. Thus
both the sunny child ("enfant blonde") and the black and
bleeding Christ are means for revelation.

Between the frame poems of *Aurore*, Léopoldine appears
in all her forms. She is child ("Mes deux filles," "L'Enfance"),
sensuous young woman ("Lise," "Vere novo," "A Propos
d'Horace," "La Coccinelle"), Eve-temptress ("Vers 1820,"
"Vieille chanson du jeune temps," xxi: "Elle était déchaussée,
...," "La Fête chez Thérèse"), suffering mother ("L'Enfance"),
and mediating angel (xxiv: "Heureux l'homme, occupé de
l'éternel destin"). Thus the presentation of the Léopoldine

[11] See chapter IV, footnote 8 for the significance of well imagery in
Hugo's work.

figure in *Aurore* reflects the metonymic and analogical relationship of that section to the whole work.

Although *Aurore* spans the total imaginative adventure, it does focus primarily upon the dawn moment, when narrator and reader set forth as "innocents." "Mes deux filles" is the poem most representative of this deceptively idyllic "aurore." The metaphorizing consciousness which we saw at work on historical reality in the first part of "Pasteurs et troupeaux" is actually figured in this poem.

iii
Mes deux filles

Dans le frais clair-obscur du soir charmant qui tombe,
L'une pareille au cygne et l'autre à la colombe,
Belles, et toutes deux joyeuses, ô douceur!
Voyez, la grande soeur et la petite soeur
Sont assises au seuil du jardin, et sur elles
Un bouquet d'oeillets blancs aux longues tiges frêles,
Dans une urne de marbre agité par le vent,
Se penche, et les regarde, immobile et vivant,
Et frissonne dans l'ombre, et semble, au bord du vase,
Un vol de papillons arrêté dans l'extase.

La Terrasse, près d'Enghien, juin 1842[12]

We know that Hugo considered the poem a key structural work, for in July of 1855, when Noël Parfait suggested a change of the position of either it or the preceding poem, "Le poète s'en va . . . ," in order to avoid a repetition, Hugo answered:

Evitons cher coopérateur, les transpositions (. . .). D'ailleurs les pièces de ce diable de recueil sont comme les

---

[12] The date of this poem, the last summer before Léopoldine's death, is probably fictitious. The handwriting on the manuscript is that of 1855. Barrère states 1855 categorically. Journet and Robert are more cautious. See *Notes*, p. 40.

pierres d'une voûte. Impossible de les déplacer. Je me borne
à changer le premier hémistiche de "Mes deux filles."[13]

The poem appears to constitute a perfectly contained and
balanced picture, like a photograph in a family album. A bouquet of white flowers curves protectively over the white forms
of two little girls against a darkening background. The father
addresses us intimately, as if we were close friends, pointing
out details we may have missed in the picture. The poem could
be said to be Parnassian, in that the objects described seem to
be molded by the single-sentence form into which they have
been poured.[14] The ten lines fall neatly into two five-line sections: the first five describe the children, the second the flowers,
and the two are connected by the running-on of lines five and
six (. . . et sur elles / Un bouquet . . .). Lines one and two and
their parallels in the second half, six and seven, are classical
alexandrines with the hemistich in the middle. Lines three
and eight radically alter the rhythm by the introduction of
Hugo's famous trimeter. The narrator and the reader themselves imitate the movement within the poem. They stand
outside the picture, but bent over it in much the same way
that the bouquet is bent over the girls. The words "oeillets"
and "Voyez" phonologically make this connection clear. Thus
the bouquet's ecstatic contemplation is our own.

Yet like the sunlit valley of "Pasteurs et troupeaux," "Mes
deux filles" contains unsettling premonitions. The narrator
would metamorphose his own daughters into symbolic birds,
the bouquet into a flight of butterflies, the symbol of meta-

[13] "A la vague lueur" is changed to "Dans le frais clair–obscur" to
avoid repetition of the word "lueur" from l. 19 of the preceding poem.
See Journet and Robert, *Notes*, p. 41.

[14] Joseph Vianey, in his edition of *Les Contemplations* (Paris, Les
Grands Ecrivains de la France, 1922), Vol. 1, p. 22, points out a possible
source for this poem in Gautier: "Une grêle de fleurs jonchait partout
le sol / Et l'on eût dit, au bout de leurs tiges pliantes, / Des papillons
peureux suspendus dans leur vol."

morphosis itself. His metaphors belong to a reality somewhere *outside* the framed picture before our eyes. We can see his suggestion only with our *mind's* eye. Thus both groups are balanced literally and figuratively on the edge of time and space ("du soir charmant qui tombe," "au seuil du jardin," "au bord du vase"). The reader who has completed *Les Contemplations* knows that at the end of *Pauca meae* both "Mors" and "Charles Vacquerie" refer to the metaphor suggested by the narrator's painterly eye in "Mes deux filles" as a new truth of existence:

> . . . elle changeait en désert Babylone,
> Le trône en échafaud et l'échafaud en trône,
> Les roses en fumier, *les enfants en oiseaux,*
> L'or en cendre, et les yeux des mères en ruisseaux.
> (xvi, "Mors," my italics)

> Il ne sera pas dit qu'il sera mort ainsi,
> Qu'il aura, coeur profond et par l'amour saisi,
>   Donné sa vie à *ma colombe,*
> (xvii, "Charles Vacquerie," my italics)

In the final poem of Book vi, even the flower imagery characteristic of a conventionalized idyllic vision will undergo such a radical change as to become both threatening: "Et la fleur implacable et féroce la mord," and threatened:

> Tout est douleur.

>   Les fleurs souffrent sous le ciseau,
> Et se ferment ainsi que des paupières closes:
> Toutes les femmes sont teintes du sang des roses;
> La vierge au bal, qui danse, ange aux fraîches couleurs,
> Et qui porte en sa main une touffe de fleurs,
> Respire en souriant un bouquet d'agonies.
> ("Bouche d'ombre")

The sacrificial overtones of certain substantives in "Mes deux filles" ("cygne," "colombe," "urne de marbre," and "ombre") seem to weigh more heavily than the reassuring descriptive adjectives of the first half of the poem ("frais," "charmant," "belles," "joyeuses"). The precariousness of the hour and of the positions, the breaking of the alexandrine into the Romantic trimeter, the warmth of feeling ("ô douceur"), and the metamorphosis suggested by the bird-butterfly metaphors help create an internal disorder by which the poem struggles free of its restrictive form. The poem itself is thus like the reader's arrested gaze: "immobile et vivant," a verbal picture of temporal beauty. The ambiguity of the final word, "extase," both worldly and mystical in its connotations,[15] beautifully completes this study in suspended animation. Like *Aurore*, then, or the first third of "Pasteurs et troupeaux," "Mes deux filles" is both seductively reassuring and unsettlingly subversive.

All the poems in *L'Ame en fleur* are addressed either directly or indirectly to the loved woman. Although the narrator's attitude toward her changes, one could say generally that in this section Léopoldine has evolved into the sensuous young woman of the earthly love experience that we saw figured as the goat girl in "Pasteurs et troupeaux."

"Le Rouet d'Omphale" illustrates on the level of theme and technique the change of perspective that has occurred from *Aurore* to *L'Ame en fleur*. It contains an image (the rape of Europa) which could be said to represent symbolically the relationship of the poet to the world of forms at this stage in the creative process. Like "Mes deux filles," it is the third poem

[15] Littré: two definitions popular in Hugo's time: 1. Terme de vie mystique. Elévation extraordinaire de l'esprit, dans la contemplation des choses divines, qui détache une personne des objets sensibles jusqu'à rompre la communication de ses sens avec tout ce qui l'environne. 2. Par extension, vive admiration, volupté intime qui absorbe tout autre sentiment (Rousseau, Chateaubriand, Lamartine).

in the section. Hugo was sensitive to occultist signals of this sort; the number three is clearly an organizing principle for the collection as a whole (1843 as the thirteenth year and triadic subdivisions of AUTREFOIS and AUJOURD'HUI).

iii
Le Rouet d'Omphale

Il est dans l'atrium, le beau rouet d'ivoire.
La roue agile est blanche, et la quenouille est noire;
La quenouille est d'ébène incrusté de lapis.
Il est dans l'atrium sur un riche tapis.

Un ouvrier d'Egine a sculpté sur la plinthe
Europe, dont un dieu, n'écoute pas la plainte.
Le taureau blanc l'emporte. Europe, sans espoir,
Crie, et, baissant les yeux, s'épouvante de voir
L'Océan monstrueux qui baise ses pieds roses.

Des aiguilles, du fil, des boîtes demi-closes,
Les laines de Milet, peintes de pourpre et d'or,
Emplissent un panier près du rouet qui dort.

Cependant, odieux, effroyables, énormes,
Dans le fond du palais, vingt fantômes difformes,
Vingt monstres tout sanglants, qu'on ne voit qu'à demi,
Errent en foule autour du rouet endormi:
Le lion néméen, l'hydre affreuse de Lerne,
Cacus, le noir brigand de la noire caverne,
Le triple Géryon, et les typhons des eaux
Qui le soir à grand bruit soufflent dans les roseaux;
De la massue au front tous ont l'empreinte horrible,
Et tous, sans approcher, rôdant d'un air terrible,
Sur le rouet, où pend un fil souple et lié,
Fixent de loin dans l'ombre un oeil humilié.

Juin 18 . .

Like "Mes deux filles," this poem describes a picture one can visualize; but this time the muse herself is absent—her presence is felt only metonymically in the abandoned spinning wheel that has a mythological story sculpted on its plinth. Signs have replaced life. Boxes of thread, needles, and a basket of brightly colored wool are next to the wheel. Shadowy figures of the mythic beasts Hercules was supposed to have conquered lurk somewhere in the background. All this is framed for the reader within the walls of the palace ("Il est dans l'atrium," "dans le fond du palais," "autour du rouet"). With the narrator as his guide, the reader again stands outside, looking into the room-frame of the poem.

There are then, in fact, two real pictures and one imaginary one within the poem: the very contained scene of the rape of Europa described in stanza two and the scene in the atrium itself. Both these "real" pictures evoke a third, unseen encounter, taking place between Omphale and Hercules somewhere in the depths of the poetic space. The repetition of certain words used to describe the scene on the plinth of the wheel (e.g., "monstrueux") reveals the interdependence of all the male-female principles in the poem. Europa, Omphale, and the wheel both enslave and are transfigured by Jupiter, Hercules, and the monsters respectively. Such is the relationship of the narrator and the loved woman in *L'Ame en fleur*, and by extension of the poet to the world of forms (Hugo to Léopoldine).

We have seen in "Mes deux filles" that, despite the Parnassian appearance of the poem, it nevertheless struggles to be free of its purely descriptive nature. The natural eye of the poet ("bouquet d'oeillets") is held transfixed by the sight of the bird-like girls; but the poem works to intensify the *fragility* of the stasis rather than the *power* of the thrall. In "Le Rouet d'Omphale" inspiration again springs from observation, but

65

the poem remains far less contained than "Mes deux filles." One sees only "à demi"; indeed, what appears at the very end of the poem is an eye ("un oeil humilié") looking out from within the shadows. Instead of an entirely innocent and naturalistic picture, then, one sees unnatural and threatening forms lurking in the background. This is an ancient theme treated by a Christian mind.

At the outset the title forces the reader to delve into his own memory in order to inform the poem with meaning. This is the same process which takes place in the second part of "Pasteurs et troupeaux" when the mythic allusion to the spinning sisters occurs. The effect of the poem depends upon our temporal reality. Before the poet paints the still-life of the wheel, the reader has an imaginary picture of Hercules seduced by Omphale. Thus the perfectly straightforward, indeed almost prose-like description of the wheel in the first stanza is charged with symbolic and erotic meaning, and the plinth is filled with a magical power. The spinning wheel is not just a beautiful object, but a hastily abandoned beautiful object. The interest shifts to the absent human consciousness rather than to the immediate object, as the Parnassian or Greek poets would have it. The scene on the plinth, of course, confirms this orientation and serves as a complex psychological commentary upon the *imaginary* picture rather than the picture at hand.

That the reader's interest has been usurped by imaginary and invisible *actions* rather than present description is technically confirmed by the shift from the use of paratactic syntax and the verb *to be* (used five times in four lines) in the first stanza to the accumulation of forceful verbs ("a sculpté," "écoute," "emporte," "crie," "s'épouvante," "voir," "baise") and the complex, artfully suspenseful syntax of the second. The whole is charged with a fearful potential by the personification of the "rouet qui dort."

Because of the Omphale-Hercules story the reader brings to the poem, and the cryptic confirmation from the picture of the rape of Europa on the plinth, a new poetic experience is born. Indeed, a second, twelve-line surrealistic picture-poem follows the first twelve-line realistic one, yet is subtly tied to it by the magical wheel upon which all eyes are focused. One is able to perceive the formless monsters lurking in the penumbra of the brightly colored wheel because of the poetic *idea* one has brought to the work. Thus in the "second" poem Hugo creates a picture with subjective descriptive adjectives ("odieux," "effroyables," "affreuse," "noir," "horrible," "terrible") or the evocation of events that have taken place outside of the context of the frame ("Cacus, le noir brigand de la noire caverne," "les typhons des eaux / Qui, le soir, à grand bruit, soufflent dans les roseaux"). The background picture thus exists within the shadows of the reader's own mind. The poem leaves the realm of perceivable reality and enters the abstract domain of signs. Objective and subjective worlds merge, "souple et lié," and our relationship to the poem echoes Europa's relationship to Jupiter (and by extension Hugo's to Léopoldine). The first perceivable picture-poem is thus contaminated by the monstrous presence of other forces. These forces, inherent in human consciousness, will be further articulated in the following section. One can already see, in the evolution from i,iii to ii,iii, the fearful doubling of the narrator into a complicated tormentor-victim relationship to his subject.

Book iii, *Les Luttes et les rêves*, is at the base of the triangle I have used to describe both the structure of *Les Contemplations* and the structure of Hugo's poetic process. It is the book in which the narrator discovers himself to be an alienated and corrupt awareness. Léopoldine's presence symbolically reflects this *felix-culpa* stage in the narrator's own evolution. Thematically she appears as the victimized prostitute of ii, the adulteress burned by society in x, the dead or martyred child of xv, xvii, xviii, xxiii, and the terrible new muse of "Insomnie" (xx).

Just as she was in *Aurore* and *L'Ame en fleur*, Léopoldine is also a figure for an evolving concept of poetic language. In poem ix, for example, the sacrificial figure of Europa becomes the subject of an entire poem. The virginal maiden stands before the reader holding an invisible lily. This *emblematic* picture represents a further step toward the allegorical mode that dominates the book. The poem, supposedly written for Juliette's child, Claire, on her seventeenth birthday (the fictitious date given the poem is "février 1843") could just as well address itself to Léopoldine on the eve of her marriage. Indeed, the lines, "Quand l'homme, spectre obscur du mal et de l'exil, / Ose approcher ton âme, aux rayons fiancée," would encourage such an interpretation. It was clearly written not in 1855 as an isolated anniversary piece, but for a specific place within the complex structure of *Les Contemplations*. Again the numerology (three times three) would support the choice of this poem as part of the Léopoldine sequence after "Mes deux filles" (i,iii) and "Le Rouet d'Omphale" (ii,iii).

ix

Jeune fille, la grâce emplit tes dix-sept ans.
Ton regard dit: Matin, et ton front dit: Printemps.
Il semble que ta main porte un lis invisible.
Don Juan te voit passer et murmure: 'Impossible!'
Sois belle. Sois bénie, enfant, dans ta beauté.
La nature s'égaie à toute ta clarté;
Tu fais une lueur sous les arbres; la guêpe
Touche ta joue en fleur de son aile de crêpe;
La mouche à tes yeux vole ainsi qu'à des flambeaux.
Ton souffle est un encens qui monte au ciel. Lesbos

Et les marins d'Hydra, s'ils te voyaient sans voiles,
Te prendraient pour l'Aurore aux cheveux pleins d'étoiles.
Les êtres de l'azur froncent leur pur sourcil
Quand l'homme, spectre obscur du mal et de l'exil,
Ose approcher ton âme, aux rayons fiancée.
Sois belle. Tu te sens par l'ombre caressée,
Un ange vient baiser ton pied quand il est nu,
Et c'est ce qui te fait ton sourire ingénu.

Février 1843.

The poem is extraordinarily baroque. Conceit is piled upon conceit to present an entirely unnaturalistic, emblematic portrait. The poet resurrects an obscure sixteenth-century genre, the "blason" of the female body. He describes the figure from head to toe and thus places, as always, a real, corporeal presence at the center of his work. A concrete, naturalistic vocabulary runs throughout the poem: "regard," "front," "passer," "nature," "arbres," "guêpe," "joue," "touche," "aile de crêpe," "mouche," "yeux," "souffle," "cheveux," "caressée," "pied," "nu," "sourire." Yet unlike "Mes deux filles" or "Le Rouet d'Omphale," the poem leaves us with no clear picture. It is impossible to see with our earthly eyes the sensuous presence.

Hugo accomplishes this "disincarnation" of the poetic figure in a variety of ways. To begin with, he includes in the emblem his own paradoxical and double consciousness. The monsters lurking in the background of "Le Rouet d'Omphale" twist and turn around the static and illuminated form of the girl. They are aspects of the evolving poetic mind as it seeks to apprehend the natural form: "Don Juan," "guêpe," "mouche," "marins d'Hydra," and "ange." The fully evolved allegorizing consciousness is also present, protecting the figure from the protean self within the poem. At particularly menacing moments it breaks in with a kind of priestly incantation: "Sois belle," "sois bénie," "Sois belle." At the end of the poem all these forms come together in the angel whose disembodied kiss fills the figure with inner light. Thus Hugo artfully dispels the subject-object antithesis, for the last lines of the emblem—"Un ange vient baiser ton pied quand il est nu, / Et c'est ce qui te fait ton sourire ingénu"—return us to the first line: "Jeune fille, la grâce emplit tes dix-sept ans." "Grâce" has taken on its mystical connotation and the erotic fascination of the various male figures is transformed into poetic creation. The sensuous form (Europa of "Le Rouet d'Omphale" and poetic language, by extension) is now infused with redemptive potential. Thus the *felix-culpa* stage in the spiritual evolution of the general narrative is reflected in the poetic figure itself.

On the level of the reader's experience, the same process of abstraction takes place. Every description within the "blason" requires some kind of active intellectual interpretation. Often, without a certain mental storehouse, one would not understand the emblem. "Matin" and "Printemps" are symbolic words which evoke a host of associations. The reader of *Aurore* is better equipped to understand them than is the reader who has not been initiated into the narrative adventure. Thus our historical reality plays a crucial role for a redemptive reading of the text. Don Juan evokes one set of cultural associations which are then destroyed by his miraculous transformation from sinner to reverent believer. In the third line the reader is asked to see something that is not there. The description literally annihilates itself before his eyes with the words "semble" and "invisible." Thus an *idea* of purity replaces the symbolic *form*. The girl's cheek is turned into a flower the instant it is touched by the very real wing of the wasp, and the moth is blinded by her flaming eyes. These images are such familiar conceits that the reader *understands* rather than *sees* their ef-

fect. In the second nine lines time and space are dissolved as
well. The girl becomes the *future* guide of an already poeticized *past*:

> . . . Lesbos
> Et les marins d'Hydra, s'ils te voyaient sans voiles,
> Te prendraient pour l'Aurore aux cheveux pleins d'étoiles.

Her incense-like breath dispels our familiar worldly boundaries. Ancient prophets (Sappho, Aristotle), heroes, and the
satyr-like exile of Jersey all look across different waters in different eras to the same illuminated abstractions for direction.

The structure of the poem also reflects this movement toward
an allegorical reading. The eighteen lines fall into two nine-
line sections, thus emphasizing internally the abstract numero-
logical symbolism which has been apparent thus far (ɪ,iii;
ɪɪ,iii; ɪɪɪ,ix). Despite the self-annihilating effect of the descriptions, the first nine lines seem to emphasize the girl's and the
poet-subject's sensual selves. In the second half, however, the
reader enters more fully into the world of the poetic imagination. The poet even permits himself a parenthetical flight of
fantasy with a series of allusions to past intellectual and heroic
ideals. As the poet-subject becomes increasingly an abstraction
himself ("ombre," "ange") the poet-allegorist dares to reveal
the erotic temptation ("caressée," "baiser," "nu") the natural
forms of "Mes deux filles" represent.

It is, however, the baroque transformation of the sensuous perceiving eye ("Don Juan") into creative imagination
("ange") that will assure the girl's eternal purity. Each part
of her body is an icon pointing toward some original and hence
less corrupt emanation of the Divine Logos. Through allegorical abstraction, the limited temporal incarnation of Beauty is
granted cosmic purity as Morning, Spring, Light, Lily, Flame,
and Star.

Léopoldine

Thus at the end of AUTREFOIS Léopoldine as perceivable form has been sacrificed to an ideal self through the intervention of the poetic imagination. This ideal self will appropriately introduce the reader into AUJOURD'HUI.

i

Pure Innocence! Vertu sainte!
O les deux sommets d'ici-bas!
Où croissent, sans ombre et sans crainte,
Les deux palmes des deux combats!

Palme du combat Ignorance!
Palme du combat Vérité!
L'âme, à travers sa transparence,
Voit trembler leur double clarté.

Innocence! Vertu! sublimes
Même pour l'oeil mort du méchant!
On voit dans l'azur ces deux cimes,
L'une au levant, l'autre au couchant.

Léopoldine is clearly a Christ figure in this introductory poem. The seductive foot of "Lise" in *Aurore*, of Europa in "Le Rouet d'Omphale" and of the emblematic figure in ix of *Les Luttes et les rêves* becomes the symbol of a new redemptive religion in AUJOURD'HUI:

Cette trace qui nous enseigne,
Ce pied blanc, ce pied fait de jour,
Ce pied rose, hélas; car il saigne,
Ce pied nu, c'est le tien, amour!

Pauca meae may seem regressive when one considers the evolution from *Aurore* through *Les Luttes et les rêves* because it contains a series of poem-flashbacks that revive Léopoldine as a real, palpable form:

Elle avait pris ce pli dans son âge enfantin
De venir dans ma chambre un peu chaque matin;

                    (iv,v)

Elle était pâle, et pourtant rose,
Petite avec de grands cheveux.

            (iv,vii)

Elle courait dans la rosée,
Sans bruit, de peur de m'éveiller;
Moi, je n'ouvrais pas ma croisée,
De peur de la faire envoler.

             (iv,ix)

But these are introduced and followed by philosophical poems that question the origins and subsequent loss of that form. Thus *Pauca meae* is a meditation upon a meditation and at two removes from immediate sense perception. It is dedicated to the *memory* of the lost form, and hence is a final imaginative leave-taking of the flesh-and-blood world.

En marche turns resolutely toward a visionary future, like the last part of "Pasteurs et troupeaux."

Ce que Dieu nous donne, il nous l'ôte.
Adieu, patrie! adieu, Sion!
Le proscrit n'est pas même un hôte,
Enfant, c'est une vision.

Il entre, il s'assied, puis se lève,
Reprend son bâton et s'en va.
Sa vie erre de grève en grève
Sous le souffle de Jéhovah.

                (v,ii, "Au fils d'un poète")

Léopoldine now becomes a ubiquitous spiritual presence. In "A Mademoiselle Louise B" the poet speaks to the roses:

Léopoldine

Où sont-ils, ces fronts purs?
N'était-ce pas vos soeurs, ces deux âmes perdues
Qui vivaient, et se sont si vite confondues
Aux éternels azurs!
(v,v, "A Mademoiselle Louise B")

She is the blue flower on the edge of the sea in "Paroles sur la dune," the angelic apparition of xviii, the magical goat girl of "Pasteurs et troupeaux," Persephone who becomes queen of the underworld in poem xxv. Just as in "Mes deux filles," "Le Rouet d'Omphale," and poem ix of Book iii, he presents the virginal maiden as the figure to be sacrificed to the fallen male consciousness:

xxv

O strophe du poète, autrefois, dans les fleurs,
Jetant mille baisers à leurs mille couleurs,
Tu jouais, et d'avril tu pillais la corbeille;
Papillon pour la rose et pour la ruche abeille,
Tu semais de l'amour et tu faisais du miel;
Ton âme bleue était presque mêlée au ciel;
Ta robe était d'azur et ton oeil de lumière;
Tu criais aux chansons, tes soeurs: 'Venez! chaumière,
Hameau, ruisseau, forêt, tout chante. L'aube a lui!'
Et, douce, tu courais et tu riais. Mais lui,
Le sévère habitant de la blême caverne
Qu'en haut le jour blanchit, qu'en bas rougit l'Averne,
Le poëte qu'ont fait avant l'heure vieillard
La douleur dans la vie et le drame dans l'art,
Lui, le chercheur du gouffre obscur, le chasseur d'ombres,
Il a levé la tête un jour hors des décombres,
Et t'a saisie au vol dans l'herbe et dans les blés,
Et, malgré tes effrois et tes cris redoublés,
Toute en pleurs, il t'a prise à l'idylle joyeuse;
Il t'a ravie aux champs, à la source, à l'yeuse,

74

Aux amours dans les bois près des nids palpitants;
Et maintenant, captive et reine en même temps,
Prisonnière au plus noir de son âme profonde,
Parmi les visions qui flottent comme l'onde,
Sous son crâne à la fois céleste et souterrain,
Assise, et t'accoudant sur un trône d'airain,
Voyant dans ta mémoire, ainsi qu'une ombre vaine,
Fuir l'éblouissement du jour et de la plaine,
Par le maître gardée, et calme, et sans espoir,
Tandis que, près de toi, les drames, groupe noir,
Des sombres passions feuillettent le registre,
Tu rêves dans sa nuit, Proserpine sinistre.

Jersey, novembre 1854.

I have said that allegory is a trope that requires the reader to experience the temporal origins of Hugo's redemptive scheme. In this poem the cryptic emblems of III,ix ("Jeune fille, la grâce emplit tes dix-sept ans") are acted out in a short allegorical drama and thus realize in a new form the dynamic value they symbolized. One could say that the three stages of poetic development reflected in the three chapters of Autrefois are now telescoped into the tripartite organization of this poem. The first few lines make it clear that Hugo is describing the evolution of his own poetry as it is reflected in the very book that contains this poem. Autrefois is figured as Persephone playing in the fields with her lyric sisters, "chansons": "O strophe du poète, autrefois, dans les fleurs." She is described as a source of light—*almost* divine—like the Léopoldine in the nostalgic flashbacks of *Pauca meae*.[16] The first, lyrical stage in the development of both poetic and human consciousness (see preface to *Cromwell*) is repeated in the regular six-six meter of many of the lines ("Jetant mille baisers à leurs mille couleurs"; "Tu semais de l'amour et tu faisais du miel"; "Ta

[16] For a discussion of light imagery in *Pauca meae*, see chapter VII, pp. 147-49.

robe était d'azur et ton oeil de lumière") and the traditional rhyme schemes.

In lines nine and ten a radical change of perspective occurs both formally and thematically. Our sense of continuity, of eternal, natural duration fostered by the use of the imperfect tense, is cut off abruptly by the three syllable hemistich which breaks the meter of line nine: "L'aube a lui!" Everything works to separate these three syllables from the preceding lines: punctuation, biblical allusion, and the absolute finality of the *passé composé* shock the reader out of his passive enjoyment of the preceding lyrical description. Line ten is divided —de-lyricized, so to speak—in the same way. Syntactic and rhythmic durations are no longer the same as they were in the first seven lines of the poem. "Mais lui" begins a new thought in the middle of the poetic line and shifts our focus from the predominately feminine nature ("strophe," "fleurs," "couleurs," "corbeille," "rose," "ruche," "âme," "robe," "lumière," "chansons," "soeurs") to the apprehending male consciousness that threatens to destroy it. The rift between referential (syntax) and non-referential (meter and sound) levels of communication is realized most effectively in the homonyme ("lui") that serves as rhyme-word to link the first two parts of the poem. The same sound functions as verb and pronoun. Thus God's light, or the light of Genesis, is poetically linked to the poet's satanic awareness, Heaven to Hell. Conflict characterizes the second stage in the poem on all levels. Masculine subject is separated from feminine object by the sheer semantic force of the verb: "Il . . . t'a saisie," "Il t'a prise," "Il t'a ravie." Antitheses abound: "en haut"-"en bas," "blanchit"-"rougit," "la vie"-"l'art," "gouffre obscur"-"idylle joyeuse." Meter, rhymes, and syntax are all richly complex.

The final eleven lines which constitute the last act of the poetic drama are reminiscent in many ways of Books

v and vi of *Les Contemplations*. All oppositions are resolved. The time shifts to a progressive present ("Et maintenant," "flottent," "t'accoudant," "Voyant . . . fuir"), which
nevertheless is simultaneously a meditation upon the past. The
symbol of natural duration is fixed once and for all at the
center of the creative, but other-worldly, consciousness. Thus
the poet's cranium is both "céleste et souterrain," masculine
and feminine, light and dark, good and evil. The Romantic
muse will be a reflection on the lost spring, and in this sense
"sinistre." The poetic experience, like the final long sentence
after the break in line ten, is an endless spiral backward to the
moment of earthly paradise before the fall.

In Book vi (*Au bord de l'infini*), opposition between male
and female principles dissolves, just as it did at the end of "O
strophe du poète . . ." or "Pasteurs et troupeaux"; and the
reader enters directly into the visionary world inside the poet's
brain. Correspondingly, Léopoldine becomes identified with
Hugo's own soul. As the poet and his language merge into a
mediating force, the reader is meant to experience supernatural
reality directly. In the opening poem, significantly entitled "Le
Pont," Léopoldine appears in the form of the poet's tear, which
in turn will become the ocean of creation itself in "Pleurs dans
la nuit." Although Hugo is careful to surround the phantom
guide figure with the attributes of the earlier Léopoldine
figures: "lys," "lumière," "blancheur," "front de vierge," "mains
d'enfant," this new, androgynous Léopoldine can now be referred to as "il."

. . .

C'était un front de vierge avec des mains d'enfant;
Il ressemblait au lys que la blancheur défend;
Ses mains en se joignant faisaient de la lumière.
Il me montra l'abîme où va toute poussière,

77

Si profond, que jamais un écho n'y répond,
Et me dit:—Si tu veux, je bâtirai le pont.
Vers ce pâle inconnu je levai ma paupière.
—Quel est ton nom? lui dis-je. Il me dit:—La prière.

(VI,i, "Le Pont")

The new poetry will be like the most ancient form of ritualized utterance: prayer. Poetic language becomes a kind of stream of consciousness, an unbroken hallucinatory incantation. Thus, Hugo moves beyond the intellectual and temporal stage of contemplation represented by the allegorical drama of "O strophe du poète . . ." to the final visionary level of supreme contemplation described in *Philosophie, commencement d'un livre*. "Observer," "penser," "prier" find their reflections in the evolving rhetorical figures of Hugo's book.

IV

AURORE

"Si je n'étais songeur, j'aurais été sylvain."

(I, xxvii)

To BEGIN at the beginning is a great challenge to the critic who would demonstrate a highly developed ordering of *Les Contemplations*. We know that, in true initiatory fashion, Hugo reserved the key to his order until the end and that he wished to establish a parallel between his own biographical adventure and the reader's experience of the book. Correspondingly, to the reader setting forth, this first section appears as a chaos of forms—an incoherent but dazzling array of separate works. Tone, point of view, mood, and theme change radically both within individual poems and within the chapter itself. The narrator is a twelve-year-old schoolboy, a lover, father, violent revolutionary, or ancient sage. A Dionysian celebration of creation directly precedes a dramatic dialogue with a dead man (iv,v). The revolutionary power of language is sadistically elaborated upon in "Suite," to be followed by naive songs of times gone by ("Vieille chanson du jeune temps"). Poems written at different times are telescoped into one synchronic rage ("Réponse à un acte d'accusation" . . . "Suite"), and poems inspired by the same *genius loci* are separated within the chapter to create a dialogue (Granville, Paris, La Terrace, etc.). One loses his footing within individual poems as well. Innocence gives way to terror ("Les Oiseaux"), playfulness to premonitions of damnation ("La Fête chez Thérèse"), and idyllic calm to religious visions ("Halte en marchant").

Aurore has frequently been characterized, however, as arcadian, optimistic, natural, naive, erotic. Indeed, there seems to be a preponderance of children, birds, bees, flowers, and sunlight if one considers the preternatural darkness and spectral forms of Book VI. As an early stage in the poetic process, this first part could be described as the awakening of a sentient being to the world outside of himself. Hugo, like Socrates (*Ion.* 534), compares the poet to a bee and the universe to a flower in a number of poems,[1] thus asserting the divine origin of his inspiration. Both in the preface and elsewhere, he describes the beginning of *Les Contemplations* as light and joyful:

La joie, cette fleur rapide de la jeunesse, s'effeuille
page à page dans le tôme premier, qui est l'espérance.

(*Préface*)

. . . le livre commencera par l'enfantillage et s'élargira
jusqu'à Dieu.[2]

Yet many of the poems of *Pauca meae*, the book that in fact corresponds to the tomb experience, appear to be more idyllic than those of *Aurore*.[3] Rather than as naive or "precontemplative" works, I read the *Aurore* poems as ironic reflections by a fully evolved visionary poet upon an early *stage* in both the

---

[1] See ii, "Suite," "Vere novo," "Quelques mots à un autre," and xxvii.

[2] From Adèle Hugo's journal, quoted by Journet and Robert in their critical edition of *Dieu* (Paris, 1960), p. 181.

[3] Jean Gaudon, *Le Temps de la contemplation* (Paris, 1969), p. 132: "Le charme déjà capté dans les poèmes virgiliens des années '30, le sens de la vie immédiate, le don de traduire la sensation simple sont là, et l'on pourrait dire que ces poèmes du souvenir sont autant de cailloux blancs sur le chemin qui conduit des idylles champêtres du passé aux frêles merveilles des *Chansons des rues et des bois* . . . elles appartiennent par leur esprit, à la période qu'elles évoquent plutôt qu'à celle de leur composition, à l'époque précontemplative que Hugo appelle 'Autrefois.' "

poetic process and the initiatory experience. Hugo's poet is not Plato's. His message is redemptive only after it has been ordered by the allegorizing consciousness. Intellect, of which allegory is the rhetorical reflection, is the medium through which divine "madness" is channeled. Poet as inspired dreamer and poet as constitutive consciousness are simultaneously present in *Aurore*. Throughout Book ɪ there exists an observing presence that sees at once the birth and the death, the beauty and the threat, the pleasure and the violence. It is this presence that informs the reader that *Aurore* is more than a sentimental description of Hugo's childhood garden of Les Feuillantines or a First Empire imitation of "rosy-fingered dawn."

This doubling of the narrator reveals at the outset that the autobiographical experience is being presented in an authenticated (poeticized) form. It states the sacrificial nature of creation and creativity. In order to grasp the universal meaning of his life, the reader must not yield to the seductive immediacy of the individual experience. The sacrificial imperative revealed in *Aurore* will be more and more clearly asserted as he progresses through the six books of the collection.

Thus, one is tempted to say that *Aurore* taken altogether is an analogical figure in its own right, for it is structured in such a way as to reflect the content of the collection as a whole. The poetic structuring is itself an emblem of the pattern of Divine Thought that dictates both the poet's life and the Cosmic Scheme within which he lives. Hugo thus fulfills his role as artful translator through visible forms of an invisible design. The title states both the beginning—the awakening of the senses to a responsive physical world—and the recurring nature of creation that carries with it the awareness of an earlier, completed poetic experience. Every "aurore" contains the memory of the night before. There can never be an innocent awakening. Book ɪ is related to the final poems of Book ᴠɪ in the same way that dawn is related to night or the sapling to the tree-cosmos. Indeed, it is this continuing relationship that constitutes the magic of the fully evolved image-making genius by which Hugo joins the natural with the supernatural in one expansive movement.

> Il marche dans la plaine immense,
> Va, vient, lance la graine au loin,
> Rouvre sa main, et recommence,
> Et je médite, obscur témoin,
>
> Pendant que, déployant ses voiles,
> L'ombre, où se mêle une rumeur,
> Semble élargir jusqu'aux étoiles
> Le geste auguste du semeur.
> (*Les Chansons des rues et des bois*,
> "Saison des semailles")

Marc Eigeldinger's discussion of the dynamics of Hugo's images helps clarify the function of Book 1 within the collection as a whole:

> Hugo veut rendre sensible le mystère de la création et son esprit foncièrement réaliste qui se refuse à considérer l'abstraction en elle-même ramène tout à la sensation.

> Au lieu de nous montrer comme Mallarmé la fleur détachée de sa tige, Hugo nous la donne avec les racines qui retiennent un peu de terre où elles plongeaient.[4]

An examination of the arrangement of the poems in *Aurore* should illustrate the function of this book within the total religio-poetic story. The juxtaposition of many of the poems will be understood if the reader keeps in mind Hugo's desire to represent all levels of creation simultaneously.

If one leaves aside the first poem, "A ma fille," which with

---

[4] *L'Evolution dynamique de l'image dans la poésie française du romantisme à nos jours* (Neuchâtel, 1943), pp. 83 and 113.

the last one, "Halte en marchant," serves as a frame to the entire section (thus reflecting the structure of the work as a whole with its two liminal poems) and more explicitly states the sacrificial message, one can distinguish certain groupings within the chapter. Poems ii-iv; and v-x; are all related thematically. The last poems, xvii-xxviii, echo and amplify the themes introduced in these three groups—they in fact synthesize what could be considered antithetical elements between the second and third groups.

Poems ii, iii, iv

Poems ii, iii, and iv introduce us into the "chaos of forms" with a tone of joy and reverence.

> Le poète s'en va dans les champs, il admire,
> Il adore, il écoute en lui-même une lyre;

Hugo's literary cosmogony appropriately both begins and ends with the creation myth. Since the poet is the new Messiah, he chooses first the celebration of artistic creation. Next, in "Mes deux filles," with equal religious reverence, he celebrates natural creation, and finally Original Creation. Poem iv is no less than the epithalamion of Heaven and Earth:

> L'hosanna des forêts, des fleuves et des plaines
> S'élève gravement vers Dieu, père du jour;

These three poems repeat on three levels of existence—artistic, biological, and cosmological—the miracle of birth. "Le navire, gonflant ses voiles" of the prefatory poem and the "firmament plein de la vaste clarté" of iv reflect the same notion.[5]

---

[5] Denis Saurat, in *La Religion de Victor Hugo* (Paris: Hachette, 1929), p. 88 points out the erotic nature of the cabalistic conception of divine creation: "La Cabale: 'Celui qui est en haut est le père de tout; c'est lui qui a tout crée; c'est lui qui a fécondé la terre, qui est devenue grasse et qui a donné naissance à des produits. Elle fut fécondée comme

All three poems are at once intimate and religious in tone:

Et, familièrement, car cela sied aux belles:
"Tiens! c'est notre amoureux qui passe!" disent-elles.
Et, pleins de jour et d'ombre et de confuses voix,
Les grands arbres profonds qui vivent dans les bois,

(ii)

Voyez, la grande soeur et la petite soeur
Sont assises au seuil du jardin . . .

. . .

Et frissonne dans l'ombre, et semble, au bord du vase,
Un vol de papillons arrêté dans l'extase.

(iii)

Le vent lit à quelqu'un d'invisible un passage
Du poème inoui de la création . . . .

(iv)

In all three poems the presence of the narrator is felt, but never explicitly stated. One becomes aware of the absence of an explicit first person when the narrator literally bursts forth in poem v: "Oui, mon vers . . . André. . . ." The religious vocabulary of solitary communion common to all three poems— "adore," "ulémas," "saluts," "vaste," "prière," "immensité"— will be shattered by the irreligious "I" language of v.

Despite the use of the self-effacing third person, however, in each poem there is a conspicuous observing presence. It is the evolution of that presence from ii to iv that again asserts the sacrificial theme of which the reader was forewarned in "A ma fille." The movement is essentially one from unity toward alienation.

In ii the observers are everywhere present—flowers, trees,

---

une femelle est fécondée par un mâle.'" One is struck by the virile, "fecondatory" nature of the poet's vision in the first line of Hugo's prefatory poem: "Un jour je vis, debout au bord des flots. . . ."

and the poet himself. There seems to be a direct flow between subjective and objective realities—the ideal communication described in Baudelaire's "Correspondances." Nature is described as a temple, with the poet-dreamer as its high priest.

> Les grands arbres profonds qui vivent dans les bois,
> . . .
> Comme les ulémas quand paraît le muphti,
> Lui font de grands saluts et courbent jusqu'à terre
> Leurs têtes de feuillée et leurs barbes de lierre,

In iii there is a significant change. The *human* presences, Hugo's daughters, are described as part of a mysterious objective reality that, although suggestive, does not speak directly to the narrator-father. They are in fact bent upon some private contemplation of their own. They are *being observed* by "un bouquet d'oeillets." Both subjects and observer must be altered metaphorically for the religious suggestiveness or potential communion to be released. The many-eyed bouquet is a projection into nature of the father's own ecstatic gaze about to take flight into a "vol de papillons," thus beautifully intensifying the fragility of the idyl by echoing the metaphor of the bird-like girls: "L'une pareille au cygne et l'autre à la colombe." The transiency of the moment is further intensified by the sacrificial allusions belonging to the swan-dove metaphor. It is echoed in the time of day: "Dans le frais clair-obscur du soir charmant qui tombe"; the position of the agents: "au seuil du jardin," "se penche," "au bord du vase"; and the rhythm of the lines.

In the fourth poem the observer is dramatically cut off from the scene described. His presence is announced abruptly, at the end, after the "poem" is over. The reader is suddenly shocked out of a sensuous projection into the poem by the coolly detached observation of the last line: "Et, pendant ce temps-là, Satan, l'envieux, rêve."

In each of these three poems the observers are heralded by the casual and prosaic "Et . . . ," and the final word of iv ("rêve") echoes the murmurings of the trees in ii: "C'est lui! C'est le rêveur!" The attentive reader becomes dimly aware that the poetic dreamer is also the ironic decipherer of meanings. Indeed he is "Satan, l'envieux" himself. The writing of poetry takes on a mysterious metaphysical significance and the reader is once and for all launched on the prolonged contemplative adventure.

POEMS V-X

With the final line of iv the reader is roughly snapped out of religious communion into a contemporary present characterized by violence and irony. Poems v through x comment explicitly upon the function of language and poetry for Hugo, now, in the nineteenth century. Thus the narrator reveals himself as Lucifer or postlapsarian man, an historic individual alienated from the apparent harmony and conventionalized rhetoric of poems ii through iv.

> Oui, mon vers croit pouvoir, sans se mésallier,
> Prendre à la prose un peu de son air familier.
> André, c'est vrai, je ris quelquefois sur la lyre.

Here one has a poet speaking to his immediate predecessor, conscious of his role in an evolving history of artistic creation. The primitive, Dionysian communion of "Pan" (*Les Feuilles d'Automne*)—"Allez, voyez, chantez! c'est Dieu qui remplit tout . . ."—is no longer possible in Chateaubriand's Christian universe. If the poetic imagination informs the universe with meaning, it also deprives it of its deceiving innocence. The poet's eye is satanic because it contaminates creation with its own alienated presence. Indeed nature—even in ii—can be described only anthropomorphically (the "sourire triste" of

"Pasteurs et troupeaux"). The poet is now a kind of "élu," "bourreau de Dieu," like the soldier of Joseph de Maistre. He will ask: "La fleur, a-t-elle tort d'écarter sa tunique?" Correspondingly, lyrical description characteristic of ii-iv will give way to the persuasive rhetoric of v-x, thus paralleling the movement we have seen in AUTREFOIS from *Aurore* through *Les Luttes et les rêves*. Since Divinity is vital and redemptive only when it is perceived (the daughters in iii are perceived as redemptive symbols, "L'une *pareille* au cygne et l'autre à la colombe"), the ephemeral experience of nature is sacrificed to a language which represents it in a set of communicable signs. Just as the children of "Mes deux filles" were transformed so as to become literary symbols, Léopoldine-child will be sacrificed in the course of the narrative to become Léopoldine-angel, mediating symbol, in AUJOURD'HUI.

The poet-dreamer of vi is no longer alone in nature's garden, as he was in ii. He now assumes the role of the poet-allegorist who says about the children clamoring for his stories:

> Que je riais comme eux et plus qu'eux *autrefois*,
> Et qu'*aujourd'hui*, sitôt qu'à leurs ébats j'assiste,
> Je leur souris encor, bien que je sois plus triste;
> (vi, "La Vie aux champs," my italics)

The story he tells them is that of the approaching apocalypse, the history of emerging Evil, which will find its fullest voice in *Les Luttes et les rêves* and which accounts for the presence of the ironic doubling in *Aurore*. The mutilated sphinx, itself a human creation, hides its divine secret from the questing pilgrim. Pantheistic communion is replaced by questioning and fragmentary explanations:

> Le voyageur de nuit, qui passe à côté d'eux,
> S'épouvante, et croit voir, aux lueurs des étoiles,
> Des géants enchaînés et muets sous des voiles.
>   (vi, "La Vie aux champs")

87

Poems vii and viii show the poet-Satan-terrorist at work, using the language of a fallen civilization, the syllables of 1793 to carry the message of future redemption.

> Oui, je suis ce Danton! je suis ce Robespierre!
> J'ai, contre le mot noble à la longue rapière,
> Insurgé le vocable ignoble, son valet,
> Et j'ai, sur Dangeau mort, égorgé Richelet.
>
> (vii, "Réponse à un acte d'accusation")

Before the mystery of "La Vie aux champs" can be wrenched from the sphinx, the modern poet must reawaken the human spirit, anesthetized by a dead and venal rhetoric, to the existence of a transcendental reality. He can do this only by inventing a new language.

> Les mots heurtent le front comme l'eau le récif;
> Ils fourmillent, ouvrant dans notre esprit pensif
> Des griffes ou des mains, et quelques-uns des ailes;
> Comme en un âtre noir errent des étincelles,
> Rêveurs, tristes, joyeux, amers, sinistres, doux,
> Sombre peuple, les mots vont et viennent en nous;
> Les mots sont les passants mystérieux de l'âme.
>
> (viii, "Suite")

Hugo's *Contemplations* are the army-deluge that invades the Bastille of Human Consciousness to liberate redemptive Freedom.[6] The creation described in poems ii through iv must in-

---

[6] Hugo, *Philosophie, commencement d'un livre*, pp. 54-55: "Liberté exigeant responsabilité, plus vous élargissez la liberté actuelle, plus vous agrandissez la responsabilité ultérieure. Plus vous donnez de choses à faire à la vie, plus vous laissez de choses à faire à la tombe. L'esclave est irresponsable; à la rigueur il pourrait mourir tout entier; la mort n'aurait rien à lui dire. Le citoyen, lui, est de toute nécessité immortel; il faut qu'il réponde. . . . Ceci est l'origine divine de la liberté. Pour que l'homme soit responsable ailleurs, il faut qu'il ait été libre ici-bas. Le sépulcre n'est pas béant pour rien. L'attente du tombeau implique la liberté de l'homme."

vade one's being; language will open the way. The poet then must sacrifice his personal experience of communion with nature to the insensitive mob, imprisoned within the institutions created by a fallen human spirit.

> Il y a des êtres qui . . . ayant l'azur du ciel, disent: c'est assez! songeurs absorbés dans le prodige, puisant dans l'idolâtrie de la nature l'indifférence du bien et du mal, contemplateurs du cosmos radieusement distraits de l'homme, qui ne comprennent pas qu'on s'occupe de la faim de ceux-ci, de la soif de ceux-là . . . esprits paisibles et terribles, impitoyablement satisfaits. Chose étrange, l'infini leur suffit. Ce grand besoin de l'homme, le fini, qui admet l'embrassement, ils l'ignorent. Le fini, qui admet le progrès, ce travail sublime, ils n'y songent pas . . . . Jamais la joie, toujours l'extase. S'abîmer, voilà leur vie . . . . C'est là une famille d'esprits, à la fois petits et grands. Horace en était, Goethe en était, La Fontaine peut-être; magnifiques égoïstes de l'infini, spectateurs tranquilles de la douleur . . . qui n'entendent ni le cri, ni le sanglot, ni le râle, ni le tocsin, pour qui tout est bien, puisqu'il y a le mois de mai, qui, tant qu'il y aura des nuages de pourpre et d'or au-dessus de leur tête, se déclarent contents, et qui sont déterminés à être heureux jusqu'à épuisement du rayonnement des astres et du chant des oiseaux.
>
> (*Les Misérables*, ed. Massin, vol. xi, pp. 851-52)

As he states in the preface to *Cromwell*, drama rather than lyric poetry is the genre most symbolic of this new concern with popular redemption.

> Le poëme éploré se lamente; le drame
> Souffre, et par vingt acteurs répand à flots son âme;
>
> (ix)

Rather than the sacred "muphti" to whom nature pays homage in ii, the poet is characterized as a sacrificial figure: Christ, pelican, Molière dying as he plays Argan, faceless Homer, Saint John, and finally Eschylus, for whom his own creation, Prometheus, becomes the vulture nailed into his cranium.

In poem x Hugo invokes the spirit of Madame de Girardin —a new muse, "morte et transfigurée" with whom he has nevertheless shared the earthly *fête* (Paris, 1840–Jersey, 1855). He invokes her spirit to carry him further on the spiritual voyage:

> Car je te sens flotter sous mes rameaux penchants;
> Car ta lyre invisible a de sublimes chants!
> Car mon sombre océan, où l'esquif s'aventure,
> T'épouvante et te plaît; car la sainte nature,
> La nature éternelle, et les champs, et les bois,
> Parlent à ta grande âme avec leur grande voix!
>
> (x, "A Madame D G de G")

The ship image of the prefatory poem is ominously merged with Léopoldine's fragile craft and the poet's own exile from France. Poetic insight and some form of expiation seem to be synonymous. Thus poems v through x of *Aurore* announce themes which will be fully developed in Books iii, iv, and v of the collection as a whole.

POEMS xi-xvi

The next grouping, poems xi-xvi, creates an abrupt change of tone and seems to refute or ignore the invocation to a transcendental reality which has just taken place. Just as poems v-x constitute an amplification in terms of nineteenth-century France upon the theme of poetic creation, poems xi-xvi are an autobiographical amplification upon the theme of biological creation presented in "Mes deux filles." Yet they too reflect the metaphysical intent of Hugo's poetics, for the apprenticeship of the senses and the consciousness of evil go hand in hand. "Dieu fit l'univers et l'univers fit le mal" ("Ce que dit la bouche d'ombre"). The awakening of our senses implies an increasing fascination with material creation. In Book II, as in this group of poems, creation will be concentrated in the woman.

She will function throughout the collection as both an alienating and a redemptive figure. It is to be remembered that within *Pauca meae*, "4 SEPTEMBRE 1843," the date of Léopoldine's death, immediately follows the poem written at the time of her wedding, "Dans l'église, 15 février 1843," and that *L'Ame en fleur*, a lyrical tribute to earthly love (Juliette's part), is immediately followed by *Les Luttes et les rêves*, the Sodom and Gomorrah of *Les Contemplations*. This group of "innocently" erotic poems, which characterizes *Aurore* for so many readers, has already been "contaminated" by the notions of sacrifice and evil present in the poems that precede them.

In "Lise" the father-daughter relationship of "Mes deux filles" is reversed. The young boy of 1811 looks adoringly at the "motherly" older child and feels the first stirrings of erotic desire:

> Elle disait de moi: C'est un enfant!
> Je l'appelais mademoiselle Lise;
> Pour lui traduire un psaume, bien souvent,
> Je me penchais sur son livre à l'église;
> Si bien qu'un jour, vous le vîtes, mon Dieu!
> Sa joue en fleur toucha ma lèvre en feu.
>
> (xi, "Lise")

The "Aurore" of a revolutionary age of poetry—characterized in the preceding group by "Suite"—yields to the "Aurore" of first love: "Comme le matin rit sur les roses en pleurs" (xii, "Vere novo"). The "bouquet d'oeillets" of "Mes deux filles" has indeed metamorphosed into "vol de papillons":

Oh! les charmants petits amoureux qu'ont les fleurs!
Ce n'est dans les jasmins, ce n'est dans les pervenches
Qu'un éblouissement de folles ailes blanches
Qui vont, viennent, s'en vont, reviennent, se fermant,
Se rouvrant, dans un vaste et doux frémissement.

(xii, "Vere novo")

In turn they are transformed into bits of torn love notes, fragmentary symbols of their original selves:

Ô printemps! quand on songe à toutes les missives
Qui des amants rêveurs vont aux belles pensives,
. . .
Aux messages d'amour, d'ivresse et de délire
Qu'on reçoit en avril et qu'en mai l'on déchire,
On croit voir s'envoler, au gré du vent joyeux,
Dans les prés, dans les bois, sur les eaux, dans les cieux,
Et rôder en tous lieux, cherchant partout une âme,
Et courir à la fleur en sortant de la femme,
Les petits morceaux blancs, chassés en tourbillons,
De tous les billets doux, *devenus papillons*.

(xii, "Vere novo," my italics)

The threat associated with this erotic awakening is present even in such "vere novo": in the very notion of an ephemeral love, in the word "rôder" or the suggestion of a lover transformed into butterfly who runs/flies "à la fleur en sortant de la femme."

The revolutionary's rage in "Suite," directed against a doddering monarchy and frigid classical aesthetic, is now echoed in a schoolboy's rage against all the impotent old men who imprison "le chant libre et joyeux" within their fossilized texts, rules of rhetoric, and *pensums*. Horace, the bard of the lascivious fawn and the beautiful slave girl—indeed, Chénier's

Horace—can be read only by the youth whose blood boils to meet the gate-keeper's daughter.

> Horace, quand grisé d'un petit vin sabin,
> Tu surprenais Glycère ou Lycoris au bain,
> Qui t'eût dit, ô Flaccus . . .
>
> . . .
>
> Que tu faisais ces vers charmants, profonds, exquis,
> Pour servir, dans le siècle odieux où nous sommes,
> D'instruments de torture à d'horribles bonshommes,
> Mal peignés, mal vêtus, qui mâchent, lourds pédants,
> Comme un singe une fleur, ton nom entre leurs dents!
> Grimauds hideux qui n'ont, tant leur tête est vidée,
> *Jamais eu de maîtresse et jamais eu d'idée!*
>
> (xiii, "A propos d'Horace," my italics)

It is in this group of adolescent love poems that the laughter he had promised Chénier emerges. Popular song rhythms, the octosyllable, and riming couplets predominate. The next three poems which complete this group, "A Granville, en 1836," "La Coccinelle," and "Vers 1820," were all, paradoxically, written at the height of the spiritist period of the turning tables, when every new poem was destined for a place in Hugo's "Book."

Poems xvii-xxviii

The remaining eleven poems (xvii-xxviii) constitute a synthesis of the preceding eleven works, whose themes center on artistic or erotic creation. Poem xvii introduces the notion of the brotherhood of the arts, the collective quest of artistic creation that will find its clearest expression in "Les Mages" of Book vi. Hugo kept the manuscript date ("22 oct. 1841") because it so beautifully represents a prophetic work that, though of minor artistic worth, nevertheless heralds the later and grander expressions of the same themes to be expressed in "Magnitudo parvi."

> Tous les penseurs, sans chercher
> Qui finit ou qui commence,
> Sculptent le même rocher:
> Ce rocher, c'est l'art immense.
>   (xvii, "A M. Froment Meurice")

Thus this poem represents the kind of dialogue that must take place on all levels in order that new and redemptive understanding may occur. The dialogue is between the contemporary poet and all his dead guide figures—Virgil, Dante, Chénier, etc.; it takes place within his own life as exemplified in prefigurative poems like this one, and it takes place between the individual poems within a given work.

Poems xviii through xxi are a radical juxtaposing of the artistic-erotic themes presented in the two groups v-x and xi-xvi. The reader is unsettled by the rapid change of tone, point of view, and genre in the remaining poems. The violence of the change from "Les Oiseaux" to "Je ne songeais pas à Rose . . ." or from "A un poète aveugle" to "Elle était déchaussée, elle était décoiffée . . ." has a disruptive effect that "Suite" had proclaimed necessary for a new awareness to be born.

"Les Oiseaux" is related to poem vi, "La Vie aux champs," and hence carries on the dialogue within *Aurore*. Both poems have old and sage narrator-poets. The message of this dialogue reflects the narrative message of the work as a whole. Both begin with solitary walks in nature—the first in a cultivated, blooming landscape, the second in a deserted cemetery. Both establish themselves with dramatic sets at the outset. Both narrators make reference to a providential reality, although with different effect:

Moi, je vais devant moi; le poète en tout lieu
Se sent chez lui, sentant qu'il est partout chez Dieu.

(vi)

Dieu veut que ce qui naît sorte de ce qui tombe.

(xviii)

The first poem is serene at first and shocks by ending on an apocalyptic note. The second is apocalyptic at the outset and, though highly ironic at the end, still gains in optimism as it progresses. In the first the poet reads directly from God's book and narrates the story of civilization to the innocent children. In the second the poet experiences a fainting-drowning-death —"Et l'ombre m'emplissait . . ."—and then mystically discovers from the birds that he is as fossilized and mean as the pedants in "A propos d'Horace":

Autour de moi, nombreux,
Gais, sans avoir souci de mon front ténébreux,
Dans ce champ, lit fatal de la sieste dernière,
Des moineaux francs faisaient l'école buissonnière.
. . .
Je pris ces tapageurs ailés au sérieux;
Je criai:—Paix aux morts! vous êtes des harpies.
—Nous sommes des moineaux, me dirent ces impies.
—Silence! allez-vous-en! repris-je, peu clément.
Ils s'enfuirent; j'étais le plus fort. Seulement,
Un d'eux resta derrière, et, pour toute musique,
Dressa la queue, et dit:—Quel est ce vieux classique?

The mocking rime, "musique"-"classique" is the shock that permits the poet new insight. Isolated from the natural world within his personal revery, he would inevitably betray his messianic function. The birds fill the cemetery-world with the light of laughter ("Nous avons besoin de ce *rayon*")—not the innocent laughter of the children in vi, to be sure, but the ironic laughter that their incongruous presence among the dead evokes in the fallen reader. The unrelieved irony of their presence forces the observer to remain outside himself, a *conscious* witness to his own mortality, in the garden-cemetery filled with the mocking presence of natural duration.

As the themes of erotic and artistic creation are repeated and juxtaposed in the remaining works, their ironical relationship is forced upon us. After "Les Oiseaux," a disturbing commentary upon man's role in the Divine Plan, Hugo throws us into the mocking sing-song rhythm of xix, "Vieille chanson du jeune temps."

> Je ne songeais pas à Rose;
> Rose au bois vint avec moi;
> Nous parlions de quelque chose,
> Mais je ne sais plus de quoi.
>
> . . .
>
> Je ne vis qu'elle était belle
> Qu'en sortant des grands bois sourds.
> "Soit; n'y pensons plus!" dit-elle.
> Depuis, j'y pense toujours.

Like xxi it echoes the naive sensuality of earlier poems— "Lise" or "La Coccinelle"—but in xix and xxi the seductive eroticism of the woman-temptress has become the focus of the narrator's attention. The hypnotic rhythm produced by "Rose, rose, rossignols," the use of the imperfect tense, and the abrupt change to present tense in the last line all reveal his fawn-like presence. The naive narrator is thus unmasked by his demonic other.

Coming directly after the priestly asceticism of "A un poète aveugle" (xx), which pays homage to the transcendental muse of x and states the superiority of spiritual insight personified in the blind bard, the first stanza of xxi is shockingly sensuous.

The irony would of course be lost if one were not to observe Hugo's narrative sequence:

Quand l'oeil du corps s'éteint, l'oeil de l'esprit s'allume.
(xx, "A un poète aveugle")

Elle était déchaussée, elle était décoiffée,
Assise, les pieds nus, parmi les joncs penchants;
Moi qui passais par là, je crus *voir* une fée,
(xxi, my italics)

Indeed, the first line of each stanza in this poem states the seductive threat of the here-and-now world. The girl's reality, at first pictorially described, "je crus voir une fée," intrudes itself more and more disturbingly as the poem progresses.

Elle me regarda de ce regard suprême
. . .
Elle essuya ses pieds à l'herbe de la rive;
Elle me regarda pour la seconde fois,
. . .
Comme l'eau caressait doucement le rivage!
. . .
Ses cheveux dans ses yeux, et riant au travers.
(xxi)

Finally, she laughs, and the poem ends with an end to innocence. Lexically, syntactically, and thematically, the last words form a rift through which the narrator may fall.

The theme of the ironic observer, which first appeared in the narrative development of poems ii-iv, constitutes the very warp and woof of the extraordinary "La Fête chez Thérèse." The conflicting notions of our fallen, erotic nature and the redemptive obligation of the poetic voice begin to merge in this "playful" poem about plays within plays. The ironical tone is felt at once by the use of polite language: "La chose fut exquise et fort bien ordonnée." In the classical language of the discriminating patrician audience whom Hugo berated in "Réponse à un acte d'accusation" and "Suite," the narrator begins to describe the Watteauesque festivities. Mask upon mask, the costumed guests observe a mock pastoral in which monkeys ride about on the backs of dogs and Columbine sleeps in a seashell hidden amongst the lattice work, an unthreatening perversion of the sardonic Plautus. A real noonday sun and a soft April breeze provide the ironic distancing.

> Le soleil tenait lieu de lustre; la saison
> Avait brodé de fleurs un immense gazon,
> Vert tapis déroulé sous maint groupe folâtre.
> Rangés des deux côtés de l'agreste théâtre,
> Les vrais arbres du parc, les sorbiers, les lilas,
> (xxii, "La Fête chez Thérèse")

Language within this idyllic masquerade has so prettified truth that God is a clown and sin a roué's charm:

> Thérèse la duchesse à qui je donnerais,
> Si j'étais roi, Paris, si j'étais Dieu, le monde,
> . . .
> Le seigneur Pantalon, dans une niche, à droite,
> Vendait des limons doux sur une table étroite,
> Et criait par instants: "Seigneurs, l'homme est divin.
> Dieu n'avait fait que l'eau, mais l'homme a fait le vin!"

The reader himself is caught up in the "charm" and does not become aware of its danger until the narrator-observer (like Satan in iv) shocks him by the isolated couplet:

> Moi, j'écoutais, pensif, un profane couplet
> Que fredonnait dans l'ombre un abbé violet.

The "profane couplet" is *this* couplet, set off as it is from the rest of the poem-idyll. It is profane in the same way that the irreligious laughter of v or the revolutionary poetics of "Suite"

98

are profane; it states the truth and rips the veils of the *bien-séances*. The sham holiness of a perverted religion must be destroyed before a new redemptive language can be effective. It is the couplet spoken by one of the legion of the sacred damned, dressed in the purple costume of an abbot. The word "pensif," rhythmically isolated from the rest of the line, states the paradox essential to Hugo's religious and poetic order. This same damned abbot will soon say of himself:

Je suis le ténébreux par qui tout dégénère.
. . .

        . . . Orateurs, écrivains,
Poëtes, nous avons, du doigt avançant l'heure,
Dit à la rhétorique: — Allons, fille majeure,
Lève les yeux! — et j'ai, chantant, luttant, bravant,
Tordu plus d'une grille au parloir du couvent;
J'ai, torche en main, ouvert les deux battants du drame.
        (xxvi, "Quelques mots à un autre")

The real profanity of the gallant language is not apparent until this unmasking, at which point the biblical overtones of the final stanza of "Thérèse" can be heard: "Les folles *en riant* entraînèrent les sages." The poet's "profane" or purely sensuous eye, symbolized by the erotic orb of the peacock's tail, is released from its thrall by his alienated consciousness:

Thérèse était assise à l'ombre d'un buisson;
Les roses pâlissaient à côté de sa joue,
Et, la voyant si belle, un paon faisait la roue.

Moi, j'écoutais, pensif, un profane couplet
Que fredonnait dans l'ombre un abbé violet.

Thus the charming fête becomes charged with metaphysical significance. "La Fête chez Thérèse" is a good example of a poem that can be correctly read only within the context of the work as a whole. The isolated couplet, "Moi, j'écoutais . . . ," does not gain its full value until the reader has understood the rôle of the ironic consciousness in the redemptive scheme.

In the following poem Hugo openly states the presence of evil in social terms with the emblematic picture of the orphaned child. This image will become the central symbol of Books III and IV and indeed of the total narrative. While the mother dies, the child sings and the Satanic narrator looks on: "Et j'écoutais ce râle, et j'entendais ce chant (xxiii, "L'Enfance")." The erotic presence of "La Fête chez Thérèse" is revealed in this poem to be Death itself.

> . . . et sur leurs gorges blanches
> Les actrices sentaient errer l'ombre des branches.
> > (xxii, "La Fête chez Thérèse")

> La mort au-dessus d'elle errait dans la nuée;
> > (xxiii, "L'Enfance")

In the remaining four poems, the distance between the poet-allegorist and the lyrical "I" seems to disappear.

> Heureux l'homme, occupé de l'éternel destin,
> Qui, tel qu'un voyageur qui part de grand matin,
> Se réveille, l'esprit rempli de rêverie,
> Et, dès l'aube du jour, se met à lire et prie!
> A mesure qu'il lit, le jour vient lentement
> Et se fait dans son âme ainsi qu'au firmament.
> Il voit distinctement, à cette clarté blême,
> Des choses dans sa chambre et d'autres en lui-même;
> Tout dort dans la maison; il est seul, il le croit,
> Et cependant, fermant leur bouche de leur doigt,
> Derrière lui, tandis que l'extase l'enivre,
> Les anges souriants se penchent sur son livre.
> > Paris, septembre 1842.
> > > (xxiv)

100

From a pictorial point of view, this poem is a companion-piece or mirror-image of "Mes deux filles." Instead of the projection of the temporal forms (daughters, father) into the enduring innocence of natural creation ("Cygne," "colombe," "oeillets," "papillons"), the opposite seems to have taken place. In xxiv the father is the "homme-voyageur" announced in the preface, but all movement takes place within his cranium. The daughters are heraldically frozen as angelic guardians of that inner voyage. Poet, child, reader are all bent over the book, like the poet over the mystery of creation in the prefatory poem "Un jour je vis. . . ." He is not merely a father-dreamer, but is like Ulysses, the *national* hero of his time, who will embark upon the great humanitarian epic announced by Ballanche. Unlike the private ecstasy expressed by the metaphoric language of iii, the new plebeian poet's ecstasy bears with it the moral responsibility of the teacher. His experience of Unity (xxv) must be narrated over and over; it must be understood by the humblest as well as by the poet-initiators themselves. Together poems xxiv and xxv describe the ultimate visionary experience characterized by the melting of opposites into a sublimely simple revelation: " 'Et moi, j'ai des rayons, aussi!' lui disait-elle!" (xxv, "Unité")

As he warned Chénier in v, Hugo is not afraid to mix prose with poetry. Since he addresses himself to the masses, his poetry must reflect the nature of that vital yet imprisoned spirit. Three more times Hugo asserts the redemptive power of the new poet-hero. "Quelques mots à un autre," like "Réponse à un acte d'accusation" and "Suite," does so in violent, historical terms:

> Certe, on me laisserait en paix, passant obscur,
> Si je ne contenais, atome de l'azur,
> Un peu du grand rayon dont notre époque est faite.
> (xxvi, "Quelques mots à un autre")

101

The next poem echoes ii and thus reaffirms the direct, Orphic powers of the poetic consciousness:

> Oui, je suis le rêveur; je suis le camarade
> Des petites fleurs d'or du mur qui se dégrade,
> Et l'interlocuteur des arbres et du vent.
> Tout cela me connaît, voyez-vous. . . .
>
> (xxvii)

Poem xxviii constitutes an *ars poetica* valid for a fully evolved poetic voice—indeed for the poet of *Au bord de l'infini* as well as for the poet of *Aurore.*

> Il faut que le poëte, épris d'ombre et d'azur,
> Esprit doux et splendide, au rayonnement pur,
> Qui marche devant tous, éclairant ceux qui doutent,
> Chanteur mystérieux qu'en tressaillant écoutent
> Les femmes, les songeurs, les sages, les amants,
> Devienne formidable à de certains moments.
>
> (xxviii)

Thus at the end of *Aurore,* the tension created by the doubling of the narrator is dissipated; but we have come a long way. It is a question not of abandoning one poetic voice for another, but rather of making the Universal Analogy heard on all levels. The problem for the nineteenth-century poet is with the communicant for whom religious expression is no longer meaningful. The prophetic voice of Saint John and the roar of the apocalyptic lion must take him unawares, "au milieu de cette humble et haute poésie."

"A ma fille" and "Halte en marchant"

The frame poems, "A ma fille" and "Halte en marchant," explicitly state the direction of the spiritual journey revealed indirectly within their enclosing panels. The first poem is apocryphally dated one year before the supreme sacrifice-drowning

102

was to take place, and the last poem describes the poet's discovery of redemption through death, at an inn in the midst
of idyllic surroundings. Like the date of the first poem,
the location of the second evokes Léopoldine's drowning, thus
reaffirming the poeticization of personal history: Hugo first
discovered her death while reading a newspaper in a country
inn, on his return from the Pyrenees.

In i, Hugo gives his daughter, and by analogy the reader, the
necessary advice for a spiritually meaningful life: "Vis du
monde éloignée." That one is supposed to identify at the outset
with the daughter is evident from the structure of this moraliz-
ing poem. There is a clear progression from the personal and
specific "mon enfant" repeated twice in the first two stanzas
to the more general "nul" and "tous les hommes" of stanzas
three to five. The universal nature of the message is further
emphasized by the use of the allgorical *persona* of "grand roi
sans amours," "penseurs" and "héros" in stanzas six to eight,
"nous" of nine and ten, and the final divine commandment in
the last stanza:

> Cette loi sainte, il faut s'y conformer,
> Et la voici, *toute âme y peut atteindre*:
> Ne rien haïr, mon enfant; tout aimer,
> Ou tout plaindre!
>
> (my italics)

While the poems placed toward the end of *Aurore* demonstrate through the use of irony the threat of sensual reality to
the poetic or religious spirit, "A ma fille" explicitly states the
value of the spiritual life. Divine light is placed within the
sacrificial child in stanza two:

> Sois bonne et douce, et lève un front pieux.
> Comme le jour dans les cieux met sa flamme,
> Toi, mon enfant, dans l'azur de tes yeux
> Mets ton âme!

The soul replaces the sun as a source of truth just as it does in poem xxiv, "Heureux l'homme, occupé de l'éternel destin." "Flamme" of stanza two is opposed to the ephemeral "flambeaux" of stanza eight. Thus very gently Hugo establishes the "univers sous un crâne" concept which will be reflected in the narrative movement from *Aurore* to *Au bord de l'infini*. The mortal time of "nos jours vains et sonores" and the repetition of "un," "un," "un," in stanza five are replaced by the eternity of a singular merciful presence: "Chaque matin, il baigne de ses pleurs / Nos aurores." The same antithesis is reflected by the isolated events of such poems as "Lise," "A Granville, en 1836," or "La Coccinelle," and the contemplative presence which arranged them in the collection. Thus the sterility of a life of personal satisfaction symbolized in "A ma fille" by the "désert immense" or "un puits où le vide toujours recommence" is replaced by the creative and sacrificial tear. Resignation, compassion, and charitable love are God's law—all the rest *vanitas vanitatum*.

"Halte en marchant"

At the end of the first chapter the pilgrim arrives at the first station. As for Juliette and Hugo on their return from the Pyrenees in September 1843, revelation takes place in a country inn.[7] It is a sacred place, revealed miraculously to the traveler, as the château of the Fisher King was to Perceval:

Une brume couvrait l'horizon; maintenant,
Voici le clair midi qui surgit rayonnant;

. . .

Un bouge est là, montrant, dans la sauge et le thym,
Un vieux saint souriant parmi des brocs d'étain,

[7] In allegorical literature the inn is often used as a holy center to which all roads lead, a place where revelation occurs. See Fletcher, *Allegory*, pp. 210 ff.

Avec tant de rayons et de fleurs sur la berge,
Que c'est peut-être un temple ou peut-être une auberge,
Que notre bouche ait soif, ou que ce soit le coeur,
Gloire au Dieu bon qui tend la coupe au voyageur!

The sacrificial child is there, at once pagan and Christian in the detail:

On croit voir l'humble toit effondré d'une crèche.
A la source du pré, qu'abrite un vert rideau,
Une enfant blonde alla remplir sa jarre d'eau,
Joyeuse et soulevant son jupon de futaine.
Pendant qu'elle plongeait sa cruche à la fontaine,
L'eau semblait admirer, gazouillant doucement,
Cette belle petite aux yeux de firmament.[8]

[8] Charles Baudouin discusses the psychoanalytic importance of well imagery in Hugo's work, *Psychanalyse de Victor Hugo*, pp. 63-6: "Nous comprendrons plus profondément cette attitude devant le mystère, lorsque nous aurons étudié le complexe de la naissance. Retenons dès maintenant que 'l'abîme des soleils' symbolise étroitement avec le 'ventre des mères.' L'abîme demeure, chez Hugo, une des expressions favorites du mystère cosmique; ne nous étonnons pas de voir souvent le premier, comme le second, représenté par l'image du puits, dont nous connaissons les résonances depuis que nous l'avons rencontrée dans les premiers souvenirs. . . . Il n'y a pas à s'y méprendre: le puits de la cour de la rue de Clichy, le puisard des Feuillantines sont devenus, par un grandissement magnifique, l'abîme métaphysique de l'inconnu, et désormais, 'Le contemplateur, triste et meurtri, mais serein. . . / . . . Se penche, frémissant, au puits des grands vertiges (*A celle qui est restée en France*).'" In *Les Misérables* Cosette meets Jean Valjean for the first time in the pitch dark at the well outside of Thénardier's inn. Soon afterward he draws her from her fetal position under the table, where she hides from abuse, and they become a questing couple. The well imagery is especially important within the context of the symbolic year, 1843. The ocean in which Léopoldine drowns will become the well-source from which Hugo draws the poem telling the story of the creative process. Thus the drowning is baptismal and redemptive:
Poëte, tu fais bien! poëte au triste front,
   Tu rêves près des ondes,

105

Just as in "Pasteurs et troupeaux," it is from the moment of encounter with the girl that the symbolic image is born:

> Et moi, près du grand lit drapé de vieilles serges,
> Pensif, je regardais un Christ battu de verges.[9]

A natural scene described in the language of pagan antiquity has evoked a supernatural awareness in just the same way that the sight of Thérèse inspired the response of the profane couplet.

> Le fait religieux ce n'est pas l'église; c'est la rose qui s'ouvre, c'est l'aube qui éclôt, c'est l'oiseau qui fait son nid. Le fait religieux, c'est la sainte nature éternelle.
> (*Philosophie, commencement d'un livre*, p. 65)

The identification between the communicant-reader and Léopoldine, suggested by the first poem, is now further intensified and complicated by the identification between the narrator-pilgrim and Christ himself.

> Plus tard, le vagabond flagellé devient Dieu;
> . . .
> Souffrez, penseurs, des pleurs de vos bourreaux baignés!
> Le deuil sacre les saints, les sages, les génies; . . .

After an elaboration upon the poet's function as martyr,

> Et tu tires des mers bien des choses qui sont
> Sous les vagues profondes!

[9] André Dumas' misreading of this poem illustrates my thesis that an understanding of the narrative order of the work as a whole helps to illuminate individual poems: "Le début et la fin du poème s'accordent mal; on a le sentiment d'une cassure. Peut-être les premiers vers, tableau virgilien d'un paysage et d'une auberge furent-ils écrits en 1837, après une promenade avec Juliette dans la banlieue parisienne, et les derniers à Jersey. On insulte les poètes, les pasteurs d'hommes, mais leur martyre fait leur force et leur gloire. Victor Hugo, attaqué par d'infatigables adversaires, a souvent développé cette idée." *Les Contemplations* (Paris, 1962), p. 375, note 157.

Hugo ends "Halte en marchant" and *Aurore* with a parable, using a strikingly *unnaturalistic* image of light as his key symbol:

Un de ceux qui liaient Jésus-Christ au poteau,
Et qui, sur son dos nu, jetaient un vil manteau,
Arracha de ce front tranquille une poignée
De cheveux qu'inondait la sueur résignée,
Et dit: 'Je vais montrer à Caïphe cela!'
Et, crispant son poing noir, cet homme s'en alla.
La nuit était venue et la rue était sombre;
L'homme marchait; soudain, il s'arrêta dans l'ombre,
Stupéfait, pâle, et comme en proie aux visions,
Frémissant!—il avait dans la main des rayons.

Thus *Aurore* is both the first step—the awakening of the senses to the universe of forms—and the entire journey, which will require the sacrifice of those natural forms to a higher level of contemplative awareness. In the same way each day (dawn to dusk) or each life (Hugo's or Léopoldine's) is a reflection of the story of Human Destiny. *Aurore*, like *Les Contemplations* as a whole, can be both a beginning and a totality, Genesis and the total Scripture; it is a remembered experience that must be communicated, ironically and dialectically, to the fallen reader.

V

L'AME EN FLEUR

IN THE preceding chapter it became clear that the relationship of the poet-narrator to the poet-allegorist provides a thematic thread that helps clarify the seemingly paradoxical presence of both idyllic and apocalyptic voices. Because of this poetic doubling, *Aurore* can be considered both part and totality of the general narrative. As part it has a particular focus that can be termed idyllic or naive. The poet-narrator and, correspondingly, the reader setting forth are, in a sense, seduced by that which evokes familiar reality in themselves.

In the second book of *Les Contemplations* this encounter between the subjective consciousness and the outside world is carried one step further. The organic universe of *Aurore* is internalized—hence the metaphor "âme en fleur." The bee-flower image representative of the *Aurore* experience is translated into explicitly human and, at first, sexual terms. The multiplicity of the garden coalesces into the symbolical loved one, just as it does in the allegorical garden of Guillaume de Lorris after the lover's gaze is channeled into the crystals in the depths of the pond.

I have already pointed out in my discussion of poems xi-xvi of *Aurore* that the focusing of natural creation in the woman indicates an increasing preoccupation with the world of forms. Paradoxically, then, Book II is moving us further from the happy innocence of Original Creation and closer to the contemplative inwardness which will make a return to that unity possible. In other words, it is one step closer to the *felix culpa* of Books III and IV.

In *L'Ame en fleur* the poet's experience of the world is ex-

pressed in a more intensely personal way. It is, correspondingly, the most consistently lyrical chapter in the collection.[1] Subjective time replaces the pseudo-journalistic time of *Aurore*.
All the poems are given months or seasons but no years: e.g.,
"mai, 18. . . ." Nature is described in human terms, as an
état d'âme:

> Les vieux antres pensifs, dont rit le geai moqueur,
> Clignent leurs gros sourcils et font la bouche en coeur;
> (i, "Premier mai")

It is not difficult to see the way *L'Ame en fleur* fits into the
general allegorical narrative on all levels. On that of Hugo's
cosmogony, it represents the ripening and perpetuation of an
imperfect creation. "Tout conjugue le verbe aimer. . . ." This
is reflected in the individual's life by an awakening sexuality
and in Hugo's own life by his encounter with Juliette Drouet.
On the level of the poetic process it is the moment when
consciousness appropriates natural forms to make them a part
of the universe inside his brain. The seizing of the innocent
but seductive maiden (Europa, Persephone) by the fallen god
figures this stage.

> Mon bras pressait ta taille frêle
> Et souple comme le roseau;
> Ton sein palpitait comme l'aile
> D'un jeune oiseau.
>
> Longtemps muets, nous contemplâmes
> Le ciel où s'éteignait le jour.
> Que se passait-il dans nos âmes?
> Amour! amour!

[1] In the preface to *Cromwell* Hugo says that lyric poetry is representative of an early stage in the cultural development of the human race.
Hunt, *The Epic*, points out Edgar Quinet's debt to Hugo for the same
idea in *Génie des religions*, where Quinet considers architecture and
lyric poetry together as early expressions of man's religious development.

Comme un ange qui se dévoile,
Tu me regardais, dans ma nuit,
Avec ton beau regard d'étoile,
    Qui m'éblouit.

                (x)

That Hugo accepted the neo-Platonic and popular Romantic notion of earthly love as a route—however perilous—toward the Divine seems evident everywhere in his work. In "Les Mages" (vi,xxiii) he lists the priests of love: Plautus, Ariosto, Catullus, Horace, Epicurus, Bion, and Moschus. In *Les Misérables* he describes the love-sick Marius as a kind of pantheistic medium through whom creation pours:

> J'ai rencontré dans la rue un jeune homme très pauvre qui aimait. Son chapeau était vieux, son habit était usé; il avait les coudes troués; l'eau passait à travers ses souliers et les astres à travers son âme.
>
>   (p. 668)

Redemption of the brutish male through love is a favorite theme in many of Hugo's novels. Quasimodo, Jean Valjean, and Gilliatt are examples. In fact, Jean Valjean's advice to Marius and Cosette at the end of *Les Misérables*: "Soyez-vous l'un pour l'autre une religion," describes Hugo's view of his own relationship with Juliette Drouet:

> Des amours . . . comme le nôtre . . . ne se désalterent qu'en Dieu. Pour vivre pleinement, il leur faut la mort. . . .
>
>   (31 Déc. 1854)

> Le jour où nous entrerons dans cette vie qu'on appelle la mort, notre chair tombera . . . et il ne restera que les âmes; ton âme, la mienne, mêlées, mariées, enlacées. . . faisant un seul rayon de l'oeil de Dieu.
>
>   (31 Déc. 1855)[2]

[2] Letters written to Juliette on the first of every year, quoted by Albouy in his notes to the Pléiade edition of *Les Contemplations*, p. 1441.

Yet because love can result in a heightened sensuality (*Aurore*, poems xix, xx), it is more than ever prey to the evils of temporal existence. Matter begets matter, imperfection begets imperfection. Love can be either redemptive as it is for Quasimodo or sinful as it is for Claude Frollo. In its highest form it is far from its sensual beginnings. Thus there are present in *L'Ame en fleur* two seemingly contradictory attitudes. The woman as sensuous form is both a seductive threat and a source of hope. On the one hand she draws the narrator away from his untroubled communion with nature. On the other, his obsessive, indeed slave-like, concentration upon her particular form can represent the first step toward a new poetry in which she will gain a redemptive significance. The mortal beauty of Léopoldine, Juliette, or Persephone will be transformed through the poetic imagination into a symbol of regeneration and eternity—the symbol of artistic creation itself.

Much ink has been spent over the question of whether certain poems in *L'Ame en fleur* were in fact addressed to Léonie d'Aunet rather than to Juliette.[3] Given Hugo's mythic perception of his own life, it seems likely that he would feel the necessity for Léonie's adulterous presence in this chapter; for his affair with her symbolized the threat of seduction by the sensual forces that had to be transcended if he and Juliette were to love religiously. It is the gradual revelation of this threat of the sensual world on the poetic dream that constitutes the thematic structure of *L'Ame en fleur*.

Generally one could say that the love within Book II becomes less and less physical and more and more idealized. Taken separately the first fourteen poems, in the main, celebrate an expanding and receptive sensuality. Poetic devices used in the

[3] See the notes in the following editions: Albouy (Pléiade), pp. 1440, 1455; Dumas (Garnier), note 163, p. 376, or note 161, p. 375; also Journet and Robert, *Notes*, p. 70; L. Guimbaud, *Victor Hugo et Juliette Drouet* (Paris, 1914), p. 421; Léon Cellier, "A propos du *Rouet d'Omphale*," *Mélanges*, 1940.

first poem, such as repetition, amplification, running on, or words in a series, translate the bursting storm of sensuality that new love and Original Creation have in common.

> A chaque pas du jour dans le bleu firmament,
> La campagne éperdue, et toujours plus éprise,
> Prodigue les senteurs, et dans la tiède brise
> Envoie au renouveau ses baisers odorants.
> Tous ses bouquets, azurs, carmins, pourpres, safrans,
> Dont l'haleine s'envole en murmurant: Je t'aime!
> Sur le ravin, l'étang, le pré, le sillon même,
> Font des taches partout de toutes les couleurs;
> Et, donnant les parfums, elle a gardé les fleurs;
> Comme si ses soupirs et ses tendres missives
> Au mois de mai, qui rit dans les branches lascives,
> Et tous les billets doux de son amour bavard,
> Avaient laissé leur trace aux pages du buvard!
>
> (i, "Premier Mai")

Nature is described anthropomorphically (i, ix, xi), the loved ones are placed in a country setting (v, vi, vii, xii, xiii), or nature is absorbed into the loved one herself, a reverse expression of the anthropomorphizing consciousness (ii, viii, x). Poem ix explicitly states the Orphic power of love to "move nature to tears."

> Amour, lorsqu'en nos coeurs tu te réfugias,
> L'oiseau vint y puiser; ce sont ces plagiats,
> Ces chants qu'un rossignol, belles, prend sur vos bouches,
> Qui font que les grands bois courbent leurs fronts farouches,
> Et que les lourds rochers, stupides et ravis,
> Se penchent, les laissant piller le chènevis,
> Et ne distinguent plus, dans leurs rêves étranges,
> La langue des oiseaux de la langue des anges.
>
> (ix, "En écoutant les oiseaux")

112

Poem xiv, at the very center of the chapter, marks a turning-point. It is the description of a dream about dead lovers in a poeticized letter. Their earthly reality is rejected as a false paradise:

Je n'ai fait que rêver de vous toute la nuit.

. . .

Oh! oui, nous étions morts, bien sûr; je vous le dis.
Nous avions tous les deux la forme de nos âmes.

. . .

Je disais: "Viens-nous-en dans les profondeurs sombres,
Vivons; c'est *autrefois* que nous étions des ombres."

(my italics)

Indeed, nature recedes from view following this very highly mediated (dream, letter, death) poem. Winter and darkness (xv, xviii, xx, xxiv, xxvi, xxviii) replace spring and sunlight, and the lovers withdraw from a world that now threatens their magical circle. This withdrawal is the main theme of most of the remaining poems (xv, xvi, xviii, xx, xxi, xxiii, xxiv, xxv, xxvii, xxviii).

"Si nous pouvions quitter ce Paris triste et fou,
Nous fuirions; nous irions quelque part, n'importe où,"

(xxi)

Love becomes a defense against another, stronger reality and the song a kind of ritual incantation to stave off its monstrous presence (xxii, xxiii, xxiv, xxv, xxvi):

Aimons toujours! aimons encore!

. . .

L'amour seul reste. O noble femme,
Si tu veux, dans ce vil séjour,
Garder ta foi, garder ton âme,
Garder ton Dieu, garde l'amour!

(xxii)

113

Cut off from the rest of the world, the lovers are reduced to a tight, self-enclosing circle, each flickeringly illuminated by the other's gaze.

> Sans relever la tête et sans me dire un mot,
> Une ombre reste au fond de mon coeur qui vous aime;
> Et, pour que je vous voie entièrement, il faut
> Me regarder un peu, de temps en temps, vous-même.
>
> (xv)

> Moi qui ne cherche dans ce monde
> Que la seule réalité,
> Moi qui laisse fuir comme l'onde
> Tout ce qui n'est que vanité,
>
> Je préfère, aux biens dont s'enivre
> L'orgueil du soldat ou du roi,
> L'ombre que tu fais sur mon livre
> Quand ton front se penche sur moi.
>
> (xxii)

> Je respire où tu palpites,
> Tu sais; à quoi bon, hélas!
> Rester là si tu me quittes,
> Et vivre si tu t'en vas?
>
> (xxv)

> Aimons! c'est tout. Et Dieu le veut ainsi.
> Laisse ton ciel que de froids rayons dorent!
> Tu trouveras, dans deux yeux qui t'adorent,
> Plus de beauté, plus de lumière aussi!
> Aimer, c'est voir, sentir, rêver, comprendre.
> L'esprit plus grand s'ajoute au coeur plus tendre.
>
> (xxviii)

Their thoughts become fixed upon their own transfigured selves in xix, xxii, xxv, xxvi. At the end of Book II the nature of

poems i-xiv is either absent or coldly indifferent. Even the
memory of a lost spring is described as lighting up only the
outside of a temple whose truth is now sealed within. The
world is no longer a mirror of man's soul, but a mocking reminder of his temporality:

> Nos coeurs battaient; l'extase m'étouffait;
> Les fleurs du soir entr'ouvraient leurs corolles . . .
> Qu'avez-vous fait, arbres, de nos paroles?
> De nos soupirs, rochers, qu'avez-vous fait?
> C'est un destin bien triste que le nôtre,
> Puisqu'un tel jour s'envole comme un autre!
>
> O souvenirs! trésor dans l'ombre accru!
> Sombre horizon des anciennes pensées!
> Chère lueur des choses éclipsées!
> Rayonnement du passé disparu!
> Comme du seuil et du dehors d'un temple,
> L'oeil de l'esprit en rêvant vous *contemple*!
>
> (xxviii, my italics)

Contemplation of the vanished past is symbolically expressed
in the last stanza through an allusion to *Faust* and the ballad
of the King of Thule that Gretchen sings as Mephistopheles
hides the jeweled casket in her room.

> Quand les beaux jours font place aux jours amers,
> De tout bonheur il faut quitter l'idée;
> Quand l'espérance est tout à fait vidée,
> Laissons tomber la coupe au fond des mers.
> L'oubli! l'oubli! c'est l'onde où tout se noie;
> C'est la mer sombre où l'on jette sa joie.

Like the King of Thule in the medieval German ballad, the
dying lover throws the cup symbolizing fidelity to his dead
loved one back into the sea so that it will never be adulterated

by the "monstre réalité" of which she was so afraid in poem
xii:

> Alors, elle me dit: "J'ai peur qu'on ne nous voie!
> Cherchons un antre afin d'y cacher notre joie!
> Vois ce pauvre géant! nous aurions notre tour!
> Car les dieux envieux qui l'ont fait disparaître,
> Et qui furent jaloux de sa grandeur, peut-être
> Seraient jaloux de notre amour!"
>
> (xii, "Eglogue")

The thematic pattern of increasing spiritualization and despair repeats and indeed intensifies the sacrificial pattern I
have noted in *Aurore* from joyous personal communion with
nature toward an ironic observation of that experience. *L'Ame
en fleur* could be said to be nothing more than a description of
the fleeting quality of earthly love, had we not read the ironic
treatment of the love theme in *Aurore*.[4]

The clear-cut pattern outlined in the preceding paragraphs
(expanded consciousness to mediated withdrawal) is however,
more complex than one may first imagine. By placing the disturbingly erotic "Le Rouet d'Omphale" at the beginning of
the love story (this poem stands out from the others in the
first half of *L'Ame en fleur* because nature is complely absent
from it), Hugo alters the reader's appreciation of all subsequent positive affirmations of an awakened sensuality. If the
reader recognizes the contaminating effect of the poems upon
one another, both as he reads for the first time and in retro-
spect, he must feel the inevitability of sacrifice that ends the
chapter (the gesture of the King of Thule). Behind the lyric
poetry there emerges early an ominous metaphysical drama
between good and evil.

We have seen in chapter iv that although "Le Rouet d'Om-

[4] See my discussion of "La Fête chez Thérèse," in chapter iv.

116

phale" describes a single tableau, a Grecian room containing only a carved spinning wheel, with shadowy figures of the twenty monsters Hercules has conquered hovering in the background, the poem is formally split in the middle. The first part is a precise, realistic description of the abandoned wheel; the second part is an emotional evocation of the roaming monsters. The painterly still-life and simple paratactic sentence structure of the first twelve lines gives way to the disturbing dreamworld atmosphere and complex syntax of the last twelve lines. This dramatic binary structure jolts the reader out of his passive appreciation of form into an attitude of defense and suspicion—precisely the movement the lovers will make in the thematic development of the section as a whole. Both the wheel and the monsters have been abandoned by the absent lovers, Omphale and Hercules; the legend depicted on the plinth of the wheel bears silent testimony to the invisible encounter taking place somewhere beyond the atrium, in the depths of the pagan palace.

Thus "Le Rouet d'Omphale" expresses the dichotomy I have already described between the seemingly timeless earthly paradise of the lovers and the ominous reality waiting just beyond their magic circle. The contracting sphere of the experience of earthly love, which ultimately ends in the physical annihilation of the lovers (the dying King of Thule throws the symbolic reminder of his dead loved one back into the formless sea), is ironically stated by the poet's focusing upon ideated representations of their being ("rouet," "monstres"; "Europe," "taureau blanc"; "roue," "quenouille"; "fil souple et lié," "massue"). The lovers are present only by their *absence*, by the marks they have left upon the reality of the atrium.

The haste with which Hercules has left the wheel and the humiliation of the half-conquered monsters eloquently express the violence of the lovers' encounter. Hugo places "Le

Rouet d'Omphale" immediately after a poem that channels the cosmic sexuality of "Premier Mai" into the poet's own experience:

> Les monts, les champs, les lacs et les chênes mouvants,
> Répètent un quatrain fait par les quatre vents.
>
> (end of "Premier Mai")

> Mes vers fuiraient, doux et frêles,
> Vers votre jardin si beau,
> Si mes vers avaient des ailes,
> Des ailes comme l'oiseau.
>
> (ii)

Thus poem iii is unsettling to the reader who finds himself docilely led into a sexual atmosphere heavy with implied condemnation. That the world of poetry (rouet) and heroic action (Hercules, slayer of monsters) must wait is particularly disturbing. The humiliation and quiescent violence of iii will indeed contaminate the reader's experience of the other poems in the first half of *L'Ame en fleur*, which, if read singly, would seem to state positively an awakened sensuality. Consequently, seemingly "innocent" and traditional love poems like vi and vii are read with the "oeil humilié" of a *voyeur*.

> Nous allions au verger cueillir des bigarreaux.
> Avec ses beaux bras blancs en marbre de Paros,
> Elle montait dans l'arbre et courbait une branche;
> Les feuilles frissonnaient au vent; sa gorge blanche,
> O Virgile, ondoyait dans l'ombre et le soleil;
>
> (vii)

The same poetic doubling that takes place between poet-narrator and poet-allegorist has taken place in the reader.

The theme of humiliation through love is a major one in *L'Ame en fleur* (see poems viii, xii, xviii) and requires further examination, because it reflects once again the sacrificial imperative of Hugo's poetics.

The humiliated lover belongs to the tradition of courtly romance later to be re-worked as a poetic conceit in the sixteenth century, and thus is a part of the "autrefois" of a French literary tradition. As we have seen by the references to Virgil and Horace in *Aurore*, Hugo wishes to establish the parallel evolution of our social, literary, and poetic consciousness. His intentional evocation of a sixteenth-century ancestry is clear in such poems as viii, for example: "Tu peux, comme il te plaît, me faire jeune ou vieux," or xxv:

> Je respire où tu palpites,
> Tu sais; à quoi bon, hélas!
> Rester là si tu me quittes,
> . . .
>
> Je suis la fleur des murailles
> Dont avril est le seul bien.
> Il suffit que tu t'en ailles
> Pour qu'il ne reste plus rien.

The woman who has usurped the power of the natural world (sun, moon, rain) to control her lover totally is a Petrarchan theme.

Yet in "Le Rouet d'Omphale," Hugo seems to be expanding the application of the theme of servile dependence of one lover upon the other in such a way as to make the love experience reflective of the more general sacrificial pattern from *Aurore* to *Au bord de l'infini*, and hence of the poetic process itself. Technically, the last twelve lines of "Le Rouet d'Omphale" are representative of the poetry of Book vi—"Pleurs dans la nuit" or "Horror." The monsters belong to the chaos of forms that poetic language will ultimately tame. If one recognizes Jupiter and Hercules as symbols of the poetic consciousness and Eu-

119

ropa and Omphale as symbols of the world to be apprehended (an extension of the bee-flower metaphor of *Aurore*), the dependence of the lovers upon one another becomes more than a mere literary conceit. That Hercules has left the world of heroic action to spin for Omphale is a positive change. Some kind of renewal through sacrifice is essential on both spiritual and artistic levels. The springtime return of Persephone to Earth and her eternal kidnapping back to Pluto's world of the dead may well represent the pattern. *Les Contemplations* both begins and ends with poems that have as their subject the world outside the poet's mind. Yet the process of interiorization—of *apprehension* by the satanic presence—is necessary for that world to be endowed with its divine—i.e., intentional—nature. The natural world of *Aurore* will grow into the supernatural (Hugo's "surnaturel") world of *Au bord de l'infini* through the intervention of the poetic mind. Both Europa and Persephone thus gain in significance after their contact with the satanic demigod:

> Et maintenant, captive et reine en même temps,
> Prisonnière au plus noir de son âme profonde,
> Parmi les visions qui flottent comme l'onde,
> Sous son crâne à la fois céleste et souterrain,
> Assise, et t'accoudant sur un trône d'airain,
>
> . . .
>
> Tu rêves dans sa nuit, Proserpine sinistre.
>
> (V,xxv)

The springtime experience, suggested by the circular, hypnotic stanza of the last poem of *L'Ame en fleur*, is always threatened by death:

> Ma bien-aimée ainsi tout bas parlait,
> Avec son front posé sur sa main blanche,
> Et l'oeil rêveur d'un ange qui se penche,

Et sa voix grave, et cet air qui me plaît;
Belle et tranquille, et de me voir charmée,
Ainsi tout bas parlait ma bien-aimée.

Nos coeurs battaient; l'extase m'étouffait;
Les fleurs du soir entr'ouvraient leurs corolles . . .
Qu'avez-vous fait, arbres, de nos paroles?
      (xxviii, "Un Soir que je regardais le ciel")

And the sensuous Arcadia of vii ("Nous allions au verger cueillir des bigarreaux") is threatened by the *carpe diem* theme of xxvi:

Aimez-vous! c'est le mois où les fraises sont mûres.
L'ange du soir rêveur, qui flotte dans les vents,
Mêle, en les emportant sur ses ailes obscures,
Les prières des morts aux baisers des vivants.

The circular interdependence of the poetic lucidity and sense perception must be constantly maintained if time is to be transformed into eternity.

A metapoetic interpretation on the theme of dependence dissipates the limiting antithesis of the world of subjective love and the waiting reality of the atrium that an isolated reading of *L'Ame en fleur* or "Le Rouet d'Omphale" would yield. The scene engraved on the plinth of the spinning wheel, symbol of poetic expression, brings the two worlds together both in theme and in diction.

Un ouvrier d'Egine a sculpté sur la plinthe
Europe dont un dieu n'écoute pas la plainte.
Le taureau blanc l'emporte. Europe, sans espoir,
Crie, et, baissant les yeux, s'épouvante de voir
L'Océan monstrueux qui baise ses pieds roses.
  . . .

Cependant, odieux, effroyables, énormes,
Dans le fond du palais, vingt fantômes difformes,
Vingt monstres tout sanglants, qu'on ne voit qu'à demi,
Errent en foule autour du rouet endormi:

The word "monstrueux" associates the "vingt monstres tout sanglants" with the powers that rape and carry away the maiden. At the same time, an identification is established between the half-defeated creatures bearing the imprint of Hercules' "massue" and the raped Europa herself. The last line of the poem, "fixent de loin dans l'ombre *un oeil humilié*," echoes the highly stressed "baissant les yeux" of line eight. Thus the monsters—like the "rouet" itself—contain *both* the absent lovers, who are in their turn double: the raped Europa and the domesticated Hercules; the god-bull Jupiter and the temptress Omphale. The distance between the two worlds is only illusory. The acting out of some primal desecration seems to symbolize the nature of man's creative experience on every level. The eventual triumph of Divine Will, reflected through human deeds is, despite the dark humiliated wait in the atrium, symbolized by the story carved on the plinth and the mace implanted in the monsters' heads.

Poem xii, ironically entitled "Eglogue," clearly reveals the cosmic scheme of which the lovers' "magical circle" experience of reality is an inferior reflection. As they wander through an Arcadian countryside, they come upon an abyss:

Pareils à deux oiseaux qui vont de cime en cime,
Nous parvînmes enfin tout au bord d'un abîme.
Elle osa s'approcher de ce sombre entonnoir;
Et, quoique mainte épine offensât ses mains blanches,
Nous tâchâmes, penchés et nous tenant aux branches,
    D'en voir le fond lugubre et noir.

                         (xii)

At the very moment when the woman dares to peer into the dark crater, an ancient Titan falls into it and vultures begin devouring him. At once she associates the fallen Titan with her own love and rushes to hide from the gods' vengeance. The Arcadian mode of the next poem, thus subverted, stresses the escapist quality of the lovers' world:

> Viens!—une flûte invisible
> Soupire dans les vergers.—
> La chanson la plus *paisible*
> Est la chanson des bergers.
> (xiii, my italics)

The "sombre entonnoir" of xii is so quietly reflected in xiii that only a narrative reading would reveal its presence:

> Le vent ride, sous l'yeuse,
> Le sombre miroir des eaux.

"Sombre miroir" echoes "sombre entonnoir" and thus tells us that the dark waters are not "miroir," but "abîme." "Penchés sur l'abîme" represents a more profound contemplative attitude than mere narcissistic lyric reverie.

The re-interpretation of the experience of earthly love is one more step toward a fully developed creative awareness. Man as lover or creator of poems is necessarily satanic. He is the fallen Titan of xii, the bird-catcher of x ("Mon bras pressait ta taille frêle"), and the humiliated monster of iii. In the following chapter, I will examine how Hugo arranges his poems to reflect man's fallen nature and will suggest an interpretation of the religious and poetic implications of that knowledge.

VI

LES LUTTES ET LES RÊVES

Whereas *Aurore* and the beginning of *L'Ame en fleur*
seem to stress the narrator's response to the sensuous
world outside himself, *Les Luttes et les rêves* reveals him thrust
into a painful awareness of his own isolation. The subjective
dating of Book II is replaced by objective, journalistic time.
The narrator's historical self—a being burdened by the weight
of his past, now represented poetically by *Aurore* and *L'Ame
en fleur*, separates him from the natural world of cyclical duration. Indeed the nature of *Aurore* recedes into a fading echo
of itself in the last lines of "Melancholia": "O forêts! bois profonds! solitudes! asiles!" or in the title of xvii: "Chose vue un
jour de printemps." The poet is no longer dreaming like some
original Adam in the midst of the lush garden of I,ii ("Le
poète s'en ve dans les champs . . ."), or II,i ("Tout conjugue
le verbe aimer . . ."). Rather he is Cain's heir, condemned to
wander in a wasteland, having only occasional mocking
glimpses of that original idyll.

> Une terre au flanc maigre, âpre, avare, inclément,
> Où les vivants pensifs travaillent tristement,
> Et qui donne à regret à cette race humaine
> Un peu de pain pour tant de labeur et de peine;
> Des hommes durs, éclos sur ces sillons ingrats;
> Des cités d'où s'en vont, en se tordant les bras,
> La charité, la paix, la foi, soeurs vénérables;
>
> (xi, "?")

The city replaces nature as the stage for most of the poems, and
the narrator looks on, uncertain of his role as observer or
participant.

124

> Ecoutez. Une femme au profil décharné,
> Maigre, blême, portant un enfant étonné,
> Est là qui se lamente au milieu de la rue.
> (ii, "Melancholia")

Since this is the book that finally unmasks the satanic presence lurking in the background of *Aurore* (iv, xxii) and *L'Ame en fleur* (iii), irony, which exists so long as there is a certain degree of ambiguity, gives way to pathos. It is not surprising that the rhetorical expression and pathetic subject matter of this book make it by far the least appealing to the modern reader, for whom these subjects have become the clichés of a conventionalized Romanticism. Some examples of an almost maudlin sentimentality are xiv, "A la mère de l'enfant mort"; xvi, "Le Maître d'études"; xvii, "Chose vue un jour de printemps"; xviii, "Intérieur"; and, perhaps worst of all, the very poem that Hugo's contemporaries admired the most, xxiii, "Le Revenant."

Les Luttes et les rêves seems to correspond to that stage of awareness that Hugo calls "penser" in the *Philosophie, commencement d'un livre* and that, alas, seems the least suitable for poetic language:

> Une fois l'éblouissement de cette quantité de soleils passé,
> le coeur se serre, l'esprit tressaille, une idée vertigineuse et
> funèbre lui apparaît . . . l'état normal du ciel, c'est la nuit
> . . . la nuit et l'hiver. . . . (p. 30)

The narrator repeatedly asks the Jobian "why," graphically expressed by the title of poem xi, which is simply a question mark, or the last lines of xvii:

> Dieu! pourquoi l'orphelin, dans ses langes funèbres,
> Dit-il: "j'ai faim!" l'enfant, n'est-ce pas un oiseau?
> Pourquoi le nid a-t-il ce qui manque au berceau?
> (xvii, "Chose vue un jour de printemps")

"Toute terre est un bagne" (xii) is a theme which recurs over and over. The world is no longer the place in which God speaks to man through his creatures, but rather a cage inhabited by a society of torturers and victims who will ultimately be judged by a punishing God. Indeed, an elaborate system of cosmic justice is outlined for us in "Saturne."

It would seem that man's erotic desire to apprehend the world outside of himself, represented by the bee-flower metaphor in *Aurore* and the lovers of *L'Ame en fleur*, has led him to the Sodom and Gomorrah described in "La Statue":

> Juvénal, qui peignit ce gouffre universel,
> Est statue aujourd'hui; la statue est de sel,
>   Seule sous le nocturne dôme;
> Pas un arbre à ses pieds; pas d'herbe et de rameaux;
> Et dans son oeil sinistre on lit ces sombres mots:
>   Pour avoir regardé Sodome.

The woman is now figured as a fallen creature, contaminated by man's predatory sensuality. The innocent girl-child of *Aurore* becomes the prostitute of "Melancholia," the sacrificial virgin of ix, or the dead child of the central poem (xv).

This concentration upon suffering society thematically echoes the poet's concern for the redemptive function of language. Self-absorption and poetic reverie without social conscience become a form of guilt:

> Et leur vitre, où pendait un vieux haillon de toile,
> Etait, grâce au soleil, une éclatante étoile
> Qui, dans ce même instant, vive et pure lueur,
> Eblouissait au loin quelque passant rêveur!
>   (xviii, "Intérieur")

This belief in the social obligation of the poet, expressed, for example, in the poet-as-teacher of "Le Maître d'études" (xvi), is crucial to Hugo's poetics. It is what distinguishes Romantics like Lamartine, Vigny, and Hugo from Baudelaire and the Parnassian poets. As early as 1823 in an article elaborating a theory of the novel, Hugo said:

> . . . peu d'écrivains ont aussi bien rempli que Walter Scott, les devoirs du romancier relativement à son art et à son siècle; car ce serait une erreur presque coupable dans l'homme de lettres que de se croire au-dessus de l'intérêt général et des besoins nationaux, d'exempter son esprit de toute action sur les contemporains, et d'isoler sa vie égoïste de la grande vie du corps social.[1]

The exemplary nature of Book III is revealed throughout in the form as well as the subject matter of the thirty poems. Satire displaces the lyrical voice, for it is the poet's *duty* to instruct.

The title itself, with its binary structure, plurals, and repetition, reflects this new divisive stage in the evolution of the spirit. It is an important change from the unity of *Aurore* or the implied unity of *L'Ame en Fleur*. In true allegorical fashion, many of the individual titles allude to earlier symbolical forms that are a part of the nineteenth-century intellectual heritage. "Melancholia" (ii) refers to an allegorical painting of the same name by Dürer; "Quia pulvis es," words spoken by the priest on Ash Wednesday, was God's warning to Adam after the commission of Original Sin; and "Magnitudo parvi" contains biblical ("Blessed are the weak . . .") or Pascalian overtones. Literary genres favored by the seventeenth-century French moralists replace the "naive" medieval and renaissance forms of *L'Ame en fleur*: "La Source" (vi), "La Statue" (vii), "La Chouette" (xiii), and "La Nature" (xxix) are fables. The satirist Juvenal figures as a prophet in "La Statue." Pascalian imagery is everywhere:

[1] "A propos de Quentin Durwood," *Oeuvres complètes*, ed. Massin, Vol. II, p. 432.

> . . . Ils n'ont qu'une pensée:
> A quel néant jeter la journée insensée?
> Chiens, voitures, chevaux! cendre au reflet vermeil!
>
> (ii, "Melancholia")

> Il voit, il adore, il s'effare;
> Il entend le clairon du ciel,
> Et l'universelle fanfare
> Dans le silence universel.
>
> (xxx, "Magnitudo parvi")

Cryptic signs or clues revealing God's invisible presence are placed here and there in Book III as if to confirm our faith in a decipherable universe. "Ecrit sur un exemplaire de la *Divina Commedia*," "Ecrit au bas d'un crucifix," "Epitaphe," "Ecrit sur la plinthe d'un bas relief antique" are a few examples. A Hugolian bestiary (lion, eagle, owl, spider, dove) emerges full-fledged.

Dramatic structuring or some form of dialogue are key poetic devices throughout this book. Certain poems, such as viii, x, xxii, xxiv, seem to reflect the naturalistic vision of *Aurore* or *Ame en fleur*, only to be subverted either explicitly from within, as in the case of viii or xxii:

> . . . Hélas! tu te trompes, oiseau.
> Ma chair, faite de cendre, à chaque instant succombe;
> Mon âme ne sera blanche que dans la tombe;
> Car l'homme, quoi qu'il fasse, est aveugle ou méchant.—
> Et je continuai la lecture du champ.
>
> (viii)

> Moi, je laisse voler les senteurs et les baumes,
> Je laisse chuchoter les fleurs, ces doux fantômes,
> Et l'aube dire: Vous vivrez!
> Je regarde en moi-même, et, seul, oubliant l'heure,
> L'oeil plein des visions de l'ombre intérieure,
> Je songe aux morts, ces délivrés!
>
> (xxii)

or implicitly by the poems that immediately surround them. "Le Maître d'études" recreates and reverses the roles of the schoolmaster and pupils of "A propos d'Horace." (Both poems were written in June of 1855.) Poem viii, which explicitly states the allegorical nature of the universe, is a new version of the poet's dialogue with the birds as he translates the Book of Nature (see vi and xviii of *Aurore*). And finally, the ominous figure of the apocalyptic lion in poems ix and xxviii of *Aurore* emerges as a dominant motif in *Les Luttes et les rêves* (see poems v, vi, xix, xxiv). One is on the very brink of the New Testament (AUJOURD'HUI). Indeed, the poet himself has become that prophetic figure whose language will destroy before it transfigures:

Sinistre, ayant aux mains des lambeaux d'âme humaine,
De la chair d'Othello, des restes de Macbeth,
Dans son oeuvre, du drame effrayant alphabet,
Il se repose; ainsi le noir lion des jongles
S'endort dans l'antre immense avec du sang aux ongles.

(xxviii, "Le Poète")

This continuing dialogue with Books i and ii attests to Hugo's belief in a progressively developing awareness on all levels. For the poet it means that he must interiorize the achievements of his predecessors and speak to his contemporaries in a thoroughly modern idiom. For the reader it means that the lessons of the past must be first understood and then transcended until heavenly justice ("Saturne," iii) and human justice ("La Nature," xxix) are no longer distinct. The final poem of Book iii, "Magnitudo parvi," systematically outlines the stages in the fully developed contemplative genius and characterizes the ideal "mage" as an isolated *spiritual* leader. A revolutionary language replaces the sword. Men will be prepared for the new era by an altered perception of being.

Thus *Les Luttes et les rêves* can be read as a poeticized

theodicy. From the revelation of Evil on Earth in "Melancholia" and man's remoteness from the forces which govern him in "Saturne," Hugo leads us to the transcendental ethic of "Magnitudo parvi." With Dante as our guide (iii,i) Book iii begins the rite of passage that will terminate in the revelation of the Divine Voice of "Ce que dit la bouche d'ombre." The paradoxical descent-ascent structure of Autrefois becomes apparent. The *Aurore* or awakening of the human spirit could never have taken place if some original rift had not occurred. Book iii announces the end of an Autrefois of personal reverie and the beginning of an exemplary poetics dedicated to the redemption of that human spirit.

> Nul de nous n'a l'honneur d'avoir une vie qui soit à lui.
> Ma vie est la vôtre, votre vie est la mienne, vous vivez ce
> que je vis; la destinée est une. . . . *Autrefois, Aujourd'hui.*
> Un abîme les sépare, le tombeau.
>
> (Préface)

"Magnitudo parvi" dramatically places Hugo and Léopoldine on the edge of the abyss into which they will both plunge in Books iv and v.

> Le jour mourait; j'étais près des mers, sur la grève.
> Je tenais par la main ma fille, enfant qui rêve,
> > Jeune esprit qui se tait!
> La terre, s'inclinant comme un vaisseau qui sombre,
> En tournant dans l'espace allait plongeant dans l'ombre;
> > La pâle nuit montait.

A closer look at the poems in Book iii reveals the artistic ordering of the themes we have just described. The subtly contaminating structures of *Aurore* and *L'Ame en fleur* give way to a lurid rhythmic struggle between hope and despair. Doubt caused by the spectacle of human cruelty (ii, vi, vii, x, xi, xii, xxix, etc.) alternates with affirmations of faith in an invisible system of Divine Justice (iii, iv, v, xxvi, etc.) that can ultimately be deciphered by the visionary mind (viii, xii, xiii, etc.). The dead child (xv, "Epitaphe") is at the center of the dilemma: "Que te sert d'avoir pris cet enfant, ô nature?"

The first poem is initiatory, and the last an act of faith. Dante introduces us into the underworld of the socially damned. The title, "Ecrit sur un exemplaire de la *Divina Commedia*," emphasizes the miraculous origins of the poem, written, as it were, by the spirit of a dead allegorist who reveals to a new prophet the order of his own symbolical and anterior lives (mountain, tree, lion, man). At the end of Book iii the highly intellectual and patrician guide gives way to the simple shepherd of "Magnitudo parvi," his nineteenth-century plebeian heir. The first is described as a black outline, defined by the divine light behind him:

> Un soir, dans le chemin je vis passer un homme
> Vêtu d'un grand manteau comme un consul de Rome,
> Et qui me semblait noir sur la clarté des cieux.
>> (i, "Ecrit sur un exemplaire . . .")

The second is illuminated by the light of the man-made fire:

> Ses brebis, d'un rien remuées,
> Ouvrant l'oeil près du feu qui luit,
> Aperçoivent sous les nuées
> Sa forme droite dans la nuit;
>> (xxx, "Magnitudo parvi")

Although both figures serve as media through which a superior level of awareness can be achieved, the second represents the power of every man to determine his own destiny. Hugo's new religion is no longer dependent upon grace or the miraculous intercession of a divine figure.

> L'homme, que la brume enveloppe,
> Dans le ciel que Jésus ouvrit,
> Comme à travers un téléscope[2]
> Regarde à travers son esprit.
>
> L'âme humaine, après le Calvaire,
> A plus d'ampleur et de rayon;
> Le grossissement de ce verre
> Grandit encor la vision.
>
> (xxx, "Magnitudo parvi")

From isolated, mute matter (mountain), to growing trees, sentient lion, and finally conscious man, there is a paradoxical movement away from nature, yet closer to God, exactly the opposite movement from the one described by Baudelaire in "L'Irrémédiable":

> Une Idée, Une Forme, Un Etre
> Parti de l'azur et tombé
> Dans un Styx bourbeux et plombé
> Où nul oeil du Ciel ne pénètre;

"Magnitudo parvi" affirms man's contemplative power to pass beyond the prison of forms onto the supreme level of awareness which Hugo calls "voyance":

[2] Hugo liked to use this rational invention as an image for the poetic eye. *Promontorium somnii*, the prose work in which he describes his visionary poetics, begins with the recollection of a time when the narrator looked through a telescope at the moon: "Peu à peu ma rétine fit ce qu'elle avait à faire, les obscurs mouvements de machine nécéssaires s'opérèrent dans ma prunelle, ma pupille se dilata, mon oeil s'habitua . . . et cette noirceur que je regardais commença à blêmir. Je distinguai, quoi? Impossible de le dire. C'était trouble, fugace, impalpable à l'oeil. . . . Si rien avait une forme, ce serait cela.

"Puis la visibilité augmenta, on ne sait quelles arborescences se ramifièrent . . . L'effet de profondeur et de perte du réel était terrible. Et cependant le réel était là. . . ." *Oeuvres complètes,* ed. Massin, Vol. xii, p. 452.

Il sent, faisant passer le monde
Par sa pensée à chaque instant,
Dans cette obscurité profonde
Son oeil devenir éclatant;

Et, dépassant la créature,
Montant toujours, toujours accru,
Il regarde tant la nature,
Que la nature a disparu!

Car, des effets allant aux causes,
L'oeil perce et franchit le miroir,
Enfant; et contempler les choses,
C'est finir par ne plus les voir.

To use Hugo's own terms from *Philosophie, commencement d'un livre*, "thought" gives way to "prayer." The truly visionary moment is a merging of the human soul (fire) with God (star) of which it is a spark. The language of this new, visionary poetry will in turn create a world consciousness that has passed beyond its slavish and destructive attachment to temporal forms. The merging of the two lights (fire-star) is literally and figuratively a dawn moment.

That the collection should begin with *Aurore* now becomes more significant. The visionary moment is somehow synonymous with recurring dawn. Indeed, the relationship of *Aurore* and the "tombeau" experience described in the preface and represented by *Pauca meae* is already hinted at in this poem which links AUTREFOIS and AUJOURD'HUI. The visionary experience, the dematerialization of forms and loss of self for a revelation of universal selfhood, is expressed both as an illumination and as a drowning:

Il plonge au fond. Calme, il savoure
Le réel, le vrai, l'élément.
Toute la grandeur qui l'entoure
Le pénètre confusément.
. . .

133

Il sent croître en lui, d'heure en heure,
L'humble foi, l'amour recueilli,
Et la mémoire antérieure
Qui le remplit d'un vaste oubli.

. . .

Oeil serein dans l'ombre ondoyante,
Il a conquis, il a compris,
Il aime; il est l'âme voyante
Parmi nos ténébreux esprits.

. . .

Son être, dont rien ne surnage,
S'engloutit dans le gouffre bleu;
Il fait ce sublime naufrage;
Et, murmurant sans cesse: —Dieu,—
(xxx, "Magnitudo parvi")

The creation is described throughout Hugo's work as a vast oceanic mass and the ultimate creative experience as a "sublime naufrage."

The star-fire or "lumière-pensée" will serve as beacon ("phare") to the fragile ship of the prefatory poem. No longer a toy of wind, waves, and tides, human destiny is guided by its own potential brilliance.

Peut-être, à son insu, que ce pasteur paisible,
Et dont l'obscurité rend la lueur visible,
    Homme heureux sans effort,
Entrevu par cette âme en proie au choc de l'onde,
Va lui jeter soudain quelque clarté profonde
    Qui lui montre le port!

Ainsi ce feu peut-être, aux flancs du rocher sombre,
Là-bas est aperçu par quelque nef qui sombre
    Entre le ciel et l'eau;

Humble, il la guide au loin de son reflet rougeâtre,
Et du même rayon dont il réchauffe un pâtre,
Il sauve un grand vaisseau!
(xxx, "Magnitudo parvi")

Thus the apocalyptic waters pushing at the underpinnings of the earthly "fête" in "Melancholia" (ii) are the source for man's ultimate salvation.

VII

PAUCA MEAE

auca meae is the book of mourning that, with Book III, marks the turning-point in Hugo's allegorical narrative. *"Autrefois, Aujourd'hui. Un abîme les sépare, le tombeau"* (*Préface*). Both III, which ends AUTREFOIS, and IV, which begins AUJOURD'HUI, stress man's suffering, mortality, and sense of alienation from God. Thus doubt constitutes the very center of the supreme contemplative experience. The narrator is torn throughout both parts by the effort to separate Providence from Fatality. He repeatedly questions the God whose divine justice seeks out the most innocent and virtuous victims. The dead child in the poem at the center of *Les Luttes et les rêves* (xv, "Epigraphe") is the central figure of *Pauca meae*, but this time the child is Hugo's own creation. Like *L'Ame en fleur*, then, Book IV is an amplification of the preceding part, dramatically focusing the reader's attention upon a specific rather than general treatment of one more phase in the evolution of the spiritual and poetic quest.

Book IV properly belongs to the new era called AUJOURD'HUI, however, because in it the poet chooses to meditate upon the *memory* of an experience rather than upon the experience itself. Books III and IV both reveal the inadequacy of a poetry that represents Being as directly present, that is to say an idyllic poetry. The world of AUTREFOIS is once and for all cut off from the narrator with the death of his child. The three years that separate "4 SEPTEMBRE 1843" from the rest of the book figuratively represent that distance between experience and recollection.

136

Pauca meae could be said, then, to reflect the stage in the poetic process when the objective world is transformed into its imagined counterpart, when man's consciousness replaces the natural world as the poetic landscape.

> Chose inouie, c'est au dedans de soi qu'il faut regarder le dehors. Le profond miroir sombre est au fond de l'homme. . . . La chose réfléchie par l'âme est plus vertigineuse que vue directement.[1]

As we have seen in "Magnitudo parvi," the drowning represents the poetic moment *par excellence*, when the imagination transforms the reality of AUTREFOIS into a symbolical reflection of itself. The child, Léopoldine, is sacrificed and transformed thereby to become a poetic image. This change is the message of "Demain, dès l'aube . . ." (xiv), where the father breaks off the natural branches of holly and broom to place them as symbols of eternity on his child's grave.

The resolution of his personal tragedy does not take place, however, until after a period of mourning. The loss of his child leaves the narrator gazing back upon an evanescent past, transfixed like Chateaubriand's René or Baudelaire's swan (chapter 1). His nostalgic recollection of the *Aurore* of Léopoldine's life makes up the central poems of the section: v ("Elle avait pris ce pli dans son âge enfantin . . ."), vi ("Quand nous habitions tous ensemble . . ."), vii ("Elle était pâle, et pourtant rose . . ."), ix ("O souvenirs! printemps! aurore! . . ."). Indeed, shining through poem vii is the image of the living child and future victim, who, with her sister (reminiscent of 1,iii—"Mes deux filles") silently runs her fingers over the biblical stories of a punishing God:

[1] Hugo, *La Contemplation suprême, Oeuvres complètes*, ed. Massin, Vol. xii, p. 112.

Le soir, elle prenait ma Bible
Pour y faire épeler sa soeur,
Et comme une lampe paisible,
Elle éclairait ce jeune coeur.

. . .

Elle lui disait: "Sois bien sage!"
Sans jamais nommer le démon;
Leurs mains erraient de page en page
Sur Moïse et sur Salomon,

Sur Cyrus qui vint de la Perse,
Sur Moloch et Léviathan,
Sur l'enfer que Jésus traverse,
Sur l'éden où rampe Satan!

(vii)

That Hugo chose a personal experience of overwhelming
emotional importance as the source of his inspiration tells the
reader a great deal about his view of the poetic function. *Pauca
meae* is "Didine's Book." The new poet is plebeian in the
sense that he is personally involved in the ritual sacrifice. He
experiences the effect of his own creation, and would have the
reader do the same. It is only in this way that the work of art
can be redemptive. In "A Villequier" he seems to envy the
drowned couple their experience of death and its resultant
knowledge.

Je dis que le tombeau qui sur les morts se ferme
Ouvre le firmament;
Et que ce qu'ici-bas nous prenons pour le terme
Est le commencement;

(xv)

Like the ship in the prefatory poem, he is forced to remain
a scribe on the surface of creation. His own tears make up
the ocean into which he is cast, starless and lost:

Je ne résiste plus à tout ce qui m'arrive
    Par votre volonté.
L'âme de deuils en deuils, l'homme de rive en rive,
    Roule à l'éternité.
                 (xv, "A Villequier")

The tear, a symbolic projection of the suffering consciousness,
will be used to describe the poetic image or by extension the
work of art in Book vi:

  . . . Un fantôme blanc se dressa devant moi
  Pendant que je jetais sur l'ombre un oeil d'alarme,
  Et ce fantôme avait la forme d'une larme;
  C'était un front de vierge avec des mains d'enfant;
                 (vi,i, "Le Pont")

This identification with the reality to be transformed is fully
realized in "Charles Vacquerie," the final poem of *Pauca meae,*
where the drowning scene is poetically recreated through the
figure of Charles, Léopoldine's husband. For Hugo Charles is
a surrogate self.

  Oh! quelle sombre joie à cet être charmant
  De se voir embrassée au suprême moment
    Par ton doux désespoir fidèle!
  La pauvre âme a souri dans l'angoisse, en sentant
  A travers l'eau sinistre et l'effroyable instant
    Que tu t'en venais avec elle!
          (xvii, "Charles Vacquerie")

In the epilogue poem, "A celle qui est restée en France," Hugo
sends his book, poeticized tears, to lie next to Léopoldine in her
grave as a fecundating principle.

  Que ce livre, du moins, obscur message, arrive,
  . . .
  Qu'il y tombe, sanglot, soupir, larme d'amour!
  Qu'il entre en ce sépulcre où sont entrés un jour

> Le baiser, la jeunesse, et l'aube, et la rosée,
> Et le rire adoré de la fraîche épousée,
> Et la joie, et mon coeur, qui n'est pas ressorti!

The poet then exchanges roles with the couple, assuming the burden of their martyrdom by the agonizing nature of his own poetic quest:

> Dors!—O mes douloureux et sombres bien-aimés!
> Dormez le chaste hymen du sépulcre! dormez!
>   Dormez au bruit du flot qui gronde,
> Tandis que l'homme souffre, et que le vent lointain
> Chasse les noirs vivants à travers le destin,
>   Et les marins à travers l'onde!
>   (xvii, "Charles Vacquerie")

This stanza will be echoed in the "berceuse d'ombre" passage of "A celle qui est restée en France" at the close of the work: "Paix à l'Ombre! Dormez! dormez! dormez! dormez!" At the end of the final poem of *Pauca meae* Charles and Léopoldine are changed into a double star that, like the fire-star of "Magnitudo parvi," serves as a guide for the floundering ship of the human spirit:

> Vivez! aimez! ayez les bonheurs infinis.
> Oh! les anges pensifs, bénissant et bénis,
>   Savent seuls, sous les sacrés voiles,
> Ce qu'il entre d'extase, et d'ombre, et de ciel bleu,
> Dans l'éternel baiser de deux âmes que Dieu
>   Tout à coup change en deux étoiles!
>   (xvii, "Charles Vacquerie")

Thus the lovers' convulsive embrace and descent-ascension can be read as the central symbol of the work. It reflects the poet's satanic apprehension of the world and its transformation into the mediating work.

La vie n'est qu'une occasion de rencontre. C'est après la
vie qu'est la jonction. Les corps n'ont que l'embrassement,
les âmes ont l'étreinte. Vous figurez-vous, ô mes bien-
aimés, ce divin baiser de l'azur quand il n'y a plus dans le
moi que de la lumière. (*La Contemplation suprême*, p. 123)

That Hugo chose Books III and IV as the central sections of
Les Contemplations and that he placed the nostalgic poems of
the lost idyll (v, vi, vii, ix) at the center of IV, reflect struc-
turally an important truth of his poetics. A fallen humanity
weeping over its own mortality is at the center of the redemptive edifice. Like Vigny's "Moïse," the "new" *poète-pâtre* is
chosen out of the mass of suffering humanity. The two horse-
men of poem xii are aspects of the same consciousness, the historical self looking forward and the constitutive self looking
backward; both must be present for art to work redemptively:

Lui regarde en avant: je regarde en arrière.
Nos chevaux galopaient à travers la clairière;
Le vent nous apportait de lointains angelus;
Il dit; "Je songe à ceux que l'existence afflige,
"A ceux qui sont, à ceux qui vivent. — Moi," lui dis-je,
    "Je pense à ceux qui ne sont plus!"
(xii, "A quoi songeaient les deux cavaliers dans la forêt")

Out of this doubling, Hugo creates a religion of continuity.
Dead pasts, instead of being agonizing reminders of a lost
paradise, as they were for Chateaubriand, are the link to a
collective experience that in his preface Hugo calls Human
Destiny. The shining star-symbol into which Léopoldine and
Charles are transformed is meaningful only so long as it is a
guide for the boat of the prefatory poem or the lost mariner
of "A Villequier." The continuity between the mortal hero
and his transcendental goal is thus maintained. It is in this
way that we should understand Hugo's statement to Baude-

141

laire: "Je n'ai jamais dit: l'art pour l'art; j'ai toujours dit: l'art pour le progrès."

The organization of the poems within Book IV formally reflects the fully developed change from idyllic immediacy to nostalgic recollection. It is fitting that a poetics that places the knowledge of human suffering at its center should find its fullest expression in the elegiac mode. Coleridge spoke of elegy as the form of poetry natural to the reflective mind. It would seem to be the Romantic form *par excellence*, for, unlike the idyll, it expresses a longing for a lost ideal.

The poet's nostalgic leave-taking of the demystified idyll ("la fraîche églogue du bel adolescent Avril," I,xvi) is eloquently expressed by the title—*Pauca meae*, an allusion to Virgil's tenth Bucolic: "Pauco meao Gallo . . ." ("I would sing some verses for my dear Gallus . . ."). The fictional dating makes every poem of Book IV a memorial written on the anniversary of a symbolic death. Eight out of the seventeen poems are for Léopoldine herself. Others are for Léopold, Hugo's first-born, and Claire, both of whom are avatars of Léopoldine herself.

The mythic-historic change from a sensuous but comprehensible pagan world to the mysterious suffering of the Christian world is revealed in the opening poem:

L'archange effleure de son aile
Ce faîte où Jéhovah s'assied;
Et sur cette neige éternelle
On voit l'empreinte d'un seul pied.

Cette trace qui nous enseigne,
Ce pied blanc, ce pied fait de jour,
Ce pied rose, hélas! car il saigne,
Ce pied nu, c'est le tien, amour!

(i)

The pink and white foot reminiscent of the nymphs of *Aurore*
("Elle était déchaussée, elle était décoiffée, / Assise, les pieds
nus . . .") is transformed into a symbol of the crucifixion. Innocence and virtue are the attributes of both Léopoldine and
Christ.

> Pure Innocence! Vertu sainte!
> O les deux sommets d'ici-bas!
> Où croissent, sans ombre et sans crainte,
> Les deux palmes des deux combats!
>
> (i)

This poem, dated the month before her marriage, the next
written in the church during the wedding ceremony, and the
heraldic "4 SEPTEMBRE 1843," followed by a line of dots,
a kind of graphic suspension of real time, introduce the reader
into *Pauca meae*. Placed as it is immediately before the date
of her drowning, the marriage ceremony is tantamount to a
sacrificial ritual.[2]

Thematically the remaining poems (iii-xvii) form a clear
elegiac pattern that in turn reverses the descending course of
the three sections of AUTREFOIS. First the poet, like Job, is
stunned and bewildered by the cruelty of divine punishment
for the absurd sin of loving God too much:

> As-tu donc pensé, fatal maître,
> Qu'à force de te contempler,
> Je ne voyais plus ce doux être,
> Et qu'il pouvait bien s'en aller?
>
> T'es-tu dit que l'homme, vaine ombre,
> Hélas! perd son humanité
> A trop voir cette splendeur sombre
> Qu'on appelle la vérité?
>
> (iii, "Trois ans après")

[2] See chap. III, note 9.

143

He abandons his role as leader of men to fix obsessively his attention upon the memory of his own dead child. Poems iv, v, vi, vii, and ix breathe life into her body by the sheer intensity of nostalgic feeling:

> Tenez! voici le bruit de sa main sur la clé!
> Attendez! elle vient! laissez moi, que j'écoute!
> Car elle est quelque part dans la maison sans doute!
>
> (iv)

> C'est là que nous vivions.—Pénètre,
> Mon coeur, dans ce passé charmant!—
> Je l'entendais sous ma fenêtre
> Jouer le matin doucement.
>
> (ix)

In the next four poems (x-xiii) the grieving father is overcome by the blackest despair: "O Seigneur! ouvrez-moi les portes de la nuit, / Afin que je m'en aille et que je disparaisse!" (xiii). It is at this point that the poet, like Christ or Job, himself seems to undergo a spiritual drowning, a loss of faith. In poems xiv ("Demain dès l'aube . . .") and xv ("A Villequier"), the despair gives way to a Jobian submission to God's will. Yet from the point of view of human destiny, God and Fatality are no different. The drowning motif grows in importance, as if the human experience of God paradoxically can be defined only by the terrifying recognition of His absence. The father breaks a branch of heather and places it on the grave of the dead child, *in memoriam*. This acceptance of the death of natural forms prepares the revelation, characteristic of elegy, which occurs in the final poems xvi and xvii. Albouy speaks aptly of Léopoldine's death as "la rançon de la vision de l'au delà permise à son père."[3] Out of the intense contemplation of death is born the shining revelatory image:

[3] "Présentation à William Shakespeare," *Oeuvres complètes*, ed. Massin, Vol. XII, p. 1539.

Je vis cette faucheuse. Elle était dans son champ.
Elle allait à grands pas moissonnant et fauchant,
Noir squelette laissant passer le crépuscule.
Dans l'ombre où l'on dirait que tout tremble et recule,
L'homme suivait des yeux les lueurs de la faulx.

. . .

Tout était sous ses pieds deuil, épouvante et nuit.
Derrière elle, le front baigné de douces flammes,
Un ange souriant portait la gerbe d'âmes.

(xvi, "Mors")

As I have already pointed out, the final poem reveals the drowned couple to us as a lasting metaphysical reality. These two stars ending the chapter complement the two worldly guides—"Innocence" and "Vertu"—of the first poem.

The two revelatory moments, and especially the general tone of the encomium to Charles Vacquerie that brings *Pauca meae* to a close, finally reverse the downward spiral that describes the structure of the first half of the book. The last poem also endows the human spirit with freedom despite the inevitability of death, and thus separates once and for all God from Fatality. What seems to be an orthodox horror of suicide in the first two stanzas is suddenly reversed into a tribute to Charles' heroic affirmation of his love.[4]

---

[4] In *Philosophie, commencement d'un livre,* Hugo is bent upon proving the existence of a soul. He says to Anatole LeRay, a priest turned materialist: "Donc . . . en restant dans le fait matériel, qui est, selon vous, la seule sagesse, un homme n'a jamais aucune raison pour se sacrifier à un autre homme?" (p. 64). LeRay says no, but later dies while heroically attempting to save the lives of three drowning women. His sacrificial death (the analogy with Charles Vacquerie is obvious) thus proves for Hugo the existence of a soul, "un moi latent," which reflects God's own Being. Thus the ethical imperative of Hugo's philosophy is expressed in sacrificial terms. Jacques Séebacher in "Poétique et politique de la paternité" has referred to this aspect of Hugo's thought as "existentialist."

Il ne sera pas dit que ce jeune homme, ô deuil!
Se sera de ses mains ouvert l'affreux cercueil
    Où séjourne l'ombre abhorrée,
Hélas! et qu'il aura lui-même dans la mort
De ses jours généreux, encor pleins jusqu'au bord,
    Renversé la coupe dorée,

Et que sa mère, pâle et perdant la raison,
Aura vu rapporter au seuil de sa maison,
    Sous un suaire aux plis funèbres,
Ce fils, naguère encor pareil au jour qui naît,
Maintenant blême et froid, tel que la mort venait
    De le faire pour les ténèbres;

Il ne sera pas dit qu'il sera mort ainsi,
Qu'il aura, coeur profond et par l'amour saisi,
    Donné sa vie à ma colombe,
Et qu'il l'aura suivie au lieu morne et voilé,
Sans que la voix du père à genoux ait parlé
    A cette âme dans cette tombe!

En présence de tant d'amour et de vertu,
Il ne sera pas dit que je me serai tu,
    Moi qu'attendent les maux sans nombre!
Que je n'aurai point mis sur sa bière un flambeau,
Et que je n'aurai pas devant son noir tombeau
    Fait asseoir une strophe sombre!

N'ayant pu la sauver, il a voulu mourir.
           (xvii, "Charles Vacquerie")

The gesture of willing self-immolation distinguishes man from beast and endows him with the power to mediate between God and the rest of suffering humanity. The disclosure of this divine principle within the human spirit is represented by the transformation of the couple into stars. The poet then

repeats the suicidal gesture, this time by drinking the cup of
life that Charles had cast aside:

> Allez des esprits purs accroître la tribu.
> De cette coupe amère, où vous n'avez pas bu,
>   Hélas! nous viderons le reste.
> Pendant que nous pleurons, de sanglots abreuvés,
> Vous, heureux, enivrés de vous-mêmes, vivez
>   Dans l'éblouissement céleste!
>   (xvii, "Charles Vacquerie")

Thus in the remaining books the poet will speak from beyond
the tomb. He condemns himself to live out his suffering in
order to immortalize their martyrdom in a redemptive work.

The emergence of light out of darkness characteristic of the
last poem and of the elegiac form is, perhaps, the primary
thematic development in Book IV and, as we shall see, of
AUJOURD'HUI generally. In poems iii-ix the living child is the
poet's source of light:

> C'était le bonheur de ma vie
> De voir ses yeux me regarder.
> . . .
> Pourquoi m'as-tu pris la lumière
> Que j'avais parmi les vivants?
>   (iii)

> Et c'était un esprit avant d'être une femme.
> Son regard reflétait la clarté de son âme.
>   (v)

> A travers mes songes sans nombre,
> J'écoutais son parler joyeux,
> Et mon front s'éclairait dans l'ombre
> A la lumière de ses yeux.
>   (vi)

147

In poem vi she is the sun, the moon, candlelight, and the flame of life. Her extinction is equivalent to the extinction of Creation:

> Toutes ces choses sont passées
> Comme l'ombre et comme le vent!
>
> (vi)

In poems x-xiii total darkness reigns.

> Pendant que le marin, qui calcule et qui doute,
> Demande son chemin aux constellations;
> Pendant que le berger, l'oeil plein de visions,
> Cherche au milieu des bois son étoile et sa route;
> Pendant que l'astronome, inondé de rayons,
>
> Pèse un globe à travers des millions de lieues,
> Moi, je cherche autre chose en ce ciel vaste et pur.
> Mais que ce saphir sombre est un abîme obscur!
> On ne peut distinguer, la nuit, les robes bleues
> Des anges frissonnants qui glissent dans l'azur.
>
> (x)

In xiv and xv the dawn world ("Demain dès l'aube . . .") is replaced by the poet's concentration upon the loss of that idyllic light; finally, poems xvi and xvii describe the transfiguration of the lost object into a shining symbol representing Divinity. Thus the natural light of day (*Aurore*, AUTREFOIS) is internalized and projected outward again in a supernatural reflection of itself. The development of the light imagery then directly parallels the elegiac pattern already outlined from lament over lost subject (iii-ix) to despair (x-xiii), to submission (xiv, xv), to revelation (xvi, xvii).

In *Pauca meae* Hugo takes us further yet on the contemplative journey. The descending movement of AUTREFOIS is reversed. The child of *Aurore*, the mistress of *L'Ame en fleur*, and the prostitute-victim of *Les Luttes et les rêves* are meta-morphosed by death into a shining symbol who will be our guide toward a superior level of awareness in the final stages of the allegorical journey.

VIII

EN MARCHE

The transformation of Léopoldine and Charles into guiding stars at the end of Book IV heralds a new level of experience which autobiographically corresponds to the exile years. Hugo the man will now become a disembodied prophetic voice speaking to his times from the other side of the shore. The first poem in Book V, "A Aug V," explicitly develops an analogy between Léopoldine's drowning and Hugo's own exile:

> Poëte, quand mon sort s'est brusquement ouvert,
> Tu n'as pas reculé devant les noires portes,
> Et, sans pâlir, avec le flambeau que tu portes,
> Tes chants, ton avenir que l'absence interrompt,
> Et le frémissement lumineux de ton front,
> Trouvant la chute belle et le malheur propice,
> Calme, tu t'es jeté dans le grand précipice!
>
> (i, "A Aug V")

Once again Hugo poeticizes history by changing the dates of the poems dedicated to the two brothers, Charles and Auguste Vacquerie, to Jersey, September 4, 1852. Thus the last poem in *Pauca meae* and the first poem in *En marche* read as if they were one continuous work written on the anniversary of Léopoldine's death. Auguste is even referred to in the first line of the poem as "*son* frère," thus forcing the reader to go back to the last poem of the preceding book.

If one accepts, then, the analogy between exile and drowning for which Hugo so clearly asks acceptance, one cannot help being struck at first by the seemingly regressive change in perspective. At the end of Book IV, Léopoldine and Charles transcend their limited historical selves to become eternal symbols of a metaphysical reality. Hugo transcends his personal grief to sing an encomium to the self-sacrificing Charles. Yet Book v, more than any other, calls forth the historical specificity of Hugo's own life. The title, *En marche*, is the here-and-now cry for progress of the revolutionary man. The chapter is filled with people, Hugo's friends and family: Auguste Vacquerie; the Marquis of C.; Louise Bertin; Claire Pradier; Jules Janin; Alexandre Dumas; Ponto, his dog; Paul Meurice; Louise Colet; Madame Hugo herself. The near-epistolary style of some of the poems further emphasizes the autobiographical reality of the individual evoked ("A Aug V," "Au fils d'un poëte," "Ecrit en 1846 . . ." "Ecrit en 1855," "A Jules J," "A Alexandre D"). Hugo takes care to give *concrete* evidence for the inspiration of these poems by adding footnotes and explanatory introductions. In a footnote to "A Jules J," for example, he says: "Voir *Histoire de la littérature dramatique*, Tome iv, p. 413 et 414"; after "A Alexandre D" he writes "(réponse à la dédicace de son drame *La Conscience*)"; after "A Paul M" he specifies, "Auteur du drame *Paris*." Nowhere else in *Les Contemplations* does Hugo represent his life so concretely. Even in the preface he goes to great pains to suppress his historical personality:

> Ma vie est la vôtre, votre vie est la mienne, vous vivez ce que je vis; la destinée est une. Prenez donc ce miroir, et regardez-vous-y. On se plaint quelquefois des écrivains qui disent moi. . . . Ah! insensé, qui crois que je ne suis pas toi. . . .

Despite this proliferation of autobiographical references, however, Hugo wishes the reader to see these people from his past as representative or allegorized figures. Like Léopoldine and Charles, they are recollections of their former selves. They exist "aujourd'hui" as characters, similar to the ones in Hugo's own novels, indeed in a book the hero himself is reading. He is careful to identify Janin, Dumas, and Meurice as *authors*, disembodied creators of *Histoire de la littérature dramatique, La Conscience*, and *Paris*. They are in fact aspects of Hugo's own writer-self. This doubling becomes very clear in "A Alexandre D" as the two poets bid goodbye to one another on the quay at Antwerp at the moment of Hugo's departure into exile.

La roue ouvrit la vague, et nous nous appelâmes;
—Adieu!—Puis, dans les vents, dans les flots, dans les lames,
Toi debout sur le quai, moi debout sur le pont,
Vibrant comme deux luths dont la voix se répond,
Aussi longtemps qu'on put se voir, nous regardâmes
L'un vers l'autre, faisant comme un échange d'âmes;
Et le vaisseau fuyait, et la terre décrut;
L'horizon entre nous monta, tout disparut;
Une brume couvrit l'onde incommensurable;
Tu rentras dans ton oeuvre éclatante, innombrable,
Multiple, éblouissante, heureuse, où le jour luit;
Et moi dans l'unité sinistre de la nuit.

(xv, "A Alexandre D")

The poet will ultimately be illuminated through his work; but the man who undergoes the experience of creativity must first lose himself as an individual. The sacrifice required by the creative voyage is reverently acknowledged by the poet on shore—that is, both by the Dumas who dedicated his poem to Hugo and by the Hugo who in turn addresses his poem to Dumas.

Merci du bord des mers à celui qui se tourne
Vers la rive où le deuil, tranquille et noir, séjourne,
Qui défait de sa tête, où le rayon descend,
La couronne, et la jette au spectre de l'absent,
Et qui, dans le triomphe et la rumeur, dédie
Son drame à l'immobile et pâle tragédie!

(xv, "A Alexandre D")

The memory of a particular, emotionally charged event, always the source for Hugo of the poetic image, constitutes the very core of the poem:

> Je n'ai pas oublié le quai d'Anvers, ami,
> Ni le groupe vaillant, toujours plus raffermi,
> D'amis chers, de fronts purs, ni toi, ni cette foule.
> Le canot du steamer soulevé par la houle
> Vint me prendre, et ce fut un long embrassement.
> Je montai sur l'avant du paquebot fumant,
> La roue ouvrit la vague, et nous appelâmes:

It becomes more and more clear as one proceeds through Book v that Hugo, the exiled and disembodied voice, is addressing himself to these particular people because they have unwittingly served as guides in his own evolution toward a superior, visionary state of mind.

Madame Hugo is present as the symbol of the weeping Virgin, "Dolorosae" (xii). Louise Bertin is the muse of a pastoral dream (v). The Marquis de C. d'E., a monarchist friend of Hugo's mother, is the representative of blind, prerevolutionary thought:

> J'ajoute un post-scriptum après neuf ans. J'écoute;
> Etes-vous toujours là? Vous êtes mort sans doute,
> Marquis; mais d'où je suis on peut parler aux morts.
>
> (iii, "Ecrit en 1855")

Thus the encounters in the poet's life are like the poems in his work: they both influence the course of his spiritual development and are influenced (transformed into symbolic meaning) by his accumulating insight. In other words, the visionary poet of AUJOURD'HUI supplies meaning to the isolated poems of AUTREFOIS (just as the exile supplies meaning to his former life), and thus earns the right to order them according to this meaning. Correspondingly, the reader-initiate

of Aujourd'hui becomes the decipherer of his naive first reading of these poem-encounters. The following lines from the
opening poem of *En marche* illustrate this biographical transformation.

> Ton frère dort couché dans le sépulcre noir;
> *Nous,* dans la nuit du sort, dans l'ombre du devoir,
> *Marchons à la clarté qui sort de cette pierre.*
> Qu'il dorme, voyant l'aube à travers sa paupière!
> *Un jour, quand on lira nos temps mystérieux,*
> *Les songeurs attendris promèneront leurs yeux*
> *De toi, le dévouement, à lui, le sacrifice.*
>
> (i, "A Aug V," my italics)

Hugo does not hesitate to make up facts just as he has not
hesitated to make up dates and places throughout the collection. At the beginning of "Ecrit en 1846," for example, he
quotes from a letter he identifies as: "(Le Marquis de C.
d'E. . . *Lettre à Victor Hugo.* Paris, 1846.)" Yet anyone reading this radically anti-monarchical poem knows that in 1846
Hugo was one of Louis-Philippe's strongest supporters and a
pair de France. In fact, the Marquis d'Espinousse had already died in 1841. To this same poem, actually written in 1854,
he adds a footnote:

> On n'a rien changé à ces vers, écrits en 1846. Aujourd'hui,
> l'auteur eût ajouté Claremont.

History is valuable, then, only when it transcends itself, and
Hugo would have us see that transformation take place. The
more fictionalized the event has become, the stronger the redemptive powers of the poetic consciousness. The transcendental potentiality of history is explained in parable form in "Le
Mendiant." Two men are separated from each other, each
within the prison of his own material surroundings (house,
overcoat):

Un pauvre homme passait dans le givre et le vent.
Je cognai sur ma vitre . . .

The poor man enters the narrator's house and places his moth-eaten coat in front of the fire to dry. Through the holes in this decaying shell the narrator sees the light of the fire. Suddenly the man and the coat, by the very fact of their fading bodies, become vessels through which God reveals himself:

> Son manteau, tout mangé des vers, et jadis bleu,
> Etalé largement sur la chaude fournaise,
> Piqué de mille trous par la lueur de braise,
> Couvrait l'âtre, et semblait un ciel noir étoilé.
> Et, pendant qu'il séchait ce haillon désolé
> D'où ruisselaient la pluie et l'eau des fondrières,
> Je songeais que cet homme était plein de prières,
> Et je regardais, sourd à ce que nous disions,
> Sa bure où je voyais des constellations.
>
> (ix, "Le Mendiant")

It would seem that Hugo is also bent upon establishing the historical validity of his subjects in order to demonstrate the universal (to use Ballanche's term, "plebeian") application of Léopoldine's and Charles' symbolical transformation. Their martyrdom functions as a kind of saint's life and the island of Jersey takes on a mythical value like the rock of Prometheus or the Thebaid.

> Je suis sur un rocher qu'environne l'eau sombre,
> Ecueil rongé des flots, de ténèbres chargé,
> Où s'assied, ruisselant, le blême naufragé.
>
> (iii, "Ecrit en 1855")

It is from this place that a new religion of personal sacrifice and social progress is preached. Those who follow Hugo into exile are the disciples of the New Order:

155

Vous, qui l'avez suivi dans sa blême vallée,
Au bord de cette mer d'écueils noirs constellée,
Sous la pâle nuée éternelle qui sort
Des flots, de l'horizon, de l'orage et du sort;
Vous qui l'avez suivi dans cette Thébaïde,
Sur cette grève nue, aigre, isolée et vide,
Où l'on ne voit qu'espace âpre et silencieux,
Solitude sur terre et solitude aux cieux;
Vous qui l'avez suivi dans ce brouillard qu'épanche
Sur le roc, sur la vague et sur l'écume blanche,
La profonde tempête aux souffles inconnus,
Recevez, dans la nuit où vous êtes venus,
O chers êtres! coeurs vrais, lierres de ses décombres,
La bénédiction de tous ces déserts sombres!

(vi, "A vous qui êtes là," my italics)

The weeping father of *Pauca meae* is transformed into the larger, symbolic father of mankind in the last poem of *En marche*. Though the work is dedicated "A mes enfants," it is clear from the final lines that his "children" are no longer Adèle and "Didine," but the entire human race:

C'étaient Eve aux cheveux blanchis, et son mari,
Le pâle Adam, pensif, par le travail meurtri,
Ayant la vision de Dieu sous sa paupière.
Ils venaient tous les deux s'asseoir sur une pierre,
En présence des monts fauves et soucieux,
Et de l'éternité formidable des cieux.
Leur oeil triste rendait la nature farouche;
. . .

Ils songeaient, et, rêveurs, sans entendre, sans voir,
Sourds aux rumeurs des mers d'où l'ouragan s'élance,
Toute la nuit, dans l'ombre, ils pleuraient en silence;
Ils pleuraient tous les deux, aïeux du genre humain,
Le père sur Abel, la mère sur Caïn.

(xxvi, "Les Malheureux")

156

Thus *En marche* states both the poet's isolation from immediate historical reality and his total commitment to it. Like the imaginary shepherd of "Magnitudo parvi," whose fire the father and child see from the shore of AUTREFOIS, he is both the lonely seer and the leader of men. As he will state in *Les Génies appartenant au peuple* in 1863:

> Ces hommes-là, qui font ces choses, ces pères des chefs-d'oeuvre, ces producteurs de civilisation, ces hauts et purs esprits, quel moi ont-ils? Ils ont un moi incorruptible, parce qu'il est impersonnel. Leur moi, désintéressé d'eux-mêmes, indicateur perpétuel de sacrifice et de dévouement, les déborde et se répand autour d'eux. Le moi des grandes âmes tend toujours à se faire collectif. Les hommes de génie sont Légion. Ils souffrent la souffrance extérieure . . . ils saignent tout le sang qui coule; ils pleurent les pleurs de tous les yeux; ils sont autrui. Autrui, c'est là leur moi. Vivre en soi seul est une maladie. *L'âme est astre, et doit rayonner.* L'egoïsme est la rouille du moi. (my italics)[1]

For Hugo the function of genius is to lead mankind beyond its historic present to a state of universal understanding. Having reached this state, mankind assumes the role of a providential God-Father for itself.

> Le penseur, poëte ou philosophe, poëte et philosophe, se sent une sorte de paternité immense. La misère universelle est là, gisante; il lui parle, il la conseille . . . il lui montre son chemin, il lui rallume son âme.—Vois devant toi, pauvre humanité. Marche!—Il souffre avec ceux qui souffrent, pleure avec ceux qui pleurent, lutte avec ceux qui luttent, espère pour ceux qui désespèrent. . . . Inépuisable compassion, tel est le fond du génie. . . . (Ibid., pp. 443-44).

It is not surprising, then, that Book v is so strikingly populated compared to Book iv.

---

[1] *Oeuvres complètes*, ed. Massin, Vol. XII, p. 444.

Once again the organization of the poems within Book v reflects Hugo's religious and poetic message. Thematically the chapter divides itself into two parts. There are twenty-six poems in all, and the three in the middle ("Dolorosae," "Paroles sur la dune," "Claire P") can be read as a separate emblematic picture around which the other poems are organized. The first eleven poems focus primarily upon incidents and people in the life of Hugo the man; the last eleven poems constitute an elaborate commentary upon the social function of poetry. Thus biographical, spiritual, and artistic allegories are linked for us in this part. Indeed, Book v seems to be structured in such a way as to intensify the parallelisms among cosmos, history, and intellectual creation. These three realms of being, described in the first poems of *Aurore* (ii, iii, iv—see chapter iv) are again emblematically reflected in the work of art itself.

That the stages in Hugo's "real" life are representative of a larger, more significant pattern is made clear at the outset. In poem iii ("Ecrit en 1846 . . . Ecrit en 1855") he explains the evolution of his political and social attitudes from childhood to the exile years, and it is clear from his choice of words that this evolution corresponds roughly to the six parts of *Les Contemplations*:

(*Aurore*)

Oui, dans le même temps où vous faussiez ma lyre,
Marquis, je m'échappais et j'apprenais à lire
Dans cet hiéroglyphe énorme: l'univers.
Oui, j'allais feuilleter les champs tout grands ouverts;
Tout enfant, j'essayais d'épeler cette bible

(*Les Luttes et les rêves*)

Puis je me suis penché sur l'homme, autre alphabet.
Le mal m'est apparu, puissant, joyeux, robuste,
. . .

158

Comme on arrête un gueux volant sur le chemin,
Justicier indigné, j'ai pris le coeur humain
au collet, . . .

(*Pauca meae*)

Oh! l'heure vient toujours! des flots sourds au loin roulent.
A travers les rumeurs, les cadavres, les deuils,
L'écume, et les sommets qui deviennent écueils,
Les siècles devant eux poussent, désespérées,
Les Révolutions, monstrueuses marées,
Océans faits des pleurs de tout le genre humain.

(*En marche*)

Seulement, un matin, mon esprit s'envola,
Je vis l'espace large et pur qui nous réclame;
L'horizon a changé, marquis, mais non pas l'âme.
Rien au dedans de moi, mais tout autour de moi.
L'histoire m'apparut, et je compris la loi
Des générations, cherchant Dieu, portant l'arche,
Et montant l'escalier immense marche à marche.
Je restai le même oeil, voyant un autre ciel.

(*Au bord de l'infini*)

Je ne vois que l'abîme, et la mer, et les cieux,
Et les nuages noirs qui vont silencieux;
Mon toit, la nuit, frissonne, et l'ouragan le mêle
Aux souffles effrénés de l'onde et de la grêle;
. . .
Ici, le bruit du gouffre est tout ce qu'on entend;
Tout est horreur et nuit.—Après?—Je suis content.

(iii, "Ecrit en 1846 . . . Ecrit en 1855")

The two sections of this poem (1846, 1855) were in reality
written a few months apart in 1854 and 1855. The effect of

the fictional time lapse is to increase the distance between experience and meaning and thus to make the providential nature of these events more striking. As we know from *Pauca meae*, three years after the drowning Hugo began the task of deciphering the meaning of his life. Thus 1846 marks the beginning of the writing of *Les Contemplations* and 1855 the finished task.

The supreme contemplative experience cannot be communicated, however, without preparing the myopic reader. The poet must somehow make the supernatural perceivable to readers accustomed only to the natural.

> La source tombait du rocher
> Goutte à goutte à la mer affreuse.
> L'Océan, fatal au nocher,
> Lui dit:—"Que me veux-tu, pleureuse?
>
> Je suis la tempête et l'effroi;
> Je finis où le ciel commence.
> Est-ce que j'ai besoin de toi,
> Petite, moi qui suis l'immense?"—
>
> La source dit au gouffre amer:
> "Je te donne, sans bruit ni gloire,
> Ce qui te manque, ô vaste mer!
> Une goutte d'eau qu'on peut boire."
>
> (iv)

His biographical experience is the drop of water necessary to the questing mariner. Yet the drop of water is in fact a microcosm of the supernatural reality in which he floats.

Poem xv, "A Alexandre D" introduces the second part of *En marche*. The biographical man is left on shore, "où le jour luit," and the poète ("être crépusculaire" of "Magnitudo parvi") moves into the supernatural light of poetic insight. Correspondingly the remaining poems in Book v form a complex metapoetic monologue.

"Lueur au couchant" (xvi), "A Paul M" (xxi), xxii, and the final poem, "Les Malheureux" (xxvi) emphasize the visionary's social obligation explained in *Les Génies appartenant au peuple*. The poet's duty to be leader, hero and prophet of his own generation is repeatedly asserted.

> Paul, il me semble, grâce à ce fier souvenir
> Dont tu viens nous bercer, nous sacrer, nous bénir,
> Que dans ma plaie, où dort la douleur, ô poëte!
> Je sens de la charpie avec un drapeau faite.
>
> (xxi, "A Paul M")

Poems xvii-xx ("Mugitusque boum," "Apparition," "Au poëte qui m'envoie une plume d'aigle," "Cérigo") stress the power of the visionary to perceive Divinity directly and to mediate between God and man through the work of art. Poems xxiii-xxv ("Pasteurs et troupeaux," "J'ai cueilli cette fleur pour toi sur la colline, . . ." and "O strophe du poëte, autrefois, dans les fleurs . . .") describe the poetic process itself, from sensuous observation to visionary insight.

Poem xvi, "Lueur au couchant," which focuses upon the poet's lonely commitment to society ("Trouvant ainsi moyen d'être un et d'être tous"), is organized in the same way that Book v as a whole is. The first nineteen lines evoke the memory of a specific historical event of symbolic power. The dreaming poet walks through masses of people celebrating a national holiday. With "Dès lors pourtant des voix murmuraient: 'Anankè,'" a new level of experience is announced and the diction becomes strikingly metaphoric.

> Je passais; et partout, sur le pont, sur le quai,
> Et jusque dans les champs, étincelait le rire,
> Haillon d'or que la joie en bondissant déchire.
>
> (xvi, "Lueur au couchant")

Past and present merge as the individual's perception expands into a cosmic awareness. The water imagery used to describe the crowd from the beginning ("répandait," "désaltérant") grows to flood proportions and pours into his expanded consciousness. An apotheosis of brotherhood in which opposites dissolve takes place. An ordered nature and the ordering poetic consciousness reflect one another in the single, protective tree image:

> . . . et, pendant que mon esprit, qui rêve
> Dans la sereine nuit des penseurs étoilés,
> Et dresse ses rameaux à leurs lueurs mêlés,
> S'ouvrait à tous ses cris charmants comme l'aurore,
> A toute cette ivresse innocente et sonore,
> Paisibles, se penchant, noirs et tout semés d'yeux,
> Sous le ciel constellé, sur le peuple joyeux,
> Les grands arbres pensifs des vieux Champs-Elysées,
> Pleins d'astres, consentaient à s'emplir de fusées.
>
> (xvi, "Lueur au couchant")

Thus a providential God is reflected in the prophetic genius himself. "Le penseur, poète ou philosophe, poète et philosophe, se sent une sorte de paternité immense."

The following four poems move beyond the social to a religious level of being.

> Qu'on sente frissonner dans toute la nature,
> Sous la feuille des nids, au seuil blanc des maisons,
> Dans l'obscur tremblement des profonds horizons,
> Un vaste emportement d'aimer, dans l'herbe verte,
> Dans l'antre, dans l'étang, dans la clairière ouverte,
> D'aimer sans fin, d'aimer toujours, d'aimer encor,
>
> . . .
>
> Qu'on sente le baiser de l'être illimité!
> Et paix, vertu, bonheur, espérance, bonté,
> O fruits divins, tombez des branches éternelles!
>
> (xvii, "Mugitusque boum")

162

Once again, as in the preceding poem, the cosmos is described as Tree—not the tree of Christian mythology, but a nurturing tree-God dispensing its fruits in the midst of a regenerative cosmos. This moment of poetic grace causes the universal analogy between "choses" and "êtres" (nature and perceiving consciousness) to be heard: "Ainsi vous parliez, voix, grandes voix solennelles; / Et Virgil écoutait comme j'écoute. . . ."

Revelation continues in "Apparition." Divinity always reveals itself to Hugo in a material, *albeit* supernatural form:

> Je vis un ange blanc qui passait sur ma tête;
> Son vol éblouissant apaisait la tempête,
> Et faisait taire au loin la mer pleine de bruit.

The beggar's coat, the tree of "Lueur au couchant," and now the angel's black wings serve as telescopes for the expanding consciousness. "Et je voyais, dans l'ombre où brillaient ses prunelles, / Les astres à travers les plumes de ses ailes." The title of the next poem, "Au poëte qui m'envoie une plume d'aigle," following as it does upon these last two lines of "Apparition," implicitly states the analogy between mediating angel and poetry itself.

> Oh! soyez donc les bienvenues,
> Plume! strophe! envoi glorieux!
> Vous avez erré dans les nues,
> Vous avez plané dans les cieux!
> (xix, "Au poëte qui m'envoie . . .")

Thus the religious and poetic allegories are more clearly brought together. The poems in *Les Contemplations* constitute another dark form through which the reader is led toward revelation.

That the following poem, "Cérigo," should be written in response to another poet's work further strengthens this association. Baudelaire's "Voyage à Cythère" was published in

the *Revue des deux mondes* June 1, 1855, and Hugo's manuscript is dated June 11, 1855. A comparison of the diction of the
two works confirms the intentionality of the dialogue. In "Cérigo" Hugo wishes to refute Baudelaire's discovery that the ideal
of love that inspires the poetic voyage is merely the creation
of an imagination eternally nourishing itself on its own im-
purities.

> Mon coeur, comme un oiseau, voltigeait tout joyeux
> Et planait librement à l'entour des cordages;
> Le navire roulait sous un ciel sans nuages,
> Comme un ange enivré d'un soleil radieux.
>
> . . .
>
> Mais voilà qu'en rasant la côte d'assez près
> Pour troubler les oiseaux avec nos voiles blanches,
> Nous vîmes que c'était un gibet à trois branches,
> Du ciel se détachant en noir, comme un cyprès.
>
> De féroces oiseaux perchés sur leur pâture
> Détruisaient avec rage un pendu déjà mûr,
> Chacun plantant, comme un outil, son bec impur
> Dans tous les coins saignants de cette pourriture;
>
>   ("Un Voyage à Cythère")

In Hugo's poem the dream of an earthly paradise is also demystified; the "flancs nus" of the island are "écueils" for the
mariner-pilgrim:

> Cythère est là, lugubre, épuisée, idiote,
> Tête de mort du rêve amour, et crâne nu
> Du plaisir, ce chanteur masqué, spectre inconnu.
> C'est toi? qu'as-tu donc fait de ta blanche tunique?
> Cache ta gorge impure et ta laideur cynique,
> O sirène ridée et dont l'hymne s'est tu!
> Où donc êtes-vous, âme? étoile, où donc es-tu?
>
>   (xx, "Cérigo")

The poet is not permitted to escape into nature as he yearns to do in "Melancholia" ("O forêts! bois profonds! solitudes! asiles!") or in "Ponto" ("O triste humanité, je fuis dans la nature!"), but in contrast to what happens in Baudelaire's poem, the sacrifice of the pastoral dream leads to the discovery of a Divine Order. Just as in "Le Mendiant," "Lueur au couchant," or "Apparition," revelation is symbolized by the emergence of a star out of crass material reality. That Hugo should choose to use traditionally "fallen" or pagan images to reveal God's presence properly reflects his revolutionary, but redemptive poetics: "Pour l'erreur, éclairer, c'est apostasier" (xxvi). In "Cérigo," the symbol of sensual lust, "Cythère, le jardin qui se change en rocher aux flancs nus," is transformed into the brightest star in the heavens.

> Le phare de toute heure, et, sur l'horizon noir,
> L'étoile du matin et l'étoile du soir!
> Ce monde inférieur, où tout rampe et s'altère,
> A ce qui disparaît et s'efface, Cythère,
> Le jardin qui se change en rocher aux flancs nus;
> La terre a Cérigo; mais le ciel a Vénus.
>
> ("Cérigo")

Poems xxi ("A Paul M"), and xxii ("Je payai le pêcheur qui passa son chemin"), if read together, bring the social and religious allegories together. Again, as in xvi, a specific autobiographical event is expanded to cosmic proportions. Paul Meurice's dedication to Hugo on the frontispiece of his play *Paris* reads: "Un nom proscrit que mord en sifflant la couleuvre." The next poem, xxii, brings this emblematic illustration alive through a dramatic monologue. A mysterious fisherman sells the poet a sea creature, a battle between the creature and the poet takes place, and just as the fisherman disappears, the creature bites the poet, who blesses it and mercifully throws it back into the sea. The bite is the constant in both poems, but in xxii it is the focus of the dramatic action. "Il tâchait de me mordre" is repeated twice, followed by "le crabe me mordit," in this relatively short (18 lines) work. It is the poet's gesture that endows the serpent's bite with redemptive significance. The fisherman who brings the fallen creature to him remains enigmatic. Like the poet he is both Judas and Christ, and the narrator is left free to condemn or forgive. Thus the static emblem on Meurice's frontispiece, which states man's betrayed and fallen condition, is freed and given both dramatic expression and redemptive significance. This is the function of art itself,[2] according to Hugo, and is reflected by the structure of his collection.

Poems xxiii-xxv are all interrelated and constitute a final commentary on the poetic process. The tension in each one is between the seemingly innocent, natural world, symbolized by some aspect of the pastoral scene, and the dark, supernatural world beyond. In each case the transference onto a supernatural level requires the intervention of the fallen consciousness. Hugo makes it very clear that this movement beyond pagan naiveté is positive and represents a superior level of understanding. I pointed out in chapter ii how he explicitly undermines the "charming" pastoral vision in "Pasteurs et troupeaux" (xxiii) to replace it by an awesome new order where God, poet, and nature are inextricably related. The sacrifice of the pastoral muse of xxiii is also the dramatic focus of xxv ("O strophe du poète, autrefois, dans les fleurs"), whose metapoetic significance was examined in chapter iii. Hugo uses Pluto's rape of Persephone as a parable for the poetic process. Like Léopoldine at the center of the volume, the nostalgic dream of a lost paradise is enthroned at the center of the dark poetic imagination. The pale flower, smelling of the sea dream,

---

[2] Thus the fisherman with his religious implications is a figure for the artist. Note the imagery of the prefatory poem: "Et tu tires des mers bien des choses qui sont / Sous les vagues profondes!"

which he picks in poem xxiv, represents the new poetry of the supreme contemplative experience.

> J'ai cueilli cette fleur pour toi sur la colline.
> Dans l'âpre escarpement qui sur le flot s'incline,
> Que l'aigle connaît seul et peut seul approcher,
> Paisible, elle croissait aux fentes du rocher.
> . . .
> Elle est pâle, et n'a pas de corolle embaumée.
> Sa racine n'a pris sur la crête des monts
> Que l'amère senteur des glauques goëmons;
>
> (xxiv)

The three poems that form an emblematic picture in the center of Book v: "Dolorosae," "Paroles sur la dune," and "Claire P," allude indirectly to the symbol of the dead child. Hugo, alone on his exile's rock ("Paroles sur la dune"), surrounds himself by the weeping mothers of his real and spiritual children. The suggestion of a triptych is created with the Virgin (Mme Hugo) and Mary Magdalene (Juliette Drouet) on either side of an elevated Christ figure (Hugo-visionary). The three figures, however, remain blind to the meaning of their sacrifice.

> Claire, tu dors. Ta mère, assise sur ta fosse,
> Dit:—Le parfum des fleurs est faux, l'aurore est fausse,
> L'oiseau qui chante au bois ment, et le cygne ment,
> L'étoile n'est pas vraie au fond du firmament,
> Le ciel n'est pas le ciel et là-haut rien ne brille,
> Puisque lorsque je crie à ma fille: "Ma fille,
> Je suis là. Lève-toi!" quelqu'un le lui défend;—
> Et que je ne puis pas réveiller mon enfant!—
>
> (xiv, "Claire P")

Not until the last poem of Book v, "Les Malheureux," will the poet-allegorist endow their loss with its redemptive significance:

> Elle était là debout, la mère douloureuse.[3]
> L'obscurité farouche, aveugle, sourde, affreuse,
> Pleurait de toutes parts autour du Golgotha.
> Christ, le jour devint noir quand on vous en ôta,
> Et votre dernier souffle emporta la lumière.
> Elle était là debout près du gibet, la mère!
> Et je me dis: Voilà la douleur! et je vins.
> —Qu'avez-vous donc, lui dis-je, entre vos doigts divins?
> Alors, aux pieds du fils saignant du coup de lance,
> Elle leva sa droite et l'ouvrit en silence,
> Et je vis dans sa main l'étoile du matin.
>
> (xxvi, "Les Malheureux")

The morning star in the Virgin's hand is the disembodied Venus of "Cérigo," a reflection of the sacrificial young virgin of ix in *Les Luttes et les rêves*, and of the dead couple of *Pauca meae*.

Like the poems on either side of it, "Paroles sur la dune" describes the experience of loss. The narrator stands alone on the wasteland shore, contemplating his own imminent death. The contrast with "Magnitudo parvi," when he held his child's hand on the opposite shore, is inevitable. Echoes of the pessimistic "A Villequier" are evoked by the alternating twelve eight-line stanzas and the repetition of the phrase "Maintenant que . . .". Thus drowning and exile are again linked. Although "Paroles sur la dune" contains two symbolic encounters, their meaning remains mysterious. Nevertheless, their presence in the poem attests to the narrator's superiority over the two women who remain frozen in their emotional grief. One such encounter is in the very center of the poem and hence of the chapter as a whole:

[3] *Stabat mater dolorosa*, liturgy of Good Friday.

Et je reste parfois couché sans me lever
    Sur l'herbe rare de la dune,
Jusqu'à l'heure où l'on voit apparaître et rêver
    Les yeux sinistres de la lune.

Elle monte, elle jette un long rayon dormant
    A l'espace, au mystère, au gouffre;
Et nous nous regardons tous les deux fixement,
    Elle qui brille et moi qui souffre.

The other occurs at the end:

Et je pense, écoutant gémir le vent amer,
    Et l'onde aux plis infranchissables;
L'été rit, et l'on voit sur le bord de la mer
    Fleurir le chardon bleu des sables.

Without the aid of the larger narrative, these signs—dead child, ascending moon, blue flower—would remain indecipherable. That the narrator supplies them with their symbolic meaning before the end of *En marche* reveals to the reader that poet-narrator and poet-seer are no longer altogether separate from one another. The "chardon bleu des sables" is the flower he picks from the dream promontory in poem xxiv: "J'ai cueilli cette fleur pour toi sur la colline." The ascension of the moon is called "triomphale" in "Pasteurs et troupeaux."[4]

En marche is thus an urgent summons to move beyond the cramped attitude of mourning that dominates *Pauca meae*, to-

---

[4] Toward the end of the final chapter of the collection, the moon will be clearly identified as a symbol of Divine Presence:

La lune à l'horizon montait, hostie énorme;
Tout avait le frisson, le pin, le cèdre et l'orme,
    Le loup, et l'aigle, et l'alcyon;
Lui montrant l'astre d'or sur la terre obscurcie,
Je lui dis:—Courbe-toi, Dieu lui-même officie,
    Et voici l'élévation.
                        (vi,xx, "Relligio")

ward the liberating acceptance of man's mortal nature. Only then does the Cosmic Order reveal itself through that decaying individuality and does the seer emerge out of the man. At the end of *En marche* the two narrative voices of *Aurore* have finally merged. The reader is now prepared for the visionary experience of Book VI, in which unity will be expressed by one poetic voice.

IX

AU BORD DE L'INFINI

At the end of Book v the reader and the narrator are ready for the special knowledge of the poet-seer. In "Ce que dit la bouche d'ombre," the final poem of the concluding section, Hugo outlines the cosmological structure within which man must operate.

> Le spectre m'attendait; l'être sombre et tranquille
> Me prit par les cheveux dans sa main qui grandit,
> M'emporta sur le haut du rocher, et me dit:

> "Sache que tout connaît sa loi, son but, sa route;
> Que, de l'astre au ciron, l'immensité s'écoute;"

Just as *Aurore* was a foreshadowing of the total scheme, Book vi is a recapitulation of the preceding five parts. The twenty-six poems move rapidly through the six stages of the general narrative from optimism through despair to revelation. As I have pointed out in chapter ii, this is the descent-ascension pattern of Hugo's religious frame of reference.

Like Dante, the narrator has a new, other-worldly guide for this last stage in the initiatory journey.

> . . .—Mon âme, ô mon âme! il faudrait,
> Pour traverser ce gouffre où nul bord n'apparaît,
> Et pour qu'en cette nuit jusqu'à ton Dieu tu marches,
> Bâtir un pont géant sur des millions d'arches.
> Qui le pourra jamais? Personne! ô deuil! effroi!
> Pleure!—Un fantôme blanc se dressa devant moi
> Pendant que je jetais sur l'ombre un oeil d'alarme,
> Et ce fantôme avait la forme d'une larme;

C'était un front de vierge avec des mains d'enfant;
Il ressemblait au lys que la blancheur défend;
Ses mains en se joignant faisaient de la lumière.

(i, "Le Pont")

The guide seems to represent both Léopoldine ("vierge," "mains d'enfant," "larme") and Hugo's own soul ("mon âme, ô mon âme," "un fantôme blanc," "il me dit"). Indeed, a series of spectral forms with characteristics of both Hugo and Léopoldine lead us through Book VI to the orphic voice of the final poem, which then reveals the parallelism between the events in the narrator's own life and the Divine Scheme within which he lives and dies.

As I have stated in chapter I, it is in this last poem that Hugo outlines his cosmogony. The diaphanous forms that inhabited the first moments of Creation are as close to God as it is possible to be. To use Ballanche's term, they are in fact *emanations* of God. These forms can be compared to the angelic Léopoldine of childhood through whom, in *Pauca meae*, the poet was able to glimpse Divinity.

Dieu n'a créé que l'être impondérable.
Il le fit radieux, beau, candide, adorable,
Mais imparfait; . . .

("Bouche d'ombre," ll. 52ff.)

Les anges se miraient en elle.
Que son bonjour était charmant!
Le ciel mettait dans sa prunelle
Ce regard qui jamais ne ment.

(IV,vi)

The future Satan, or fallen angel, is however, potentially present, just as he was in *Aurore*, for Creation and imperfection are synonymous.

172

La créature étant égale au créateur,
Cette perfection, dans l'infini perdue,
Se serait avec Dieu mêlée et confondue,
Et la création, à force de clarté,
En lui serait rentrée et n'aurait pas été.
La création sainte où rêve le prophète,
Pour être, ô profondeur! devait être imparfaite.

("Bouche d'ombre," ll. 54ff.)

Le firmament est plein de la vaste clarté;
Tout est joie, innocence, espoir, bonheur, bonté.
. . .
Et, pendant ce temps-là, Satan, l'envieux, rêve.

(I,iv)

Tumbling down the great chain of Being, imperfection fosters imperfection. Creation becomes weightier and weightier until God's presence is completely obscured. The angelic-satanic love of *L'Ame en fleur* creates the evil and imprisoned forms of *Les Luttes et les rêves*.

L'âme tomba, des maux multipliant la somme,
Dans la brute, dans l'arbre, et même, au-dessous d'eux,
Dans le caillou pensif, cet aveugle hideux.
. . .
Le mal, c'est la matière. Arbre noir, fatal fruit.

("Bouche d'ombre," ll. 76ff.)

. . .
Donc, la matière pend à l'idéal, et tire
L'esprit vers l'animal, l'ange vers le satyre,
Le sommet vers le bas, l'amour vers l'appétit.
Avec le grand qui croule elle fait le petit.

("Bouche d'ombre," ll. 187ff.)

> L'étang mystérieux, suaire aux blanches moires,
> Frissonne; au fond du bois la clairière apparaît;
> Les arbres sont profonds et les branches sont noires;
> Avez-vous vu Vénus à travers la forêt?
>
> (ii,xxvi, "Crépuscule")

Léopoldine becomes the erotic temptress of Book ii and then the prostitute or abandoned child, symbols of a fallen world, in Book iii.

Yet all is not lost, the specter explains: man stands midway between the mute stone and the angelic forms through which God shines. Indeed, he is free to choose between a life devoted to material reality, as do the actors in "La Fête chez Thérèse," or a life dedicated to the contemplation of such abstract virtues as Progress, Love, or Suffering.[1] This is the choice that the poet makes when he goes into exile and that is the focus of *En marche.*

> L'homme ne voit pas Dieu, mais peut aller à lui,
> En suivant la clarté du bien, toujours présente;
> Le monstre, arbre, rocher ou bête rugissante,
> Voit Dieu, c'est là sa peine, et reste enchaîné loin.
> L'homme a l'amour pour aile, et pour joug le besoin.
>
> ("Bouche d'ombre," ll. 430ff.)

The first step toward redemption comes with doubt. This stage can be compared to the despair that dominates Books iii and iv (*Les Luttes et les rêves* and *Pauca meae*). Hugo temporarily loses sight of God when his child drowns:

[1] In *Les Mages* (vi,xxiii) Hugo does in fact arrange the great seers of humanity into such categories: "prêtres du rire," "prêtres de la souffrance," "prêtres de l'amour," etc. These are the categories Ballanche names for individual regeneration. See Roos, *Les Idées philosophiques,* p. 83.

Or, je te le redis, pour se transfigurer,
Et pour se racheter, l'homme doit ignorer.
Il doit être aveuglé par toutes les poussières.
. . .
Il faut qu'il doute! Hier croyant, demain impie;
Il court du mal au bien; il scrute, sonde, épie,
Va, revient, et, tremblant, agenouillé, debout,
Les bras étendus, triste, il cherche Dieu partout;
Il tâte l'infini jusqu'à ce qu'il l'y sente;
Alors, son âme ailée éclate frémissante;
L'ange éblouissant luit dans l'homme transparent.
Le doute le fait libre, et la liberté, grand.
                    ("Bouche d'ombre," ll. 489ff.)

Finally, the Léopoldine of *Aurore* is transformed into her angelic other self in Book vi, and the end of "Ce que dit la bouche d'ombre" rejoins the beginning of *Au bord de l'infini*. In the first poem, "Le Pont," the poet calls upon his soul to cross the abyss separating him from God. The soul is materialized in the form of a tear-child-virgin. Thus creation and creator are nearly synonymous. The fusion that characterized the beginning of the world takes place in the structuring of Hugo's book.

Tout sera dit. Le mal expirera; les larmes
Tariront; plus de fers, plus de deuils, plus d'alarmes;
        L'affreux gouffre inclément
Cessera d'être sourd, et bégaiera: Qu'entends-je?
Les douleurs finiront dans toute l'ombre; un ange
        Criera: Commencement!
                    ("Bouche d'ombre," ll. 781ff.)

Thus the narrative proper ends with the announcement of a new social era when evil will be abolished and universal love will reign. The last stone of the ideal edifice is in place and we are returned to a new *Aurore* (the final poem ends with "Commencement") infused with the visionary understanding that the Romantic imagination is able to offer to the living reader.

> The rehabilitation postulated both in ("Ce que dit la bouche d'ombre") . . . and in Hugo's philosophy of history as expressed elsewhere is then at once collective and individual; it involves not only the reinstatement of particular souls, but also a total reintegration of the universe with God implying the eventual extinction of evil; and so, whichever aspect of the final consummation be envisaged, "La Bouche d'Ombre" can quite appropriately wind up with the convenient and effective metaphor—
> > "Et Jésus, se penchant sur Bélial qui pleure,
> > Lui dira: C'est donc toi!"[2]

This arrival at an Ideal Order through authenticated experience is characteristic of Romantic theory in general and may be responsible for the autobiographically oriented works that proliferate after Rousseau.

> Romanticism is both idealistic and realistic . . . it conceives of the ideal as existing only in conjunction with the real and the real as existing only with the ideal. The two are brought into conjunction only in the act of perception when the higher or imaginative rationality brings the ideal to the real by penetrating and possessing the external world as a way of knowing both itself and the external world.[3]

[2] Hunt, *The Epic* . . . , p. 306.
[3] Robert Langbaum, *The Poetry of Experience* (New York, 1957), p. 23.

From a lyrical, autobiographical poetry of the first person, *Les Contemplations* evolves into a dramatic narrative of the third person. The redemptive sacrifice of self through a poeticization of experience (1843 and the loss of a personal future) is the turning point. For Hugo, as for Coleridge, then, imagination is the medium for the reconciliation of the subject-object antithesis. The poeticizing consciousness becomes "a truth self-grounded, unconditional and known by its own light . . . one which is its own predicate."[4] Hugo can thus say in his preface that this book is both autobiographical ("Mémoires d'une âme") and impersonal:

> On se plaint quelquefois des écrivains qui disent moi. Parlez-nous de nous, leur crie-t-on. Hélas! quand je vous parle de moi, je vous parle de vous. Comment ne le sentez-vous pas? Ah! insensé, qui crois que je ne suis pas toi!

The moral and religious meaning of nature is perceived only through the medium of an awakened imagination—feeling and reason fused into one creative faculty. This exalted apprehension of reality by the imagination, metaphorically expressed by the bee-flower or Jupiter-Europa relationship, engenders an immense Presence, which Hugo calls God and to which he attributes a Divine Order.[5] That this God may actually be a projection of his own powerfully structuralizing consciousness, and the Divine Order a subsequent utopian construct is, perhaps, more nearly the truth. The poet bent over the ocean in the prefatory poem can be said to be the poet bent over his own receptive consciousness and by extension over his own creative process. Hugo's awareness that his God was a cosmic reflection of self is, perhaps, implicit in the imagery of his preface:

[4] *Biographia Literaria*, Vol. I, p. 181.
[5] See note 6, Introduction.

L'auteur a laissé . . . ce livre se faire en lui. La vie, en filtrant goutte à goutte à travers les événements et les souffrances, l'a déposé dans son coeur. Ceux qui s'y pencheront retrouveront leur propre image dans cette eau profonde et triste, qui s'est lentement amassée là, au fond d'une âme.

The reader, in turn, may stare into the poet's mythologized image and see himself both fetus and drowned child.

The arrangement of the poems to point up the moral nature of his poetics is further evidence that Hugo considered his theory of poetic consciousness the basis for a new religion. One could almost say that the victory of Unity over multiplicity—the ultimate religious experience—is achieved by the necessity of reading the six books of *Les Contemplations* as a whole. In true messianic style, he "imagines himself a Creator superior to God, and destined to transform life into something more ordered than the meaningless botch he sees around him."[6] This rhetorical and hortatory work is designed to be a new scripture. The Promethean figure of "Ibo" would indeed steal divine fire and in turn transform reality by liberating the imaginative faculty in the reader to do the same. Hugo does not let the reader go before he has fully understood his very powerful role in a revitalized metaphysical structure.

As I have already observed, Book vi in its entirety reflects the religious doctrine more explicitly stated in the last poem. Dates and locations reinforce the messianic tone. Except for one notable exception—"Claire," December, 1846—the poems are all dated from the time of exile: 1852-1856, that is, from "beyond the tomb." The place locations are mystical centers: the Dolman of Rozel,[7] the island of Jersey, the island of Sark,

---

[6] Robert Brustein, *The Theatre of Revolt* (Boston, 1962), p. 17.

[7] Journet and Robert point out that there is no "Dolman de Rozel," *Notes*, p. 169. Hugo liked the name for its sacred, Druidic associations.

etc. The fact that Hugo changed the date of "Claire" from 1854, an exile year, to 1846, reveals his desire to link the inception of the poetic work (in 1846 he conceived of *Les Contemplations* as a work) with the ultimate revelation of Book VI. Significantly, it is the only poem in Book VI that re-introduces the poet's historical self, and thus breaks an otherwise continuous monologue by the faceless seer. The basis in reality for the supreme contemplative experience is thus reaffirmed.

The narrative direction of Book VI is emphatically defined by certain poems that stand out either because of their rhythmic thrust as in the case of "Ibo," or because of their sheer magnitude. "Ibo" (33 four-line stanzas, 9,4,9,4), "Pleurs dans la nuit" (112 six-line stanzas, 12,12,6; 12,12,6), "Les Mages" (72 ten-line, octosyllabic stanzas), and "Ce que dit la bouche d'ombre" (over 750 alexandrines plus sixteen six-line stanzas of the "Pleurs dans la nuit" type) are like architectural blocks that determine the superstructure of the entire chapter. These poems again reflect, in exaggerated proportions, the basic Lucifer-Creator paradox upon which the work as a whole rests: man's potential to apprehend the pure creative principle from which he has sprung ("Ibo") and the terrible alienation of the flesh in which his material self condemns him to live ("Pleurs dans la nuit").

> Je suis celui que rien n'arrête,
>   Celui qui va,
> Celui dont l'âme est toujours prête
>   A Jéhovah;
>
> . . .
>
> Le songeur ailé, l'âpre athlète
>   Au bras nerveux,
> Et je traînerais la comète
>   Par les cheveux.
>
> (ii, "Ibo")

179

Nous rampons, oiseaux pris sous le filet de l'être;
Libres et prisonniers, l'immuable pénètre
    Toutes nos volontés;
            (v, "Pleurs dans la nuit," ll. 25ff.)

Oui, mon malheur irréparable,
C'est de pendre aux deux éléments,
C'est d'avoir en moi, misérable,
De la fange et des firmaments!
        (xv, "A celle qui est voilée")

"Les Mages," like *En marche*, states the power of man's
consciousness to mediate between the imperfect world of mute
substance and Original Creation when God could be heard
breathing through the thin veil of transparent forms. The
"mages" are described as actors in a cosmic drama already
written by an Original Genius, a drama that can be observed
by and instructive to the rest of humanity:

Ah! ce qu'ils font est l'oeuvre auguste.
Ces histrions sont les héros!
Ils sont le vrai, le saint, le juste,
Apparaissant à nos barreaux.
Nous sentons, dans la nuit mortelle,
La cage en même temps que l'aile;
Il nous font espérer un peu;
Ils sont lumière et nourriture;
Ils donnent aux coeurs la pâture,
Ils émiettent aux âmes Dieu!
        (xxiii, "Les Mages," ll. 331ff.)

One could say that it is ultimately the power of the creative
imagination that invests the world with meaning. Without the
communication of that Ideal Meaning, the world would be a
mass of separate, imprisoned forms, like the lyric poems before their mythic dating, cut off from their larger meaning.

Hugo's metaphysical poetics seems to reverse the apparent meaning of the prefatory poem, in which the ship of human destiny is held up by divine powers. Indeed in Book VI the poetic imagination becomes the oceanic space in which God is suspended. The fallen consciousness in fact determines its own course.

> Donc, les lois de notre problème,
>> Je les aurai;
> J'irai vers elles, penseur blême,
>> Mage effaré!
>
> Pourquoi cacher ces lois profondes?
>> Rien n'est muré.
> Dans vos flammes et dans vos ondes
>> Je passerai;
>
> J'irai lire la grande bible;
>> J'entrerai nu
> Jusqu'au tabernacle terrible
>> De l'inconnu,
>
> Jusqu'au seuil de l'ombre et du vide,
>> Gouffres ouverts
> Que garde la meute livide
>> Des noirs éclairs,
>
> Jusqu'aux portes visionnaires
>> Du ciel sacré;
> Et, si vous aboyez, tonnerres,
>> Je rugirai.
>
>> (ii, "Ibo")

The arrangement of the remaining poems in Book VI complements the direction established by these larger guiding works. Poems i-v express confidence in both the power of the questing spirit and the reality of an Ideal Presence (*Aurore, L'Ame en fleur*). Poems vi-xx fluctuate between despair and

181

optimism (*Les Luttes et les rêves, Pauca meae*). The final poems xxi-xxvi assert the power of an altered visionary consciousness to apprehend that remote Ideal (*En marche, Au bord de l'infini*).[8]

I have done little more than summarize the general thematic direction of the individual poems in Book VI because message in this book gives way once and for all to its formal articulation. Unlike the isolated lyric experiences of the preceding books—and especially of *Aurore*—thematic interrelationships are obvious. This chapter illustrates better than any other Jean Gaudon's thesis in *Le Temps de la contemplation* that it is, in a sense, a betrayal of Hugo's visionary genius to study him within the confines of a single poem or even a single collection, that "poésie" rather than "poème" characterizes the visionary experience because it is based upon the very nature of creation itself, ceaselessly self-proliferating, accumulative, contradictory and incomplete: "fuite," "ècroulement," "évanouissement," "éclosion," . . . "tas de mots qui n'est pas même un livre . . . grand poème béant . . . (p. 410)." Book VI is particularly interesting, then, as a study in poetic technique, since Hugo has set himself the awesome task of describing immateriality and of delineating the stages in an abstract journey. Above all,

---

[8] Until as late as May, 1855, Hugo intended to use *Solitudines coeli* (later called *Dieu*) as the final book. *Dieu* is a series of dialogues between narrator and emblematic animals representing different religions: bat-Shiva, atheism; owl-Hermès, skepticism; etc. The beginning of each dialogue, "Et, je vis au dessus de ma tête, un point noir," complements the opposing direction of the prefatory poem: "Un jour, je vis, debout au bord des flots mouvants / . . . Et j'entendis, penché sur l'abîme des cieux. . . ." The narrator and reader will discover that God can be found by looking down, into their own human experience; thus the alternative title for "Solitudines coeli"—"L'Ocean d'en haut"—in which the "abîme-ciel" opposition is resolved. The narrative movement of the poems Hugo ultimately chose for Book VI reflects the same development from despair to hope as does the series of religions (from skepticism through Romanticism) described in "Solitudines coeli."

he wishes the reader not to be constrained or seduced by the appeal of individual poems. It is in this book that he must demonstrate the mediating power contained within the structure of poetic language itself.

Hugo directs the reader through this unfamiliar, poeticized landscape by giving him a figure to follow on the allegorical voyage. In true dream fashion, the narrator seems to assume various masks: demi-god, poet, father, political exile, saint, and ultimately Everyman. He does, however, remain an identifiable persona throughout.

> Je suis le poète farouche,
> L'homme devoir,
> Le souffle des douleurs, la bouche
> Du clairon noir;
> ("Ibo")

> Je suis l'être incliné qui jette ce qu'il pense;
> Qui demande à la nuit le secret du silence;
> ("Pleurs dans la nuit")

> Et je suis l'habitant tranquille
> De la foudre et de l'ouragan.

> Je suis le proscrit qui se voile,
> Qui songe, et chante, loin du bruit,
> ("A celle qui est voilée")

> Nous vivons, debout à l'entrée
> De la mort, gouffre illimitée,
> Nous, tremblants, la chair pénétrée
> Du frisson de l'énormité.
> ("Les Mages")

> J'ai perdu mon père et ma mère,
> Mon premier né, ...
> ("En frappant à une porte")

He describes the hallucinatory trip in concrete terms. There is a cosmic geography we can actually perceive. The title itself is a paradoxical spatial designation: "Au *bord* de l'infini," and the title of the first poem, "Le Pont," immediately announces the impossible possibility of moving beyond the edge of infinity. The first verses of "Le Pont" sketch a vast visionary landscape with a minimum of specific details: bridge, star of light, and shining angel. What would otherwise be an opaque black canvas is transformed into a cosmic way because of a pinpoint of light at its center. Thus a blind tunnel becomes a kind of telescopic eye, enabling us to see beyond our natural limitations.

> J'avais devant les yeux les ténèbres. L'abîme
> Qui n'a pas de rivage et qui n'a pas de cime,
> Etait là, morne, immense; et rien n'y remuait.
> Je me sentais perdu dans l'infini muet.
> Au fond, à travers l'ombre, impénétrable voile,
> On apercevait Dieu comme une sombre étoile.
>
> (i, "Le Pont")

We know from the beginning of *Promontorium somnii* and the symbolical landscape of "Magnitudo parvi" that the setting is that of the contemplative experience itself. By the end of the book, the pinpoint of light will gain in luminosity (note such titles as "Claire" and "Eclaircie") until it is *all* the narrator sees. In true mystical tradition God, Light, Thought are synonymous. "Spes" ends with the observation, "Cette blancheur est plus que toute cette nuit." In "Ce que dit la bouche d'ombre," Hugo resolves the good-evil opposition by a startling neologism: "On verra . . . / Les monstres *s'azurer*!" Architectural images are everywhere:

> Je gravis les marches sans nombre.
>
> . . .

184

Que j'irai jusqu'aux bleus pilastres,
  Et que mon pas,
Sur l'échelle qui monte aux astres,
  Ne tremble pas!

. . .

J'irai lire la grande bible;
  J'entrerai nu
Jusqu'au tabernacle terrible
  De l'inconnu,

Jusqu'au seuil de l'ombre et du vide,
  Gouffres ouverts

. . .

Jusqu'aux portes visionnaires
  Du ciel sacré;

                              (ii, "Ibo")

Un spectre m'attendait dans un grand angle d'ombre,
                              (iii)

L'infini, route noire et de brume remplie,
Et qui joint l'âme à Dieu, monte, fuit, multiplie
    Ses cintres tortueux,
Et s'efface . . .—et l'horreur effare nos pupilles
Quand nous entrevoyons les arches et les piles
    De ce pont monstrueux.
            (vi, "Pleurs dans la nuit," ll. 541ff.)

Hélas! tout est sépulcre. On en sort, on y tombe:
La nuit est la muraille immense de la tombe.
                              (xviii)

Often a landscape is created by the definition of a perspective:

Je suis l'être incliné qui jette ce qu'il pense;
. . .

185

Dans une ombre sans fond mes paroles descendent,
Et les choses sur qui tombent mes strophes rendent
        Le son creux du cercueil.

Mon esprit, qui du doute a senti la piqûre,
Habite, âpre songeur, la rêverie obscure
        Aux flots plombés et bleus,
Lac hideux où l'horreur tord ses bras, pâle nymphe,
                            ("Pleurs dans la nuit")

Dramatic tension is maintained by the series of spectral figures which emerge from the darkness and speak to the narrator.

. . .—Un fantôme blanc se dressa devant moi
. . .
Et ce fantôme avait la forme d'une larme;
                            (i, "Le Pont")

Ecoutez, je suis Jean. . . .
                                        (iv)

Passant, qu'es-tu? je te connais.
Mais, étant spectre. . . .
                                        (xii)

Sors du nuage, ombre charmante.
O fantôme, laisse-toi voir!
                                        (xv)

Nous sommes là; nos dents tressaillent, nos vertèbres
Frémissent; on dirait parfois que les ténèbres,
        O terreur! sont pleines de pas.
Qu'est-ce que l'ouragan, nuit?—C'est quelqu'un qui passe.
Nous entendons souffler les chevaux de l'espace
        Traînant le char qu'on ne voit pas.
                            (xvi, "Horror")

Une nuit, un esprit me parla dans un rêve,
Et me dit:—Je suis aigle en un ciel où se lève
    Un soleil qui t'est inconnu.
J'ai voulu soulever un coin du vaste voile;
J'ai voulu voir de près ton ciel et ton étoile;
    Et c'est pourquoi je suis venu;

                        (xviii)

The narrator's moods of despair or elation are projected outward into a kind of psychomachia, reflected in such iconographical titles as "Spes," "Dolor," "Horror." Indeed, "Relligio"
is a dramatic monologue between Hermann, the skeptic of
"Horror," and the Jobian voice of "Dolor," both aspects of
the same consciousness.

Book vi is very much like a protracted and somewhat mo-
notonous dream whose meaning is constantly being pointed
out to the sleeping *voyeur*, but that nevertheless holds him
an emotional prisoner by the startlingly realistic description
of the supernatural:

Sois la bienvenue, ombre! ô ma soeur! ô figure
Qui me fais signe alors que sur l'énigme obscure
    Je me penche, sinistre et seul;
Et qui viens, m'effrayant de ta lueur sublime,
Essuyer sur mon front la sueur de l'abîme
    Avec un pan de ton linceul!

              (xvi, "Horror")

Chaque fois qu'ici-bas l'homme, en proie aux désastres,
Rit, blasphème, et secoue, en regardant les astres,
    Le sarcasme, ce vil lambeau,
Les morts se dressent froids au fond du caveau sombre,
Et de leur doigt de spectre écrivent—DIEU—dans l'ombre,
    Sous la pierre de leur tombeau.

             (xvii, "Dolor")

Mais, ô Dieu! le navire énorme et frémissant,
Le monstrueux vaisseau sans agrès et sans voiles,
Qui flotte, globe noir, dans la mer des étoiles,
Et qui porte nos maux, fourmillement humain,
Va, marche, vogue et roule, et connaît son chemin;
Le ciel sombre, où parfois la blancheur semble éclore,
A l'effrayant roulis mêle un frisson d'aurore,
De moment en moment le sort est moins obscur,
Et l'on sent bien qu'on est emporté vers l'azur.

(xix, "Voyage de nuit")

It is in Book VI that Hugo's language seems to fulfill the revolutionary promises of "Suite" or "Réponse à un acte d'accusation." Michael Riffaterre has brilliantly analyzed many of the devices by which Hugo disorients the reader and inspires him with a metaphysical *malaise* preparatory to revelation.

> L'hallucination consiste à percevoir une sensation alors qu'il n'y a là aucun objet extérieur capable de la produire. J'appelle donc vision hallucinatoire le mode de vision par lequel Victor Hugo voit et fait voir à son lecteur le surnaturalisme . . . c'est à dire, "la partie de la nature qui échappe à nos organes."[9]

The certitude of our everyday life is removed. Instead of looking at the world, the world looks at us ("Et tout est l'oeil d'où sort ce terrible regard"). Hidden consciousnesses reveal themselves by unexpected movements. Dreams float about, outside the narrator's mind, entangling themselves with "reality." Descriptions move rapidly from the natural world into the psychological world of the poet's brain and back into the world again. Riffaterre points out that this kind of transition suggests that the reader exists inside a divine brain, the "Moi énorme

[9] "La Vision hallucinatoire chez Victor Hugo," *MLN*, Vol. 78, May, 1963, pp. 225-41.

de l'univers." Above all, Hugo's poetics reflects a dynamics of becoming. Solids flow into liquids, eyes stick out like probing fingers, oppositions melt away. "La tâche du poète selon Hugo, c'est de prolonger, de continuer la création: 'la vaste anxiété de ce que peut être. . . .'" Hugo's new language, Riffaterre goes on to say, is the metaphoric process dramatized. In other words, we experience the creative process with the creator.

> Les affinités, les analogies secrètes que le réel cache aux regards, elle les révèle en substituant l'un à l'autre des éléments qu'une vision fondée en raison continuerait à séparer. C'est le mécanisme de la métaphore. Mais la métaphore est un transfert terminé, une substitution déjà accomplie: on ne voit du rapprochement révélateur que le résultat. . . . Alors que la technique de Hugo, mettant en relief le processus même de la substitution, est en somme métaphore en mouvement; comme celle-ci, elle est un outil à sonder l'universelle analogie. (Ibid., pp. 233-35)

At the same time that Hugo's visionary style effects man's power to reunite himself dynamically with a lost God, it also states the presence of that Absolute Unity. Journet and Robert have demonstrated that in Book VI substantives take on an important rôle, whereas verbs tend to weaken.[10] Endings in *ment* are especially favored: "éboulissement," "flamboiement," "frémissement," "écroulement," etc. Indeed, the last word of Book VI—"Commencement"—is effective because it substantively asserts the self-proliferating verbal momentum of the last stanza:

> Tout sera dit. Le mal expirera; les larmes
> Tariront; plus de fers, plus de deuils, plus d'alarmes;
>   L'affreux gouffre inclément

---

[10] *Notes*, pp. 24ff.

> Cessera d'être sourd, et bégaiera: Qu'entends-je?
> Les douleurs finiront dans toute l'ombre: un ange
> Criera: Commencement!
>
> ("Bouche d'ombre")

The verbs of this passage express cessation and the final abstract noun an eternity of becoming.

Adjectives are also frequently transformed into substantives: "les exécrables," "le charmant," "la noirceur," "le ténébreux." New or exotic nouns proliferate: "puiseurs d'ombre," "éclaireurs," "l'agitateur," "du grand linceul," "pilône," "rune," "hiérophante," etc.

Strange or defamiliarizing effects are achieved in a variety of ways. Journet and Robert have shown that abstractions often appear in the midst of a series of concrete words:

> Abîme, espoir, asile, écueil,
> ("Horror")

> L'orage, l'horreur, la pluie,
> ("Les Mages")

> Prunelle énorme d'insomnie,
> De flamboiement et de bonté.
> ("Les Mages")

> Ils le portent aux vers, au néant, à Peut-Etre!
> ("Pleurs dans la nuit")

> On dirait qu'en tous lieux, en même temps, la vie
> Dissout le mal, le deuil, l'hiver, la nuit, l'envie,
> (x, "Eclaircie")

Or abstractions assume the threatening power of immediacy by the use of concrete modifiers:

> Comme si nous sentions se fermer sur nos âmes
> La main de la géante nuit.
> (xvi, "Horror")

Le problème muet gonfle la mer sonore.
>   (vi, "Pleurs dans la nuit")

Muraille obscure où vient battre le flot de l'être.
>   (ix, "A la fenêtre pendant la nuit")

La porte, affreuse et faite avec de l'ombre, est lourde;
>   ("Bouche d'ombre")

Conversely, familiar reality is expanded into limitless abstractions:

Ne verrons-nous jamais sous ces grands haleines
D'autres fleurs de lumière éclore dans les plaines
>   De l'éternel avril?
>   (ix, "A la fenêtre pendant la nuit")

>   . . . l'être sombre et tranquille
Me prit par les cheveux dans sa main qui grandit,
>   (xxvi, "Bouche d'ombre")

La petite bouche des roses
A l'oreille immense des cieux.
>   (xxiii, "Les Mages")

There are often abrupt and disturbing reversals:

Le moineau d'un coup d'aile, ainsi qu'un fol esprit,
Vient tacquiner le flot monstrueux qui sourit;
>   (x, "Eclaircie")

Or hallucinatory piling up of metaphoric effects:

A l'âge où la prunelle innocente est en fleur.
>   (viii, "Claire")

As words lose their conceptual value, a correspondingly greater emphasis is placed on affective devices: In "Le Pont," for example, the word "abîme" is rhythmically isolated:

J'avais devant les yeux les ténèbres. L'abîme,
Qui n'a pas de rivage et qui n'a pas de cime,
Etait là, morne, immense; et rien n'y remuait.

(i, "Le Pont")

In "Ibo" the upward surge of the creative genius is articulated
by the running on of verses and stanzas:

> Vous savez bien que l'âme est forte
> Et ne craint rien
> Quand le souffle de Dieu l'emporte!
> Vous savez bien
>
> Que j'irai jusqu'aux bleus pilastres,
> Et que mon pas,
> Sur l'échelle qui monte aux astres,
> Ne tremble pas!

(ii, "Ibo")

The visionary experience makes itself felt through sound as
well as rhythm:

> L'océan resplendit sous sa vaste nuée,
> L'onde, de son combat sans fin exténuée,
> S'assoupit, et, laissant l'écueil se reposer,
> Fait de toute la rive un immense baiser.

(x, "Eclaircie")

> Le flot huileux et lourd décompose ses moires
> Sur l'océan blêmi;

(ix, "A la fenêtre pendant la nuit")

The poems are arranged so as to create rhythmic variations
and echoing. One is carried through the chapter on receding
and progressing waves. The main architectural block-poems:
"Ibo," "Pleurs dans la nuit," "Les Mages," and "Ce que dit
la bouche d'ombre" all have very different rhythmic patterns;
yet at the end of the last poem, the rhythm associated with the

despair of "Pleurs dans la nuit," "Horror," and "Dolor," is echoed in a triumphant hymn to man's transcendental powers. Thus a dissolution of opposites is effected directly through our almost physical apprehension of the text.

Journet and Robert describe the synthesizing effects which these techniques have:

> Ainsi s'effacent les frontières entre la nature et l'esprit. Les notions et les choses s'interpénètrent. Le poète saisit simultanément l'aspect visible et le sens caché. Rien n'est séparé dans l'univers. Tout se recueille ou frissonne également dans le même mystère. La même âme religieuse vit dans le poète et dans les choses, qu'elles demeurent muettes, qu'elles interrogent ou qu'elles prient. Les mêmes mots s'appliquent donc à elles et à l'homme: les astres sont "effarés," "éperdus," le caillou est "pensif"; comme le poète, le taillis est "sacré," la nature est "farouche." Comme lui, "l'abîme est un prêtre." (*Notes*, p. 25)

Poetically, then, Book vi is an appropriate ending to the contemplative adventure, for this fusion of reader and narrator through vertigo creates the illusion of unity essential to Hugo's cosmogony. The mediating power of language must be experienced if one is to believe that language is divine ("le Verbe, c'est Dieu"). The transformation of the narrator from a historic to an emblematic figure, which constituted the main thematic drive of Book v and of the collection in general, is complete. The poet's prefatory claims to universality are confirmed: "La destinée est une." Thus Book vi completes Hugo's story of the poetic imagination and, like all allegory, reveals the written text as the incarnation of a universal truth outside itself.

X

A CELLE QUI EST RESTEE

EN FRANCE

Hᴜɢᴏ did not end his collection with "Ce que dit la bouche d'ombre." In April of 1855 he decided to add an epilogue entitled "L'Absent à l'absente,"[1] later changed to "A celle qui est restée en France." This final poem does not seem to reflect the new voice of *Au bord de l'infini*; indeed, in many respects it is more reminiscent of the nostalgic voice of *Pauca meae*. The narrator reassumes the role of a flesh-and-blood father and speaks to a specific child rather than to an abstract phantom.

> Mets-toi sur ton séant, lève tes yeux, dérange
> Ce drap glacé qui fait des plis sur ton front d'ange,
> Ouvre tes mains, et prends ce livre: il est à toi.

These first lines call forth Léopoldine's plastic form and hence have been said to be more "classical" than "Romantic." Jean Gaudon goes so far as to suggest that this poem represents a regression to a neoclassical fiction after Book vɪ and hence a kind of betrayal of the collection as a whole:

> Mais de même que le poète a, en projetant dans le monde extérieur les signes de l'immobilité sépulcrale et en évitant de les intérioriser, écarté pour lui-même les conséquences ultimes de sa mort symbolique, de même le père de Léopoldine se refuse à intégrer sa fille endormie au cycle atroce de la vie et de la mort. Pour donner le mouvement au beau

---

[1] The title is a reference to *The Aeneid*: IV,83: "Illum absens absentem auditque videtque. . . ."

gisant de marbre blanc figé dans le sommeil éternel, le père a recours à une fiction néoclassique et fait une infidelité significative à son propre univers poétique: "Mets-toi sur ton séant, lève tes yeux, dérange. . . ."[2]

"A celle qui est restée en France" appears less contradictory if it is considered in the light of the total narrative rather than as a further affirmation of Book VI. Like the introductory poem, "Un jour je vis, debout au bord des flots . . . ," it is not given a number, so one may assume that it was intended to stand *outside* the six subdivisions.[3] Since the poem is addressed to Hugo's daughter, it should also be considered within the context of the other Léopoldine poems. I have pointed out in several of the preceding chapters that Hugo's child appears to be an evolving metaphor for the work of art itself. These first and last poems, then, would complement one another and would appropriately be considered as larger statements of the poetic evolution contained within their panels. In the first poem,

Un jour je vis, debout au bord des flots mouvants,
  Passer, gonflant ses voiles,
Un rapide navire enveloppé de vents,
  De vagues et d'étoiles;

Et j'entendis, penché sur l'abîme des cieux,
  Que l'autre abîme touche,
Me parler à l'oreille une voix dont mes yeux
  Ne voyaient pas la bouche:

the poet is presented bent over the oceanic mystery of creation. Like the title of one of the photographs Hugo was fond of

---

[2] *Le Temps de la contemplation*, p. 355.

[3] All editions have not observed this separation and hence have encouraged confusion of the epilogue with Book VI.

having François-Victor take of him on the promontory of Jersey, this emblematic picture could be called "Victor Hugo écoutant Dieu." The poet is the sacred translator of Divine Thought. Out of the chaos of forms he will extract *figurae* which mediate between alienated humanity and that invisible Ideal.

> Poëte, tu fais bien! poëte au triste front,
> Tu rêves près des ondes,
> Et tu tires des mers bien des choses qui sont
> Sous les vagues profondes!

Léopoldine is one of those mediating forms. Her death by drowning in 1843 was symbolic of her sacred destiny. The allegorist of *Les Contemplations* will draw her back out of the cosmic darkness and endow her with poeticized life, just as he does in the first lines of the epilogue poem. Her various forms, all of which are to be found in "A celle qui est restée en France" are iconographical representations of the Divine Logos the poet sets out to make visible to the myopic reader. The epilogue poem could be said to be a final summing up of the evolution of the Léopoldine figure and of the narrative in general. Its analysis will thus provide an appropriate ending for this study.

The poem refers to all three stages of supreme expression ("sentir," "penser," "prier") and not just the first lyrical stage the opening lines might suggest. In the first of the eight sections of the poem the visionary consciousness sends the work, reality transmuted into thought, back to its fallen origins across the chaos of forms ("forêt," "prè," "mer," "vents") that separates the universal and ideal (visionary as God) from the particular and real (Léopoldine, father, reader). That the book is a form of illumination, containing the Divine Logos, is made clear:

196

D'où sort le blême éclair qui déchire la brume?
Depuis quatre ans, j'habite un tourbillon d'écume;
Ce livre en a jailli. Dieu dictait, j'écrivais;

(ll. 9ff.)

The poet dedicates it to "la tombe," symbol both of man's fallen nature and of the transition from contingent to mystical levels of existence. "*Autrefois, Aujourd'hui.* Un abîme les sépare, le tombeau."

In the second section the poet laments the past (the section begins: "Autrefois, quand septembre, en larmes revenait . . .") when a more direct expression of personal feeling seemed possible. He specifically evokes the poems of *Pauca meae* in this part.

Je me la rappelais quand elle était petite,
Quand elle m'apportait des lys et des jasmins,
Ou quand elle prenait ma plume dans ses mains,
Gaie, et riant d'avoir de l'encre à ses doigts roses;
Je respirais les fleurs sur cette cendre écloses,
Je fixais mon regard sur ces froids gazons verts,

(ll. 70ff.)

These were the poems inspired by and addressed to a particular, limited human experience. Yet he now can state that this form of nostalgic lament was not mediating, did not transcend the temporality to which it referred:

Pourquoi donc dormais-tu d'une façon si dure
Que tu n'entendais pas lorsque je t'appelais?

(ll. 58-9)

In section three he continues to emphasize the limitations of the lyrical voice symbolized by the bouquet of natural flowers he used to bring to Léopoldine's grave on the September anniversary of her death. "O mon Dieu, tout cela, c'était donc du bonheur!" The descriptive *Pauca meae* poems are as power-less to transcend death as the tears or flowers of the lamenting father.

> Lazare ouvrit les yeux quand Jésus l'appela;
> Quand je lui parle, hélas! pourquoi les ferme-t-elle?
> Où serait donc le mal quand de l'ombre mortelle
> L'amour violerait deux fois le noir secret,
> Et quand, ce qu'un dieu fit, un père le ferait?
>
> (ll. 116ff.)

Léopoldine remains a dead form sunk into oblivion like the ship of the prologue poem: "Et t'es-tu recouchée ainsi qu'un mât qui sombre?" We know, however, that the allegorical book, the "bouquet sinistre" (l. 112),[4] unlike the individual poem-flower, has this mediating power, for in the opening lines we see Léopoldine's form rise out of the grave:

> Mets-toi sur ton séant, lève tes yeux, dérange
> Ce drap glacé qui fait des plis sur ton front d'ange,
> Ouvre tes mains, et prends ce livre: il est à toi.

Section four describes the redemptive quality of this fully evolved poetic expression.

> Ce livre, légion tournoyante et sans nombre
> D'oiseaux blancs dans l'aurore et d'oiseaux noirs dans l'ombre,
> Ce vol de souvenirs fuyant à l'horizon,
> Cet essaim que je lâche au seuil de ma prison,
> Je vous le confie, air, souffles, nuée, espace!
> Que ce fauve océan qui me parle à voix basse,

---

[4] Note a similar use of "sinistre" in "Pasteurs et troupeaux": "La laine des moutons sinistres de la mer."

Lui soit clément, l'épargne et le laisse passer!
Et que le vent ait soin de n'en rien disperser,
Et jusqu'au froid caveau fidèlement apporte
Ce don mystérieux de l'absent à la morte!

(ll. 133ff.)

The book is life-giving rather than death-reflecting. Just as he did in some of the Léopoldine poems analyzed in chapter iii (iii,ix; v,xxv), the poet assumes the role of a generative consciousness.

Que ce livre, du moins, obscur message, arrive,
Murmure, à ce silence, et, flot, à cette rive!
Qu'il y tombe, sanglot, soupir, larme d'amour!
Qu'il entre en ce sépulcre où sont entrés un jour
Le baiser, la jeunesse, et l'aube, et la rosée,
Et le rire adoré de la fraîche épousée,
. . .
Qu'il soit comme le pas de mon âme en sa nuit!

(ll. 121ff.)

At the end of section four the reader discovers that poetic language has bridged the gulf between perception and the world of temporal forms.

Qu'il tombe au plus profond du sépulcre hagard,
A côté d'elle, ô mort! et que, là, le regard,
Près de l'ange qui dort, lumineux et sublime,
Le voie épanoui, sombre fleur de l'abîme![5]

(ll. 163ff.)

The tomb contains both poet and subject, luminous perception and perceived luminosity. This is the mid-point of the poem.

[5] The final line of this section recalls the title Baudelaire chose, but with an entirely different purpose. The flower as poem in Hugo's work is a symbol for rebirth, whereas in Baudelaire's work it is an ironic reminder of the natural origins of idealism.

Sections five and six correspondingly describe the orphic poet of Aujourd'hui who is able to resurrect dead forms.

> J'ai le droit aujourd'hui d'être, quand la nuit tombe,
> Un de ceux qui se font écouter de la tombe,
> Et qui font, en parlant aux morts blêmes et seuls,
> Remuer lentement les plis noirs des linceuls,
> Et dont la parole, âpre ou tendre, émeut les pierres,
> Les grains dans les sillons, les ombres dans les bières,
> La vague et la nuée, et devient une voix
> De la nature, ainsi que la rumeur des bois.
>
> (ll. 169ff.)

The transformation from a particular father holding his child's hand in "Magnitudo parvi" to the universal shepherd ("pâtre") has taken place.

> Oh! que ne suis-je encore le rêveur d'autrefois,
> Qui s'égarait dans l'herbe, et les prés, et les bois,
> Qui marchait souriant, le soir, quand le ciel brille,
> Tenant la main petite et blanche de sa fille,
>
> (ll. 199ff.)

Section five appropriately evokes the exiled "mage" of *En marche*, and section six the visionary experience of *Au bord de l'infini*. The imagery changes and hallucinatory effects characteristic of Book VI appear. Humble reality expands suddenly to cosmic proportions:

> Je ne puis plus aller où j'allais; je ne puis,
> Pareil à la laveuse assise au bord du puits,
> Que m'accouder au mur de l'éternel abîme;
>
> (ll. 215ff.)

The objective world of forms is internalized into a subjective mood or abstraction:

> La haute Notre-Dame à présent, qui me luit,
> C'est l'ombre ayant deux tours, le silence et la nuit,
>
> (ll. 219-20)

Disturbing rhythmic ("Contemple, s'il te faut de la cendre, les mondes") and incantatory effects ("penche-toi," "penche-toi," etc.) are used. This apotheosis of the contemplative experience brings the poet back to the word "tombe," the same word that began the narrative digression at the end of section one.

> Laisse là ton vil coin de terre. Tends les bras,
> O proscrit de l'azur, vers les astres patries!
> Revois-y refleurir tes aurores flétries;
> Deviens le grand oeil fixe ouvert sur le grand tout.
> Penche-toi sur l'énigme où l'être se dissout,
> Sur tout ce qui naît, vit, marche, s'éteint, succombe,
> Sur tout le genre humain et sur toute la tombe!
>
> (ll. 240ff.)

With this word he crashes back to the reality of earthbound forms. The eternal circle of creation is complete.

> . . . Ah! l'étendue a beau
> Me parler, me montrer l'universel tombeau,
> Les soirs sereins, les bois rêveurs, la lune amie;
> J'écoute, et je reviens à la douce endormie.
>
> (ll. 251ff.)

Sections seven and eight bring together one last time the beginnings and the end of poetic creation. Seven returns obsessively to the elegiac lament over earthly forms that is the origin of inspiration. His language becomes once again sentimental and charged with personal emotion:

201

> Des fleurs! oh! si j'avais des fleurs! Si je pouvais
> Aller semer des lys sur ces deux froids chevets!
>
> (ll. 255-56)

Eight, the final section added months after the completion of the rest of the poem, projects us back to the visionary universe of *Au bord de l'infini*. The *felix-culpa* paradox that is the key to this new religion of language is described once again:

> O chute! asile! ô seuil de la trouble vallée
> D'où nous apercevons nos ans fuyants et courts,
> Nos propres pas marqués dans la fange des jours,
> . . .
> Toujours nous arrivons à cette *solitude*,
> Et, là, nous nous taisons, sentant la *plénitude*!
>
> (ll. 302ff., my italics)

Thus the ending of the epilogue poem does indeed correspond to the ultimate message of "Ce que dit la bouche d'ombre." Lucifer (Belial) and Christ are reunited: "Que les enfers dormants rêvent les paradis." The poet, like God at the moment of Creation, calms the chaos of forms with the "berceuse d'ombre" passage:

> Paix à l'Ombre! Dormez! dormez! dormez! dormez!
> Etres, groupes confus lentement transformés!
> Dormez, les champs! dormez, les fleurs! dormez les tombes!

Hugo leaves us with the final vision of this universe of drowning, evanescent forms, totally encompassed by the contemplative gaze of the poet.

> Qu'assis sur la montagne en présence de l'Etre,
> Précipice où l'on voit pêle-mêle apparaître
> Les créations, l'astre et l'homme, les essieux
> De ces chars de soleils que nous nommons les cieux,

Les globes, fruits vermeils des divines ramées,
Les comètes d'argent dans un champ noir semées,
Larmes blanches du drap mortuaire des nuits,
Les chaos, les hivers, ces lugubres ennuis,
Pâle, ivre d'ignorance, ébloui de ténèbres,
Voyant dans l'infini s'écrire des algèbres,
Le contemplateur, triste et meurtri, mais serein,
Mesure le problème aux murailles d'airain,
Cherche à distinguer l'aube à travers les prodiges,
Se penche, frémissant, au puits des grands vertiges,
Suit de l'oeil des blancheurs qui passent, alcyons,
Et regarde, pensif, s'étoiler de rayons,
De clartés, de lueurs, vaguement enflammées,
Le gouffre monstrueux plein d'énormes fumées.

        Guernesey, 2 novembre 1855, jour des morts.

Thus the final, dedicatory poem to Léopoldine follows the same trajectory as does the collection as a whole. Whereas the evocation of her corporeal self at the beginning is reminiscent of her presence in *Aurore*, her transformation into a spectral form at the end returns us to the visionary world of *Au bord de l'infini*. The Léopoldine poems from the first to the last book reflect the changing function of language from the descriptive, nearly Parnassian imagery of the observer ("Mes deux filles," I,iii) through the emblematic language of the alienated thinker ("Jeune fille, la grâce emplit tes dix-sept ans," III,ix), ending with the surrealistic universe of the mystic ("Le Pont," VI,i). "A celle qui est restée en France" sums up this development in one final tribute standing outside the six books, thus making clear the analogy between Léopoldine and the work of art itself. Like Lazarus she has been reborn in the form of poetic language that contains the mystery of human destiny. Her father's creative mind takes the place of the watery chaos into which she disappeared. The disturbing imagery of the preface, where the poet describes himself as an oceanic womb into which the reader can find reflected a universalized self, is thus made clear through the transformation of his flesh and blood child into a medium for redemptive experience.

L'auteur a laissé, pour ainsi dire, ce livre se faire en lui. La vie, en filtrant goutte à goutte à travers les événements et les souffrances, l'a déposé dans son coeur. Ceux qui s'y pencheront retrouveront leur propre image dans cette eau profonde et triste, qui s'est lentement amassée là, au fond d'une âme.

CONCLUSION

THE SHEER immensity and willfully digressive nature of Victor Hugo's works would seem at first to preclude any attempt to define too closely the structure of his universe. Yet it is certain that although he wanted the task of decipherer to be a difficult one, the reader has failed to enter Hugo's world if he does not seek to discern a providential order behind the formal irregularity that characterizes Hugo's art. If the design of Hugo's work is obscure, it is because for him the divinity at its center has become invisible to modern man. Hugo repeatedly uses architectural analogies to describe his literary creations, and readers familiar with his thought know that "hasard" was as hateful to him as "symétrie." Monstrous and deformed heroes hold the key to his novels' unfolding. The grotesque Quasimodo is organically related to his structural surroundings —he is the heart and voice, so to speak, of the cathedral of Notre Dame de Paris, which gives its name to Hugo's novel. The classically beautiful Captain Phoebus, on the other hand, is pure superficiality, a temporary seducer who disappears early from the plot.

In certain of his later works Hugo emphasizes the reader's religious and moral obligations more insistently than in others. *Les Contemplations*, begun almost immediately after his flight into exile, is one of these works of special initiatory value for Hugo. It is not merely a collection of separate lyric poems, but rather an allegorical narrative that must be read temporally, in a progressive sequence, for the reader to perceive the informed nature of Hugo's vision. The order of the poems represents the poet's own creative process, which in turn reflects the relatedness of all creative processes: linguistic, historical, biological, and cosmological. Thus, his apprehension of *Les Contemplations* is meant to initiate the reader into the visionary universe of the poet himself, to alter human perception through a reenactment of the poet's own creative experience.

The event Hugo inscribed into the very center of his work unites biological, historical, and artistic levels of reality, for the drowning of his daughter in 1843 paradoxically supplied the source of inspiration for his own poetic rebirth when he moved into exile in 1851. The historic date, September 4, 1843, represents the sacrificial imperative that governs for Hugo all levels of creativity. Divine Presence, as the birdlike child who once entered the young poet's study to ruffle his papers, is replaced by signs of its absence; language substitutes itself for a now invisible natural order. The poet's role is to reveal the pattern of this lost or invisible design through visible, indeed decipherable, forms. Thus, Hugo consciously seeks to be "créateur par la forme," as Valéry so aptly observed. His text has a purely linguistic life of its own, a self-proliferating, vital presence that transforms the abstraction of language—of empty, tomblike words—into a dynamic experience through which the reader gains new and visionary insight. This development away from naturalistic to visionary perception is reflected thematically as well as formally throughout the book. Just as Léopoldine's childish presence in "Mes deux filles" (Book I) is replaced by the memory of that presence in *Pauca meae* (Book IV), and finally by her spiritual and mediating form in *Au bord de l'infini* (Book VI), the naturalistic setting of Books I and II is replaced by the emblematic landscapes to be deciphered by the intellect in Book III and finally by the cosmic "univers sous le crâne" of Book VI. Thus Hugo's fecundating imagination replaces the oceanic chaos into which Léopoldine disappeared in 1843. When, in the epilogue poem, Hugo sends his book rather than a bouquet of natural flowers to his daughter's tomb at Villequier, the dead child rises from her grave as if she had been brought back to life by the sheer energy of this new poetic language.

> Mets-toi sur ton séant, lève tes yeux, dérange
> Ce drap glacé qui fait des plis sur ton front d'ange,
> Ouvre tes mains, et prends ce livre, il est à toi.

My approach to *Les Contemplations* has been determined in part by Hugo's peculiarly Romantic vision. A sequential reading of the text is especially appropriate to Hugo's messianic view of the function of poetic language and of allegory in particular; indeed, an isolated reading of the individual poems that make up *Les Contemplations* may easily lead to misreadings, even though each poem, in the long run, can be revealed as a microcosm or structural paradigm of the whole work. The critic must remain double, in the same way that Hugo as poet remains double throughout his own text. He must be aware of the way the work affects and controls his reactions as he moves through the text for the first time, and of the way the intricate patternings of the text as a whole point to a single, unifying design. Thus, the emotional effect of the poetic order in *Les Contemplations* has been given as much consideration as the purely formalistic miracle of Hugo's art.

There are, then, three principal actors in the drama of *Les Contemplations*: the narrator who is both poet and grieving father; the subject of his narration who is both muse and dead child, and the reader who is both informed critic and myopic participant. Hugo's art, like his religion, is dependent for its ultimate meaning not upon grace or the miraculous intercession of a divine figure, but rather upon the active, engaged relationship of the reader with the other two protagonists in this tale of human destiny.

For the Christian believer, the heresy in Hugo's art is that the visionary scribe, whose duty it is to translate the revealed word of God, has substituted the inspired workings of his own imagination for those of the Divine Logos. It is this heresy, however, that determines the greatness of Hugo's achievement. One could go so far as to say that the life of Hugo's art overcomes the vision that informs it. Poetic language in *Les Contemplations* makes us aware of itself as such and not only as a medium pointing toward some other, higher order. His particular use of allegory as the controlling rhetorical figure in his later works, a figure that had been drained of vitality in the eighteenth century and had come to be associated with the separation of form and content, indicates his effort to move beyond his predecessors' use of the trope by exploiting in a revolutionary way the temporal, sequential nature of the figure. The poet who wished to revolutionize language ("mettre un bonnet rouge au vieux dictionnaire") chose quite consciously a form of poetic discourse which is historical by its very structure.

Hugo's vision of himself in the epilogue poem of *Les Contemplations* as a generative and informing consciousness has been dramatically realized by the great number of poetic heirs who see in his work an expression of their own preoccupation with form. The lexical, syntactic, and rhythmic innovations Hugo brought to French prosody, as well as the increased formal complexity of his later works, demonstrate his effort to revitalize the structures by which the poet seeks to make himself heard. Indeed, his legacy to modernist poetics could be said to be his discovery of the power inherent in the structure of language itself to signify—to inform the reader of truths that scientific discourse has failed to name.

A SELECTED BIBLIOGRAPHY

A. WORKS BY VICTOR HUGO

Oeuvres complètes de Victor Hugo, ed. Paul Meurice, Gustave Simon, Cécile Daubray. 45 vols. Paris: Imprimerie Nationale, 1901-1952.

Oeuvres complètes, ed. Francis Bouvet. 4 vols. Paris: Pauvert, 1961-1964.

Oeuvres complètes, ed. Jean Massin. 18 vols. Paris: Club français du livre, 1967-1970.

Oeuvres poétiques, ed. Pierre Albouy. Vol. I. *Avant l'exil* (1802-1851), Vol. II. *Châtiments, Les Contemplations*. Paris: Gallimard, *Bibliothèque de la Pléiade*, 1964 and 1967.

Les Contemplations, ed. Joseph Vianey. 3 vols. Paris: Hachette, *Les Grands Ecrivains de la France*, 1922.

Les Contemplations, ed. André Dumas. Paris: Garnier, 1962.

Les Contemplations, ed. Jacques Seebacher. 2 vols. Paris: Armand Colin, *Bibliothèque de Cluny*, 1964.

Les Contemplations, ed. Léon Cellier. Paris: Garnier, 1969.

Dieu (fragments), ed. René Journet and Guy Robert. Paris: Flammarion, 1969.

Dieu (L'Océan d'en haut), ed. René Journet and Guy Robert. Paris: Nizet, 1960.

Dieu (Le Seuil du gouffre), ed. René Journet and Guy Robert. Paris: Nizet, 1961.

Lettres de Victor Hugo aux Bertin. 1827-1877. Paris: Plon, 1890.

Correspondance entre Victor Hugo et Paul Meurice. Paris: Fasquelle, 1909.

Lettres à Juliette Drouet, 1833-1883. Le Livre de l'anniversaire, ed. Jean Gaudon. Paris: Pauvert, 1964.

B. Critical Works on Hugo

Albouy, Pierre. *La Création mythologique chez Victor Hugo*. Paris: José Corti, 1963.

Aragon, Louis. *Avez-vous lu Victor Hugo?* Paris: Pauvert, 1964.

———. *Hugo, poète réaliste*. Paris: Editions Sociales, 1952.

Ascoli, Georges. "A Propos du *Rouet d'Omphale* de Victor Hugo." *Mélanges de philologie et d'histoire littéraire offerts à Edmond Huguet*, 1940.

Barbéris, Pierre. "A Propos de *Lux*: la vraie force des choses (sur l'idéologie des *Châtiments*)." *Littérature*, Fév., 1971.

Barrère, Jean-Bertrand. *La Fantaisie de Victor Hugo*. 3 vols. Paris: José Corti, 1949, 1950, 1960.

———. *Hugo, l'homme et l'oeuvre*. Paris: Boivin, 1952.

———. *Victor Hugo à l'oeuvre. Le poète en exil et en voyage*. Paris: Klincksieck, 1966.

Baudouin, Charles. *Psychanalyse de Victor Hugo*. Geneva: Editions du Mont Blanc, 1943.

Berret, Paul. *La Philosophie de Victor Hugo (1854-1859)*. Paris: Paulin, 1910.

———. *Victor Hugo*. Paris: Garnier, 1939.

Biré, Edmond. *Victor Hugo après 1830*. 2 vols. Paris: Perrin et Cie., 1891.

———. *Victor Hugo après 1852, l'éxil, les dernières années et la mort du poète*. Paris: Perrin et Cie., 1894.

———. *Victor Hugo avant 1830*. Paris; J. Gervais, 1883.

Brombert, Victor. "Victor Hugo, la prison et l'espace." *Revue des sciences humaines*. Jan.-Mars, 1965, pp. 59-79.

Buche, J. "Ballanche et Victor Hugo, une source des *Misérables*." *Revue d'histoire littéraire de la France*, 34, 1927, pp. 173-188.

Cargo, Robert T. "A Further Look at Baudelaire's *Le Cygne* and Victor Hugo." *Romance Notes*, 10, pp. 277-285.

Cellier, Léon. "A Propos du *Rouet d'Omphale.*" *Mélanges de philologie et d'histoire littéraire offerts à Edmond Huguet*, 1940.

———. *Baudelaire et Hugo*. Paris: José Corti, 1970.

———. *L'Epopée romantique*. Paris: Presses universitaires de France, 1954.

Chahine, Samia. *La Dramaturgie de Victor Hugo (1816-43)*. Paris: Nizet, 1971.

Clancier, G.-E. "Note sur la poétique de l'oeil chez Hugo." *Cahiers du sud*, 368, 1962, pp. 87-96.

Clarac, Pierre. "Quelques remarques sur les relations de Chateaubriand et de Victor Hugo." *Revue d'histoire littéraire de la France*, 68, 1968, pp. 1005-1017.

Delteil, Yvon. *La Fin tragique du voyage de Victor Hugo en 1843 d'après le Journal de Voyage autographe de Juliette Drouet (1843)*. Paris: Nizet, 1970.

Ditchy, Jay Karl. *La Mer dans l'oeuvre littéraire de Victor Hugo*. Paris: Les Belles lettres, 1925.

Drouet, Juliette. *Mille et une lettres d'amour à Victor Hugo*, ed. Paul Souchon. Paris: Gallimard, 1951.

Emery, Léon. *Trois poètes cosmiques*. Lyon: Les Cahiers libres, 1964.

———. *Vision et pensée chez Victor Hugo*. Lyon: Audin, 1939.

Fongaro, Antoine. "Mallarmé et Hugo." *Revue des sciences humaines*, Oct.-Déc., 1965, pp. 515-527.

Gaudon, Jean. "Digressions hugoliennes." *Oeuvres complètes*, ed. Massin, Vol. XIV, pp. I-XVII.

———. *Hugo, dramaturge*. Paris: L'Arche, 1955.

———. *Le Temps de la contemplation. L'Oeuvre poétique de Victor Hugo des 'Misères' au 'Seuil du gouffre' (1845-1856)*. Paris: Flammarion, 1969.

———. "Présentation" (to *Les Contemplations*). *Oeuvres complètes*, ed. Massin, Vol. IX, pp. 33-49.

Gely, Claude. "Baudelaire et Hugo: influences réciproques." *Revue d'histoire littéraire de la France*, 1962, pp. 592-595.

Glauser, Alfred. *Victor Hugo et la poésie pure.* Geneva: Droz, 1957.

Glotz, R. *Essai sur la psychologie des variantes des 'Contemplations.'* Paris: Presses universitaires, 1924.

Grant, Elliott. *A Select & Critical Bibliography.* Chapel Hill: University of North Carolina Press, 1967.

———. *The Career of Victor Hugo.* Cambridge: Harvard University Press, 1945.

Grant, Richard. *The Perilous Quest; Image, Myth, and Prophecy in the Narratives of Victor Hugo.* Durham: Duke University Press, 1968.

Grillet, Claudius. *La Bible dans Victor Hugo.* Lyon: Vitte, 1910.

Guillemin, Henri. *Hugo et la sexualité.* Paris: Gallimard, 1954.

———. *Victor Hugo par lui-même.* Paris: Seuil, 1951.

Guimbaud, Louis. *Victor Hugo et Juliette Drouet, d'après les lettres inédits de Juliette Drouet à Victor Hugo et avec un choix de ces lettres.* Paris: Blaizot, 1914.

———. *Victor Hugo et Madame Biard, d'après des documents inédits.* Paris: Blaizot, 1927.

Heiss, H. "Victor Hugo Gedicht vom Spinnrod der Omphalé." *Archiv für das Studium der neueren Sprachen,* 165, Band N.S. 65, Band 1934, pp. 60-70.

Houston, John Porter. *The Demonic Imagination: Style and Theme in French Romantic Poetry.* Baton Rouge: Louisiana State University Press, 1969.

———. *Victor Hugo.* New York: Twayne, World Authors Series, 1974.

Hugo, Adèle. *Le Journal d'Adèle Hugo,* ed. Frances Guilles. 2 vols. Paris: Minard, 1968, 1970.

Hugo, Adèle-Victor. *Victor Hugo raconté par un témoin de sa vie*. Paris: Librairie Internationale, 1863.

Huguet, Edmond. *La Couleur, la lumière et l'ombre dans les métaphores de Victor Hugo*. Paris: Hachette, 1905.

———. *Le Sens de la forme dans les métaphores de Victor Hugo*. Paris: Hachette, 1904.

Hunt, Herbert J. *The Epic in Nineteenth-Century France. A Study in Heroic & Humanitarian Poetry from 'Les Martyrs' to 'Les Siècles morts.'* Oxford: Blackwell, 1941.

Hyslop, Lois B. "Baudelaire on *Les Misérables*." *French Review*, 41, Oct. 1967, pp. 23-29.

Jacoubet, H. "Sur Quelques passages des *Mages*." *Revue d'histoire littéraire de la France*, 43, 1936, pp. 291-299.

Journet, René, and Guy B. Robert. "Autour des *Contemplations*." *Annales littéraires de l'Université de Besançon*, 2e série, Vol. ii, fasc. 6, 1955.

———. "Le Manuscrit des *Contemplations*." *Annales littéraires de l'Université de Besançon*, Vol. iii, fasc. 5, 1956.

———. "Notes sur *Les Contemplations*, suivies d'un index." *Annales littéraires de l'Université de Besançon*, Vol. 21, 1958.

Lejeune, Philippe. "L'Ombre et la lumière dans *Les Contemplations*." *Archives des lettres modernes*, 7, 1968.

Maillon, Jean. *Victor Hugo et l'art architectural*. Paris: Presses universitaires de France, 1962.

Maurois, André. *Olympio ou la vie de Victor Hugo*. Paris: Hachette, 1954.

Meschonnic, Henri. "Le Poème Hugo." *Oeuvres complètes*, ed. Massin, Vol. xiv, pp. xix-lxvi.

———. "Vers le roman poème." *Oeuvres complètes*, ed. Massin, Vol. iii, pp. i-xx.

Pommier, J. "Baudelaire et Hugo. Nouvelles glanes." *Revue des sciences humaines*, 1967, pp. 337-349.

Pruner, Francis, "*Les Contemplations* 'pyramide-temple,'

ébauche pour un principe d'explication." *Archives des lettres modernes*, 43, 1962.

Py, Albert. *Les Mythes grecs dans la poésie de Victor Hugo.* Geneva: Droz, 1963.

————. "Hugo le mage." *Génies de la France. Les Cahiers du Rhône*, 4. Neuchâtel: La Baconnière, 1942, pp. 161-189.

Renouvier, Charles. *Victor Hugo, le philosophe.* Paris: Colin, 1890.

————. *Victor Hugo, le poète.* Paris: Colin, 1902.

Richard, J.-P. "Paysage et langage chez Hugo." *Critique,* 25, pp. 387-407.

Richer, Jean. "Comment Victor Hugo apprit le drame de Villequier." *Arts*, 10 juillet, 1952.

Riffaterre, Michael. "La Poésie métaphysique de Victor Hugo; style, symboles, et thèmes de *Dieu*." *Romanic Review*, Vol. 51, 1960, pp. 268-276.

————. "La Vision hallucinatoire chez Victor Hugo." *Modern Language Notes*, Vol. 78, 1963, pp. 225-241.

————. "Le Poème comme représentation." *Poétique*, 4, 1970, pp. 401-418.

————. "Victor Hugo's Poetics." *The American Society Legion of Honor Magazine*, 32, 1961, pp. 181-196.

Rochette, Auguste. *L'Alexandrin chez Victor Hugo.* Paris: Hachette, 1911.

Roos, Jacques. *Les Idées philosophiques de Victor Hugo: Ballanche et Victor Hugo.* Paris: Nizet, 1958.

Saurat, Denis. *La Religion de Victor Hugo.* Paris: Hachette, 1929.

————. *Victor Hugo et les dieux du peuple.* Paris: La Colombe, 1948.

Savey-Casard, Paul. *Le Crime et la peine dans l'oeuvre de Victor Hugo.* Paris: Presses universitaires de France, 1956.

Scott, S. J. "The Mythology of the Tree in *Les Contempla-*

tions." *Journal of the Australasian Universities Language & Literature Assoc.,* 10, May 1959, pp. 120-127.

Seebacher, Jacques. "Poétique et politique de la paternité." *Oeuvres complètes,* ed. Massin, Vol. XII, pp. XLX-XXXIV.

————. "Présentation à *Philosophie, commencement d'un livre.*" *Oeuvres complètes,* ed. Massin, Vol. XII, pp. 3-9.

————. "Sens et structure des *Mages (Contemplations* VI, 23)." *Revue des sciences humaines,* Juillet-Sept. 1963, pp. 347-370.

Simon, Gustave. *Les Tables tournantes de Jersey, Procès-Verbaux des séances.* Paris: Conard, 1923.

Spitzer, Leo. "Zu V. Hugo's *Le Rouet d'Omphale.*" *Romanische literatur Studien,* 1936-1956, pp. 277-285.

Swinburne, Algernon Charles. *A Study of Victor Hugo.* London: Chatto & Windus, 1886.

Ubersfeld, Anne. "Hugo et Baudelaire: une lettre inédite." *Revue d'histoire littéraire de la France,* 68, pp. 1047-1052.

————. *Le Roi et le bouffon.* Paris: José Corti, 1973.

Uitti, Karl D. "The Vision of Lilith in Hugo's *La Fin de Satan.*" *The French Review,* Vol. XXXI, No. 6, May 1958, pp. 479-486.

Vacquerie, Auguste. *Les Miettes de l'histoire.* Paris: Pagnerre, 1863.

————. *Profils et grimaces.* Paris: Pagnerre, 1864.

Venzac, Géraud. *Les Origines religieuses de Victor Hugo.* Paris: Bloud et Gay, 1955.

————. *Les Premiers maîtres de Victor Hugo.* Paris: Bloud et Gay, 1955.

Viatte, Auguste. *Les Sources occultes du romantisme, illuminisme, théosophie, 1770-1820.* 2 vols. Paris: Champion, 1928.

————. *Victor Hugo et les illuminés de son temps.* Montreal: Editions de l'Arbre, 1942.

Villiers, Charles. *L'Univers métaphysique de Victor Hugo.* Paris: J. Vrin, 1970.

Zumthor, Paul. "Le Moyen Age de Victor Hugo." *Oeuvres complètes,* ed. Massin, Vol. IV, pp. X-XXXI.

———. *Victor Hugo, poète de Satan.* Paris: Laffont, 1946.

C. OTHER

Abrams, M. H. *The Mirror and the Lamp.* New York: W. W. Norton & Co., 1958.

———. *Natural Supernaturalism: Tradition and Revolution in Romantic Literature.* New York: W. W. Norton & Co., 1971.

Auerbach, Eric. *Dante, Poet of the Secular World,* trans. by Ralph Manheim. Chicago: University of Chicago Press, 1961.

———. *Scenes from the Drama of European Literature.* New York: Meridian Books, 1959.

Austin, Lloyd James. *L'Univers poètique de Baudelaire; symbolisme et symbolique.* Paris: Mercure de France, 1956.

Bachelard, Gaston. *L'Eau et les rêves: essai sur l'imagination de la matière.* Paris: José Corti, 1942.

Balzac, Honoré de. *La Comédie humaine,* Vol. X. *Louis Lambert,* ed. M. Bouteron. Paris: Gallimard, *Bibliothèque de la Pléiade,* 1955.

Baudelaire, Charles. *Oeuvres complètes,* ed. Le Dantec. Paris: Gallimard, *Bibliothèque de la Pléiade,* 1963.

Béguin, Albert. *L'Ame romantique et le rêve.* Paris: José Corti, 1939.

Bloom, Harold. *The Anxiety of Influence, a Theory of Poetry.* New York: Oxford University Press, 1973.

———, ed. *Romanticism and Consciousness.* New York: Norton, 1970.

———. *The Visionary Company: A Reading of English Romantic Poetry.* Ithaca: Cornell University Press, 1971.

Brustein, Robert. *The Theatre of Revolt*. Boston: Little, Brown, 1964.

Campbell, Joseph. *The Hero with a Thousand Faces*. New York: Bollingen, Series XVII, Pantheon Books, 1949.

Charity, A. C. *Events and Their Afterlife: The Dialectics of Christian Typology in the Bible and Dante*. New York: Cambridge University Press, 1966.

Chateaubriand, François Auguste René, Vicomte de. *Atala, René, Le Dernier Abencérage*, ed. Letessier. Paris: Garnier, 1962.

———. *Mémoires d'outre-tombe*, ed. Maurice Levaillant. 2 vols. Paris: Flammarion, 1947.

Cirlot, J. *A Dictionary of Symbols*. New York: Philosophical Library, 1962.

Cohen, Jean. *La Structure du langage poétique*. Paris: Flammarion, 1968.

———. "Théorie de la figure." *Communications*, 16, 1970, pp. 3-25.

Curtius, Ernst Robert. *European Literature and the Latin Middle Ages*, trans. Willard R. Trask. New York: Bollingen, 1953.

Dante, Alighieri. *The Divine Comedy*, trans. John D. Sinclair. New York: Oxford University Press, 1961.

De Man, Paul. *Blindness and Insight*. New York: Oxford University Press, 1971.

———. "The Rhetoric of Temporality." *Interpretation, Theory, and Practice*, ed. Charles S. Singleton. Baltimore: The Johns Hopkins University Press, 1969.

Derrida, Jacques. *De la Grammatologie*. Paris: Editions de Minuit, 1967.

———. *L'Ecriture et la différence*. Paris: Seuil, 1967.

Draper, John W. *The Funeral Elegy and the Rise of English Romanticism*. New York: Octagon Books, 1967.

217

Bibliography

Eigeldinger, Marc. *Le Dynamisme de l'image dans la poésie française*. Neuchâtel: La Baconnière, 1943.

Eliade, Mircea. *Cosmos and History; the Myth of the Eternal Return*, trans. by Willard R. Trask. New York: Harper, 1959.

———. *Rites and Symbols of Initiation: The Mysteries of Birth and Rebirth*, trans. by Willard R. Trask. New York: Harper Torchbooks, 1958.

Fletcher, Angus. *Allegory: Theory of a Symbolic Mode*. Ithaca: Cornell University Press, 1964.

Fontanier, Pierre. *Les Figures du discours* (1821). Paris: Flammarion, 1966.

Friedrich, Hugo. *The Structure of Modern Poetry: from the Mid-nineteenth to the Mid-twentieth Century*, trans. by Joachim Neugroschel. Evanston: Northwestern University Press, 1974.

Frye, Northrop. "Allegory." *Princeton Encyclopedia of Poetry and Poetics*, ed. Alex Preminger. Princeton: Princeton University Press, 1965.

———. *The Anatomy of Criticism*. New York: Atheneum, 1957.

———. *A Study of English Romanticism*. New York: Random House, 1968.

Gautier, Théophile. *Histoire du romantisme*. Paris: Charpentier, 1874.

Genette, Gérard. *Figures*. Paris: Seuil, 1966; *Figures II*, 1969; *Figures III*, 1972.

Gilman, Margaret. *Baudelaire, the Critic*. New York: Columbia University Press, 1943.

Hartman, Geoffrey H. *Beyond Formalism*. New Haven: Yale University Press, 1970.

———. *The Unmediated Vision, an Interpretation of Wordsworth, Hopkins, Rilke, & Valéry*. New Haven: Yale University Press, 1954.

218

Heller, Erich. *The Artist's Journey into the Interior and other Essays*. London: Secker & Warburg, 1959.

Hirsch, E. D., Jr. *Validity in Interpretation*. New Haven: Yale University Press, 1967.

Hollander, Robert. *Allegory in Dante's "Commedia."* Princeton: Princeton University Press, 1969.

Honig, Edwin. *Dark Conceit: The Making of Allegory*. Evanston: Northwestern University Press, 1959.

Jakobson, Roman. *Questions de poétique*. Paris: Seuil, 1973.

———, and Morris Halle. *Fundamentals of Language*. The Hague: Janua Linguarum, Mouton, 1956.

Jameson, Frederic. *The Prison-House of Language*. Princeton: Princeton University Press, 1972.

———. "La Cousine Bette and Allegorical Realism." *PMLA*, 86, 1971, pp. 241-254.

Johansen, Svend. *Le Symbolisme. Etude sur le style des symbolistes français*. Copenhagen: Einar Munksgaard, 1945.

Kermode, Frank. *The Romantic Image*. New York: Vintage, 1957.

———. *The Sense of an Ending*. New York: Oxford University Press, 1966.

Lamartine, Alphonse de. *Oeuvres poétiques complètes*, ed. Marius-François Guyard. Paris: Gallimard, *Bibliothèque de la Pléiade*, 1963.

Langbaum, Robert. *The Poetry of Experience*. New York: Norton, 1957.

Lemon, Lee T., and Marion J. Reis, eds. *Russian Formalist Criticism, Four Essays*. Lincoln: University of Nebraska Press, 1965.

Lewis, C. S. *The Allegory of Love: A Study in Medieval Tradition*. New York: Oxford University Press, 1936.

Lovejoy, A. O. *Essays in the History of Ideas*. Baltimore: The Johns Hopkins University Press, 1948.

Mallarmé, Stéphane. *Oeuvres complètes*, ed. Henri Mondor

and F. Jean-Aubry. Paris: Gallimard, *Bibliothèque de la Pléiade*, 1945.

Martz, Louis L. *The Poetry of Meditation*. New Haven: Yale University Press, 1954.

Milton, John. *Complete Poems and Major Prose*, ed. Merritt Y. Hughes. New York: The Odyssey Press, 1957.

Mornet, Daniel. *Le Sentiment de la nature en France de J.-J. Rousseau à Bernardin de Saint-Pierre*. Paris: Hachette, 1907.

Potts, Abbie Findlay. *The Elegiac Mode, Poetic Form in Wordsworth & Other Elegists*. Ithaca: Cornell University Press, 1967.

Poulet, Georges. *La Distance intérieure*. Paris: Plon, 1952.

Praz, Mario. *The Romantic Agony,* trans. by Angus Davidson. Cleveland/New York: The World Publishing Company, 1963.

Raymond, Marcel. *De Baudelaire au surréalism, essai sur le mouvement poétique contemporain*. Paris: Corrêa, 1933.

Riffaterre, Michael. "Describing Poetic Structures: Two Approaches to Baudelaire's 'Les Chats.'" *Yale French Studies*, 36-37, 1966, pp. 200-242.

Rousset, Jean. *Forme et signification*. Paris: José Corti, 1964.

Sainte-Beuve, Charles A. *Oeuvres (Premiers lundis, Portraits littéraires, Portraits de femmes)*, ed. Maxime Leroy. 2 vols. Paris: Gallimard, *Bibliothèque de la Pléiade*, 1949, 1951.

Singleton, Charles S. *"Commedia": Elements of Structure*. Cambridge: Harvard University Press, 1954.

——. *Dante Studies 2. Journey to Beatrice*. Cambridge: Harvard University Press, 1954.

Smith, Barbara H. *Poetic Closure: A Study of How Poems End*. Chicago: University of Chicago Press, 1968.

Staël, Germaine de. *De la Littérature, considérée dans ses rapports avec les institutions sociales*, ed. Paul van Tieghem. Paris: Droz-Minard, 1959.

Bibliography

Tuve, Rosemond. *Allegorical Imagery*. Princeton: Princeton University Press, 1966.

Uitti, Karl D. *Linguistics and Literary Theory*. Englewood Cliffs: Prentice-Hall, 1969.

——. "Remarques sur la langue 'moderniste.'" *Le Français moderne*, Jan., 1972, pp. 25-39.

——. "Remarques sur la langue 'moderniste': Bonald." *Le Français moderne*, Oct., 1972, pp. 313-324.

Vigny, Alfred de. *Oeuvres complètes*, ed. F. Baldensperger. 2 vols. Paris: Gallimard, *Bibliothèque de la Pléiade*, 1948.

Weber, Jean-Paul. *Genèse de l'oeuvre poétique*. Paris: Gallimard, 1960.

Wellek, René. *A History of Modern Criticism*. Vol. ii. "The Romantic Age." New Haven: Yale University Press, 1953.

QUEEN MARY COLLEGE LIBRARY

Index

Journet, René, and Guy Robert, viii, 13, 16n, 60n, 61n, 80, 111n, 178n, 189-93
Judas, 166
Jupiter, 65, 119, 122
Juvenal, 127

Karr, Alphonse, 55
King of Thule, 115, 116, 117

La Fontaine, Jean de, 44, 89
Lake Gaube, 53-54, 55
Lamartine, Alphonse de, 6, 17, 63n, 127
Lamennais, Félicité de, 17
Langbaum, Robert, 176n
Lazarus, 203
Lévi-Strauss, Claude, 21n
Louis-Philippe, 154
Lucifer, 36, 37, 38, 86, 172, 202

Mallarmé, Stéphane, 10, 82
Marius, 110
Mary Magdalene, 167
Massin, Jean, viii, 14 passim
Maurois, André, 52n
Mephistopheles, 115
Meurice, Paul, 151, 152, 165, 166
Milton, John, 18, 38
Molière, Jean-Baptiste Poquelin, 90
Moschus, 110
Moses, 18n
Musset, Alfred de, 6

Napoléon, 53

Oedipus, 18n
Omphale, 47, 65, 66, 67, 117, 120, 122

Parfait, Noël, 60
Pascal, Blaise, 127
Perceval, 104

Persephone, 74, 75, 109, 111, 120, 166
Phidias, 29
Plato, 81
Plautus, 98, 110
Plotinus, 23n, 57n
Pluto, 120, 166
Ponto, 151
Pradier, Claire, 68, 142, 151
Prometheus, 18n, 38, 90, 155, 178
Pruner, Francis, 16n

Quasimodo, 25, 110, 111, 205
Quinet, Edgar, 109n

Riffaterre, Michael, viii, 188-89
Rimbaud, Arthur, 4
Robert, Guy: see Journet, René, and Guy Robert
Roos, Jacques, 18n, 34n, 174n
Rousseau, Jean-Jacques, 21, 53, 63n, 176; *Confessions*, 26; *La Nouvelle Héloïse*, 33n
Les Ruines de Babylone, 53

Saint John, 90, 102
Saintsbury, George, vii
Sappho, 71
Satan, 172
Saurat, Denis, 83n
Schiller, Friedrich, 17
Scott, Walter, 129
Seebacher, Jacques, viii, 57n, 145n
Servius Tullius, 18n
Shakespeare, William, 17, 56
Shattuck, Roger, 3, 7
Shklovsky, Victor, 49n
Le Siècle, 55
Singleton, Charles, 10n, 25n, 58n
Socrates, 80
Souday, Paul, 7n
Swedenborg, Emmanuel, 23n
Swinburne, Charles, vii

228

Index

Tennyson, Alfred, Lord, vii
Thénardier, 105n

Ulysses, 101

Vacquerie, Auguste, 16, 56, 57n, 150, 151
Vacquerie, Charles, 55, 56, 57, 141, 145, 150, 151, 155
Valéry, Paul, 4, 6, 7, 206

Venus, 168
Vianey, Joseph, viii, 61n
Vigny, Alfred de, 6, 17, 127, 141
Villemain, François, 31n
Villequier, 50, 55, 56, 206
Virgil, 18n, 94, 119, 142
Virgin, 167, 168

Wellek, René, 6n
Wordsworth, William, 33n

Library of Congress Cataloging in Publication Data

Nash, Suzanne.
  Les contemplations of Victor Hugo.

  Bibliography: p.
  Includes index.
  1. Hugo, Victor Marie, comte, 1802–1885. Les
contemplations.   I. Title.
PQ2285.C83N3   1976   841'.7   76–3273
ISBN 0–691–06313–3